The Selected Soyer

Alexis Soyer, by his wife

The Selected
SOYER

The writings of
the legendary Victorian Chef
Alexis Soyer

❦

Compiled by Andrew Langley

Absolute Press
in association with
The Reform Club

Published by Absolute Press (publishers)
14 Widcombe Crescent, Bath, Avon

in association with

The Reform Club, Pall Mall, London

First published April 1987

© Absolute Press

Phototypeset by
Sulis Typesetting, 2 Gay Street, Bath BA1 2PH

Printed by
WBC Print, Barton Manor, St. Philips, Bristol

Bound by
WBC Bookbinders, Maesteg, Mid-Glamorgan

ISBN 0 948230 10 X

Contents

Prologue

In the autumn of 1850, the journalist George Augustus Sala was walking with his brother through Hungerford Market. His eye was caught by a singular figure bargaining animatedly for lobsters:

'The stranger was a stoutish, tallish gentleman, a little past middle age, with closely cropped grey hair and a stubbly grey moustache . . . He wore a kind of paletot of light camlet cloth, with voluminous lapels and deep cuffs of lavender watered silk; very baggy trousers, with lavender stripes down the seams; very shiny boots and quite as glossy a hat; his attire being completed by tightly-fitting gloves of light yellow. An extra-ordinary oddity was added to his appearance by the circumstance that every article of his attire, save I suppose his gloves and boots, was cut on what dressmakers call a 'bias', or as he himself, when I came to know him well, used to designate as à la zoug-zoug.'

Sala asked his brother who this flamboyant gentleman might be. 'Who is that?' came the astonished reply. 'Why, of all people, who could it be but Soyer?'

Even though he had not seen the man before, Sala must surely have heard of him. For more than a decade Alexis Soyer had been one of the landmarks of fashionable London. He was without doubt the most celebrated cook of the period, whose culinary exploits at the new Reform Club in Pall Mall had thrilled not only the aristocratic members but, through adoring and minutely-detailed reports in the press, the general public as well. And had he not, that very summer, prepared a banquet for twelve hundred people which had been so lavish that the scraps had provided a meal for seven hundred paupers the next day?

Yet he was much more than simply a great chef. He was a friend to the poor of London and Ireland, for whom he had organized soup kitchens and devised nourishing and cheap recipes. He was a compulsive inventor. Stewing pans, alarm clocks, tendon separators, vegetable drainers and table stoves flew from his drawing board, not to mention other devices which were nothing to do with food, such as a transformation scene for a pantomime, a contrivance for rescuing drowning skaters, and a suit of clothes which could be changed by the pull of a string. He was a best-selling author, whose books sold not in tens but hundreds of thousands. Beyond all this, he was a charmer, a 'character', a dandy, a wit, a prankster, a life and soul of any party, a fine singer and a wonderful raconteur. For all his vanities and excesses, his friends loved him unreservedly and his staff worshipped him.

The word 'genius' sits easily on Soyer's camlet-covered shoulders. His incandescent energy, his unflagging ingenuity and his mastery of his trade remind us irresistibly of two more celebrated contemporaries, Charles Dickens and Isambard Kingdom Brunel. Indeed, in his own time he was reckoned to be at least their equal. As *The Globe* had put it in 1841: 'The impression grows on us that the man of his age is neither Sir Robert Peel, nor Lord John Russell, nor even Ibrahim Pasha, but Alexis Soyer.'

Alexis Benoit Soyer was born on 14th October 1809 in Meaux-en-Brie, a small town to the east of Paris renowned (as it is today) for its cheeses. His father was a shopkeeper, though it appears to have been his mother who ordered family matters. It was she who decided that her youngest child should be trained for the priesthood. Accordingly, at the age of nine, Alexis was packed off to the Cathedral School of Meaux.

He made a promising chorister, for he had a pleasing voice and a good ear for music, but (as his first biographers delicately put it) 'the confined life that accompanied the vocation was far from agreeable to his disposition'. The 'disposition', which was to turn him into one of the distinctive characters of the century, found the regimentation of the cloisters irksome. He complained to his parents, but they refused to take him away. The only alternative was to get himself expelled, and Alexis plunged joyfully into a campaign of annoying the authorities. This culminated in the ringing of the church's great bell at midnight, an alarm which woke the whole town and roused the local garrison. Alexis departed next day.

What was to be done with him? In exasperation, his mother sent him to Paris to stay with his elder brother Philippe, who was training to be a chef. The twelve year-old Alexis tried his hand at various jobs, but in the end was persuaded to become a cook like his brother. He was apprenticed at Grignon's in the Rue Vivienne, and in 1826 was taken on by the celebrated Douix, of the Boulevard des Italiens. Although he seemed to have fallen into the trade by chance, Alexis soon showed a remarkable flair for cookery. At the tender age of seventeen he was appointed head of Douix's kitchen, with no less than a dozen cooks in his charge. Several of the older hands were naturally peeved at this, but Soyer's charm and easy competence quickly won them round.

Soyer himself had been charmed by the delights of Paris. As well as being a born chef, he was a born townsman, and the focus of his joy was the theatre – the Théâtre des Variétés in particular. He was intoxicated by the glamorous costumes, the extravagant postures, the laughter and applause. Being a brilliant mimic and a gifted singer, he was able to entertain his colleagues with all he heard and saw. Poor Philippe had the greatest difficulty in keeping his brother from a career on the stage.

Soyer's unquenchable sociability made him the centre of attention on almost any occasion. One characteristic incident is described by his devoted biographers Volant and Warren:

'In the early part of Alexis's apprenticeship, a grand ball was given by a rich banker of the Chaussée d'Antin, and his master had to supply the refreshments, while Alexis himself was deputed to superintend the dessert. On these occasions, china and other ornaments are generally supplied by the restaurateur, and brought back in wooden trays by the apprentices and second cooks. Alexis Soyer, being a jovial fellow, was solicited by the household for a song, and of course treated liberally at the expense of the feast-giver. So he supped and drank to his heart's content until about one o'clock on a cold snowy morning when, loaded with his tray filled with valuable ornaments, etc., he went off. As soon as he left the hall, and breathed the cold air, he began to feel jollier than ever; he sang and sang again, and whilst he was repeating the chorus of –

> 'Ah! voilà la vie, la vie, la vie, suivie,
> Ah! voilà la vie, que les moines font –
> V'là – v'là – v'là – v'là – v'là – v'là,
> Ah!' etc. etc. –

all at once his head began to swim, and his road became an unfathomable mystery to him. He walked on thus for an hour or so, and at last dropped down into an enclosure, china and all, where some buildings were in progress, and went fast asleep. At the end of another hour he woke, rubbed his eyes, and started off without the china; and, after a great deal of trouble, found himself at the door of his master, Douix, just as the other cooks arrived, all staring at him, laughing, joking, and pulling him about. Well they might, for poor Alexis had left his nether garments behind him! He could not account for it, and much less for the trayful of china, valued by the master at 150 francs. However, the name of Douix being on the tray, it was brought home uninjured, some hours afterwards, by the police, together with the pair of nether garments left behind, to the great delight and merriment of the whole establishment. Of course Alexis was for many weeks after the laughing-stock of his companions, for this first attempt at bivouacking in the open field.

By 1830, Soyer's reputation was sufficient for him to be chosen as a second chef for a grand entertainment at the Foreign Office. Unfortunately the entertainment coincided with the July Revolution, sparked off by the passing of repressive measures by Charles X. Some of the mob broke into the kitchens, driving away most of the cooks and shooting down two others. Terrified though he must have been, Soyer improvised the performance of his life. Leaping onto a table, he sang La Marseillaise and other patriotic numbers, and ended up being chaired by the rioters in a triumphal procession.

Shortly after his unnerving experience, Soyer decided that England might be a safer country for a chef. He joined Philippe, who was already over the Channel, in the kitchens of the Duke of Cambridge. London, he soon found, was a headier city even than Paris. So it is something of a surprise to find that he readily accepted the post of head chef to a Mr Lloyd, of Aston Hall, near Oswestry. Shropshire must have seemed far from London's glitter, but Soyer was as eager to enjoy himself in the sticks as anywhere else. His fame spread rapidly, and the local aristocrats were frequently begging for the loan of his services. He also found a ready audience for his songs and monologues in the sitting room of the nearby Queen's Hotel.

After four years, however, the lure of the big city proved too strong. Soyer returned to London, or at least to Isleworth, where he became chef to the eccentric gourmet Marquis of Ailsa. One thing was needed to complete his happiness: a wife. Being Alexis Soyer, he set about his search in an unabashedly extravagant manner. He would, he decided, have his portrait painted and sent to an old flame in Paris with a written proposal of marriage. Accordingly he rambled about London in search of a good portrait painter, and was eventually referred to a Monsieur Simonau. He hastened to Simonau's studio, where he met Emma Jones, the artist's step-daughter. It was love, precipitate and overwhelming, at first sight. The old flame was forgotten. Soyer flung himself heart and soul into the wooing of Emma Jones.

She seems to have been the perfect match for him. At twenty-six years old, she was not only pretty, vivacious and witty, but a highly talented artist. Her crayon sketches were enjoying something of a vogue amongst the aristocracy, and in later years her oil paintings—of sentimental subjects suitable to the period, such as 'Children With Rabbits', 'The Crossing Sweeper' and 'The Centenarian Scotch Knitter'—were widely exhibited and keenly sought after. Soyer bombarded her with gifts, flowers and passionate verses (in French), and it was not long before she was swayed by his ardour. The only damper on proceedings was her step-father, who would have preferred her to give her hand to 'anybody rather than a cook'. His disapproval was swept away by the cook in question, who married Emma on April 12th 1837 at St George's, Hanover Square.

By this time, Soyer had reached another, and even more momentous, decision. He had left the Marquis with much regret and accepted the post of chef de cuisine at the newly-established Reform Club in Pall Mall.

Chef at the Reform
The Gastronomic Regenerator

By 1832, the Great Reform Bill had completed its long and tortuous passage through Parliament and become law. The jubilant Whigs decided to celebrate by founding their own Reform Club at 104, Pall Mall. The original premises soon proved to be much too small, however, and a design for a grander and far more spacious edifice was commissioned from the architect Sir Charles Barry. Meanwhile, the members took up temporary residence at nearby Gwydyr House, and it was here that Alexis Soyer began his long reign over the palates and stomachs of the Liberal aristocracy.

It was like a dream come true. Not only was he chef to more than a thousand of the most distinguished men in the land, but he also had the enthralling opportunity of planning his own kitchens. In collaboration with Barry, he designed nothing less than a private kingdom below stairs, which was described at the time as 'the finest kitchens that London, and possibly Europe, have ever seen': one could add 'and the world', without stretching the point.

The kitchens were completed in 1841, and were swiftly recognized as being the true seat of power in the new club. The ecstatic Soyer surpassed himself time and again, producing such a succession of novel and sumptuous dishes that he was hailed as 'the glory of the edifice, the genius loci'. Indeed it seemed at times that it was food rather than politics which kept the Liberals united. The chef received a daily stream of visitors—members, guests and journalists, all of whom were anxious to inspect his legendary domain. They became so numerous that the tours were usually conducted by an underling, for Soyer was not a man to neglect his work. Only the nobler arrivals were given his personal attention:

'It was curious to watch him, with his red velvet cap and spoon in hand, explaining to elegantly dressed ladies, and to the best blood of the aristocracy and nobility, his various methods of concocting soups of exquisite flavour, or his different styles of producing his dishes of fish, game, poultry, etc., at the same time giving full proof of his power over the art, by handing round either some properly made mulligatawny, or a basin of sole à la maitre d'hôtel, sending home the tasters positively rabid for their dinner, and wishing Soyer could be divided into as many pieces as a calf's head for his mock-turtle, that they might each have a bit of him in their cookery department. Sometimes he would suddenly plunge his finger, diamond ring and all, into what appeared to be a boiling cauldron of glue, pass it across his tongue, wink his eye, and add either a little more salt, pepper, or some mysterious dust, known possibly only to great artistes, to make it palatable. Then, again, he would whisper, chucklingly, "I've a dish for Lord M——— H———, for six o'clock, or a potage for Sir J. So-and-so at eight o'clock; let us taste it." '

It was at the height of all this glory that tragedy struck. In August 1842 Soyer was summoned overseas to advise no less a personage than the King of the Belgians on the design of his kitchens. He left Emma reluctantly, for she was in an advanced state of pregnancy. While he was away, a violent thunderstorm broke over London, and the terrified Emma gave birth prematurely. Both she and the baby died the same night. The dreadful news was carried to Brussels, and Soyer was at first so shocked that he attempted suicide. Back in London, he found his home now bleak and empty, and the flood of tributes and kind words from friends was almost more than he could bear. Characteristically, he found some immediate relief in his work. Another diversion was the designing of a grandiose monument for his wife's grave in Kensal Green Cemetery, which bore the simple but heart-felt inscription: 'To her'.

After Emma's death, Soyer seems to have driven himself to ever greater heights of flamboyance. His clothes grew more extravagant, tailored in slanting lines with waistcoats of velvet and satin. His cravats, tied in ever more complex patterns, were adorned with glittering scarf pins. His fingers bulged with rings. His hats were specially made so that they sat at a jaunty angle on his head. His dress boots were fitted with hollow heels to hold his loose change. His insistence on having everything *à la zoug-zoug* was extended even to his visiting cards, which were not rectangular but rhomboidal.

Among the many to be charmed and astounded by Soyer's excesses was William Makepeace Thackeray, a frequent visitor to the Reform Club. He grew to be very fond of the Frenchman, but this did not prevent him from placing an easily recognizable caricature of Soyer in his novel *Pendennis*, which began serialization in 1848. M. Alcide Mirobolant is the chef at Clavering Park—'a very good cook, but he is not quite right in the head', remarks someone. Thackeray gives us a delicious description of Mirobolant stunning the local villagers on his afternoon off:

'He walked among them quite unsuspiciously upon the afternoon of a summer day . . . in his usual favourite costume, namely, his light green frock or paletot, his crimson velvet waistcoat, with blue glass buttons, his pantalon Ecossais of a very large and decided check pattern, his orange satin neck-cloth, and his jean-boots, with tips of shiny leather—these, with a gold-embroidered cap, and a richly-gilt cane . . . formed his usual holiday costume, in which he flattered himself there was nothing remarkable (unless, indeed, the beauty of his person should attract observation), and in which he considered that he exhibited the appearance of a gentleman of good Parisian *ton.*'

Mirobolant is, of course, a figure of fun and far too pompous and stupid to have been anything more than a faint reflection of Soyer. Indeed, Thackeray repeatedly expressed his admiration of Soyer, both as a chef and as a witty companion. Yet it seems strange that the caricature did not cause offence, and it is an indication of the social position of a chef that someone observes later in the novel: 'them French cooks has as much pride and hinsolence as if they was real gentlemen'.

One wonders what Soyer thought when he read that.

As Soyer's appearance and behaviour grew ever more extraordinary, so did his cooking. One of his greatest nights was July 3rd, 1846, when the Reform Club gave a grand banquet for Ibrahim Pacha, the celebrated Ottoman general. The monstrous menu is worth giving in full:

'Dinner for 150, given to his Highness Ibrahim Pacha, by the Members of the Reform Club, July 3rd, 1846.

SEIZE POTAGES

Quatre à la Victoria.
Quatre à la Louis Philippe.
Quatre à la Colbert.
Quatre à la Comte de Paris aux Légumes printaniers.

SEIZE POISSONS.

Quatre de Turbots Sauce à la Mazarin.
Quatre de Saumons de Severn à la Crème.
Quatre de Buissons de Filets de Merlans à la Egyptienne.
Quatre de Truites Saumonée en Matelote Marinière.

SEIZE RELEVES.

Quatre de Chapons à la Nelson.
Quatre de Saddleback of Southdown Mutton rôti à la Soyer.
Quatre de Poulardes en Diadême.
Quatre de Saddleback d'Agneau rôti à la Sévigné.

CINQUANTE-QUATRE ENTREES.

Six de Poussins printaniers à l'Ambassadrice.
Six de Côtelettes de Mouton à la Réforme.
Quatre de Ris de Veau piqués en Macédoine de Légumes.
Quatre de Petits Vol-au-Vents aux Laitances de Maquereaux.
Quatre de Timballes de Riz aux Queux d'Agneau.
Quatre de Jambonneaux braisées au Vin de Madère.
Quatre de Volailles farcies à la Russe aux Légumes verts.
Quatre de Pâtés chauds de Cailles à la Banquièr.
Quatre de Rissolettes à la Pompadour.
Quatre de Grenadins de Boeuf à la Beyrout.
Six de Côtelettes d'Agneau à la Vicomtesse.
Quatre de Turbans Epigramme de Levereau au fumée.

SEIZE RÔTS.

Quatre de Turkey Poults piqués et bardes.
Quatre de Cannetons au Jus de Bigarades.
Quatre de Levereaux au Jus de Groseilles.
Quatre de Gros Chapons au Cresson.

CINQUANTE-QUATRE ENTREMETS.

Six de Gelées Macédoine de Fruits au Dantzic.
Quatre de Turbans de Meringues demi glacées.
Quatre de Charlottes Prussienne.
Six de Croquantes d'Amandes aux Cérises.
Quatre de Galantines à la Volière.
Quatre de Mirotons de Homard à l'Indienne.
Quatre de Salades de Volaille à la Soyer.
Quatre de Haricots verts au Beurre Noisette.
Six de Tartelettes Pralinées aux Abricots.
Quatre de Pain de Pêches au Noyeau.
Quatre de Petits Pois à l'Anglo-Française.
Quatre de Gelées cristalisées à l'Ananas.

RELEVES DE RÔTS.

La Crème d'Egypte, à l'Ibrahim Pacha.
Le Gâteau Britannique à l'Amiral.

Quatre de Jambons glacées en Surprise.
Quatre de Manivaux de Champignons au Curaçao en Surprise.
Quatre de Côtelettes en Surprise à la Réforme.
Deux de Meringues Chinoise-Pagoda aux Fraises.'

Baron of Beef à l'Anglaise.

Entre Pagodatique de Riz à la Luxor.

The climax of this triumphant feast was the dessert, named *La Crème d'Egypte à l'Ibrahim Pacha*. It was described next day in the *Morning Post*:
    'A pyramid about two and a half feet high, made of light meringue cake, in imitation of solid stones, surrounded with grapes and other fruits, but representing only the four angles of the pyramid through sheets of waved sugar, to show, to the greatest advantage, an elegant crème à l'ananas, on the top of which was resting a highly-finished portrait of the illustrious stranger's father, Mehemet Ali, carefully drawn on a round-shaped satin carton, the exact size of the top of the cream.'
    Balked of a secondary career on the stage, Soyer also turned his attention to writing. His first book, which appeared in 1845, was a slim volume under the title of *Délassements Culinaires* ('Culinary Recreations'), an arch

collection of essays, conceits and verses, most of which seem today to be jejune or obscure or both. The only item worth recalling is *La Fille de l'Orage* ('Daughter of the Thunderstorm')—probably the only ballet to have been penned by a great chef. This singular work shows Soyer at his most fearless, launching out into a new genre with typical gusto. The plot of Act One concerns a hero who is struck by lightning, miraculously revived by a goddess, and transported into the clouds. Besides calling for some astonishing theatrical effects, it was (wrote Volant and Warren) 'replete with choreographic difficulties, and not entirely suited to the London boards. In consequence, it was never performed . . . ' All the same, one can scarce forebear to cheer at the man's audacity.

However, Soyer had a far more ambitious—and practical—project in mind. 'He began to think seriously of writing a cookery book,' recorded his faithful secretaries. 'He set to work in earnest, and, to go on quicker with the receipts, he employed a very clever first kitchen-maid who had been some years under his tuition, and knew well the composition of all his soups, sauces, entrees, etc. He therefore requested her to write, in regular order, how she would proceed to make the various dishes. He did the same with the apprentice, who also wrote a certain series of receipts, which were afterwards revised, corrected, and some altogether put aside. Thus, in the course of ten months, the illustrated volume called *The Gastronomic Regenerator* came to light, and was very successful.'

This massive book, over six hundred pages long and containing more than two thousand recipes, was published in 1846, and was hailed by 'numerous and extraordinary reviews from the Press', all of which were full of praise. In less than a year the whole of the first edition was sold, and by 1852 a seventh edition had appeared. *The Gastronomic Regenerator* describes cooking on the grandest scale, using both the humblest and the most recherché of ingredients, but its huge popularity was largely due to the clarity with which Soyer (and his minions) gave their instructions. It also contained numerous appendices, which Soyer could not resist adding as each new edition went to the press. Above all, the book is shot through with unmistakeable traces of its author's charm and energy, even in the most unlikely places.

Selections from
The Gastronomic Regenerator (1846)

Preface

At the request of several persons of distinction; who have visited the Reform Club,— particularly the ladies, to whom I have always made it a rule never to refuse anything in my power, for indeed it must have been the fair sex who have had the majority in this domestic argument to gain this gastronomical election,—Why do you not write and publish a Cookery-book? was a question continually put to me. For a considerable time this scientific word caused a thrill of horror to pervade my frame, and brought back to my mind that one day, being in a most superb library in the midst of a splendid baronial hall, by chance, I met with one of Milton's allegorical works, the profound ideas of Locke, and several chefs-d'œuvre of one of the noblest champions of literature, Shakespeare; when all at once my attention was attracted by the nineteenth edition of a voluminous work: such an immense success of publication caused me to say, "Oh! you celebrated man, posterity counts every hour of fame upon your regretted ashes!" Opening this work with intense curiosity, to my great disappointment what did I see,—a receipt for Ox-tail Soup! The terrifying effect produced upon me by this succulent volume made me determine that my few ideas, whether culinary or domestic, should never encumber a sanctuary which should be entirely devoted to works worthy of a place in the Temple of the Muses.

But you must acknowledge, respected readers, how changeable and uncertain are our feeble ideas through life; to keep the promise above mentioned, I have been drawn into a thousand gastronomic reflections, which have involved me in the necessity of deviating entirely from my former opinion, and have induced me to bring before the public the present volume, under the title of 'The Gastronomic Regenerator', throughout which I have closely followed the plain rules of simplicity, so that every receipt can not only clearly be understood, but easily executed.

I now sincerely hope, Ladies, that I have not only kept my promise, but to your satisfaction paid tribute to your wishes.

You have not forgotten, dear reader, the effect that monstrous volume, the said nineteenth edition, produced upon me, therefore I now sincerely beg of you to put my book in a place suited to its little merit, and not with Milton's sublime Paradise, for there it certainly would be doubly lost.

Description of the Composition of this Work.

To sustain and deserve the title of 'Gastronomic Regenerator,' nothing but an entire change from the system of any other publication on the art of cookery would be admissible, it is now in the hands of my readers to judge for themselves, and to stamp its character according to its merits, either as an original or a copy; to avoid the last, however, I have closely studied to introduce the greatest novelty in every department, and have entirely omitted all unnecessary confusion, which, in many previous works, have rendered them unintelligible to the uninitiated, and almost impracticable to the initiated, however, many old and useful receipts, too good to be omitted, will be found much simplified—to reduce them to a practical point.

My readers will probably also feel interested in knowing that although for some time it has been my intention to write a work upon gastronomy, the laborious and difficult duties which I had to fulfil at the Reform Club, added to the terrific effect produced upon me by the 19th edition of that monstrous volume mentioned in the preface, have often been the cause of my giving up such an idea, and having destroyed my old manuscripts, it is only within the last ten months that I in reality commenced afresh this work; in which lapse of time I had to furnish 25,000 dinners for the gentlemen of the Reform Club, and 38 dinner parties of importance, comprising above 70,000 dishes, and to provide daily for 60 servants of the establishment, independent of about 15,000 visitors who have seen the kitchen department in that lapse of time.

How Everything Should Be in Cooking.

All clear soup must not be too strong of meat, and must be of a light brown, sherry, or straw colour.

All white or brown thick soups must be rather thinnish, lightly adhering to the back of the spoon.

All purées must adhere a little more to the back of the spoon.

Any Italian paste must be very clear, rather strong, and the colour of pale sherry.

All kinds of fish sauce should be thicker for boiled fish than for broiled or fried.

Brown sauce should be a little thinnish, and the colour of a horsechesnut.

White sauce should be of the colour of ivory, and thicker than brown sauce.

Cream, or Dutch sauce, must be rather thickish, and cannot be too white.

Demi-glace requires to be rather thin, but yet sufficiently reduced to envelop any pieces of meat, game, poultry, &c., with which it is served.

Every description of fish should be well done, but not over-boiled, broiled, stewed, or fried.

Beef and mutton must be underdone even for joints, removes, and entrées.

Lamb requires to be more done.

Veal and pork must be well done.

Venison must be underdone, red in the middle, and full of gravy, but not raw.

Poultry, either broiled, stewed, boiled, or roasted, must be done thoroughly, not cutting in the least red, but must still be full of gravy.

Pheasants and partridges must be well done through, yet full of gravy.

Grouse, black cocks, gray hens, and ptarmigans, must cut reddish, with plenty of gravy but not too much underdone.

All kinds of water-fowl must be very much underdone, so that the blood and gravy follow the knife in carving.

Plovers must be rather underdone, but done through.

Rabbits and pigeons must be well done.

Second-course savoury dishes must be rather highly seasoned, but with a little moderation.

Pastry should, when baked, be clear, light, and transparent, and of a beautiful straw colour; the body of a croustade the same.

Large pies, timbales, and casseroles of rice must be of a yellowish brown colour.

Jellies require to be very white and transparent for fruits, and not too firm, but better so than too delicate.

Orange jellies should be of a deep orange colour, and all fruit jellies as near as possible to the colour of the fruit.

Creams should be very light and delicate, but fruit creams must be kept of the colour of the fruits they are made of.

For all the demi-glacé removes the ice must be firm, but not the least hard.

All kinds of soufflé or fondu must be well done through, or they would be very indigestible, clog the delicate palate, and prevent the degustation of the generous claret which flows so freely after dinner on the table of the real epicure.

I recommend sugar in almost all savoury dishes, as it greatly facilitates digestion and invigorates the palate, but always increase or diminish the quantity according to the taste of your employer.

I often introduce onions, eschalots, or even a little garlic in some of my most delicate dishes, but so well blended with other flavours that I never have a single objection even by those who have a great dislike to it.

Horseradish and herbs of every description may always be used with discretion to great advantage.

Contrary to the expressed opinion of every other previous publication, I say that too much seasoning is preferable to too little, as your employer can correct you by saying there is too much of this or that, and you can soon get it to his taste; but while you fear over-seasoning you produce no flavour at all: by allowing each guest to season for himself, your sauce attains a diversity of flavours. The cook must season for the guest, not the guest for the cook.

I have always found great advantage in dressing the greatest part of my entrées on a thin roll of mashed potatoes; this has never been found objectionable, as it is so thin that it is imperceptible when covered with the sauces, and serves to prevent any entrées dressed in crown from being upset, before going on table, by the carelessness of the servant; For large removes, as turkey à la Nelson, &c., after forming the ship egg, bread-crumb, and set in a moderate oven to brown, fix in your croustade, and dish up; the potatoes may be eaten, but not the croustade, which is merely an embellishment. Borders may also be made of forcemeat, as for ris de veau, but gives much more trouble without being better; also of rice, by preparing it as for casserole au riz; it may be used as mashed potatoes. Make but few preserves, only those that are indispensable; you will have a continual enjoyment of earlier stock, as Nature closely watches our wants and liberally supplies our wishes. The real gourmet, though anxious to produce novelty, never attempts to over-force the produce of the various seasons.

Recipes.

Sauce à la Réform.

Cut up two middling-sized onions into thin slices and put them into a stewpan with two sprigs of parsley, two of thyme, two bay-leaves, two ounces of lean uncooked ham, half a clove of garlic, half a blade of mace, and an ounce of fresh butter; stir them ten minutes over a sharp fire, then add two tablespoonfuls of Tarragon vinegar, and one of Chili vinegar, boil it one minute; then add a pint of brown sauce, or sauce Espagnole, three tablespoonfuls of preserved tomates, and eight of consommé; place it over the fire until boiling, then put it at the corner, let it simmer ten minutes, skim it well, then place it again over the fire, keeping it stirred, and reduce until it adheres to the back of the spoon; then add a good tablespoonful of red currant jelly, and half do. of chopped mushrooms; season a little more if required with pepper and salt; stir it until the jelly is melted, then pass it through a tammie into another stewpan. When ready to serve, make it hot, and add the white of a hard-boiled egg cut into strips half an inch long, and thick in proportion, four white blanched mushrooms, one gherkin, two green Indian pickles, and half an ounce of cooked ham, or tongue, all cut in strips like the white of egg; do not let it boil afterwards. This sauce must be poured over whatever it is served with.

Mock Turtle Soup.

Put a quarter of a pound of butter at the bottom of a large stewpan, then cut up twenty pounds of knuckles of veal in large dice, with two pounds of uncooked ham; put them into a stewpan with six onions, two carrots, two heads of celery, twenty peppercorns, two blades of mace, two ounces of salt, and a pint of water; set it over a sharp fire, stirring it round occasionally until the bottom of the stewpan is covered with a light brown glaze, then lay in the half of a scalded calf's head, the cheek downwards, and fill up the stewpan with fourteen quarts of water; when boiling, place it at the corner of the fire, where let it simmer two hours and a half, keeping it well skimmed, but taking out the half head as soon as it becomes flexible to the touch, (which will take about the time the stock requires to simmer), remove all the bone and press the head flat between two dishes until cold, then pass the stock through a cloth into a basin, put a pound of butter into another stewpan, with four sprigs of winter savory, four of thyme, four of marjoram, four of basil, and four bay-leaves, fry them a few minutes in the butter, but do not let it change colour, then mix in a pound and a half of flour, stir it a few minutes over the fire until becoming slightly tinged, take it from the fire, stirring it round occasionally until partly cold, when pour in the stock, place it again upon the fire, keeping it stirred until it boils, then place it at the corner and let it simmer for half an hour, keeping it well skimmed, season with a little cayenne pepper, and more salt if required, and pass it through a tammie into a basin until wanted. When the calf's head is cold take off all the meat and fat, leaving nothing but the glutinous part, which cut into pieces an inch square; when ready to serve the soup put about three quarts (to each tureen), into a stewpan with twenty of the pieces of head and a glass of sherry, boil altogether fifteen minutes, when skim and serve very hot. This soup may likewise be thickened without a roux, as directed for brown sauce. Forcemeat and egg-balls were formerly served in this soup, the latter in imitation of turtles' eggs, but better imitations of bullets, and almost as indigestible; the omission of them will, I am certain, prove beneficial, for whether the stomach be strong or delicate it will not bear loading with ammunition of that description. The above soup requires to be a light brown colour, and for thickness it must adhere lightly to the back of the spoon.

Brill à la Billingsgate.

Broil the fish as for brill à la meùnière and dish it without a napkin; then have ready the following sauce;—blanch a pint of muscles, beard them and take out the black spots, then put two chopped eschalots in a stewpan with one ounce of butter, pass it over the fire five minutes, then add half a tablespoonful of flour, mix with it the liquor from the muscles, half a pint of milk, and half a gill of cream, a saltspoonful of salt, a little white pepper, and some grated nutmeg, boil it until rather thick, pass it through a tammie, then add two pats of butter, a few drops of essence of anchovy and the muscles; pour over the fish and serve very hot.

Filets de Soles à la Réform.

Fillet two soles, beat each fillet flat; have ready a dozen oysters, blanched and chopped, which mix with four tablespoonfuls of forcemeat of whitings and a little chopped eschalots; spread some on one fillet, then cover another over it, and so on till they are all done; put a little oil in a sauté-pan, with a little chopped eschalots, and a glass of white wine; lay your fillets in, season with a little pepper and salt, and put them in a moderate oven until tender; turn them over, and cut each into large diamonds, dress them round (points upwards) upon a dish, and put them in the hot closet; put ten tablespoonfuls of melted butter, and six do. of milk into the sauté-pan; place it over the fire, and when it boils pass it through a tammie; place it again on the fire, boil it a few minutes, add two pats of butter, and stir it till quite smooth; pour the sauce over the fillets, sprinkle some gherkins and ham (cut in strips half an inch long) over, and serve very hot.

Pike à l'Egyptienne.

Cut two onions, two turnips, one carrot, one head of celery, and one leek into slices; put them into a large stewpan with some parsley, thyme, bay-leaves, and a pint of port wine; then have your fish ready trussed, with its tail in its mouth; put it into the stewpan, with the vegetables; add three pints of broth, and set it on a slow fire to stew, with some live charcoal upon the lid; try, when done, by running the knife close in to the back bone; if the meat detaches easily, it is done; take it out, and place on a baking sheet; dry it with a cloth, then egg and bread-crumb it; put it in the oven, and salamander it a light brown; then put twenty tablespoonfuls of white sauce in a stewpan, with eight of milk, and reduce it five minutes; then add four gherkins, the whites of four hard-boiled eggs, and two truffles, cut in very small dice; finish with two tablespoonfuls of essence of anchovies, the juice of half a lemon, and four pats of butter; dress the fish without a napkin, and sauce over.

Turkey à la Nelson.

Make a croustade resembling the head of a ship; procure a very white nice young turkey, truss it as for boiling, leaving as much of the skin of the neck attached to the breast as possible, have ready the following stuffing: scrape an ounce of fat bacon (with a knife), put it into a stewpan, with a teaspoonful of chopped eschalots, pass five minutes over a moderate fire, then add twenty tablespoonfuls of white sauce, let it reduce till thick, add twenty small heads of mushrooms, six French truffles cut in slices, and twelve cockscombs; mix all well together over the fire, season with a teaspoonful of powdered sugar, half ditto of salt, and a little white pepper; finish with the yolks of two eggs, stir over the fire a minute to set the eggs, and lay it out on a dish to get cold, then detach the skin on the breast from the flesh without breaking, and force some of the stuffing under the skin; put the remainder in the interior of the breast, roast it in vegetables as described for fillet of beef, but just before it is done take away the paper and vegetables, and let it remain before the fire till of a fine gold colour. Fix the croustade at the head of the dish with a paste made of white of egg and flour, make a border of mashed potatoes round the dish, place the turkey in the centre, and have ready the following garniture: fillet three fowls, lard and braise the fillets, form the legs into little ducklings, prepare six slices of tongue of the size and shape of the fillets, and dress them round the turkey upon the mashed potatoes to form a ship. For the sauce put two glasses of Madeira wine in a stewpan, with a tablespoonful of Chili vinegar, two minced apples, a small bunch of parsley, a spoonful of chopped mushrooms, and half an ounce of glaze; let it boil a few minutes, add then tablespoonfuls of tomato sauce, a quart of brown sauce, and a pint of consommé, let it boil quickly until it adheres to the spoon, stirring it the whole time, finish with a tablespoonful of red currant jelly, pass it through a tammie into another stewpan, season with a little salt and pepper, boil it another minute, glaze the turkey, pour the sauce in the dish, glaze the pieces of tongue and serve.

Haunch of Venison.

May be decidedly called the second great pedestal; turtle soup and haunch of venison certainly being the two great pedestals, or Gog and Magog of English cookery. It is appreciated from the independent citizen to the throne; for where is there a citizen of taste, a man of wealth, or a gourmet, who does not pay due homage to this delicious and recherché joint, which ever has and ever will be in vogue; but even after all that nature has done in point of flavour, should it fall into the hands of some inexperienced person to dress, and be too much done, its appearance and flavour would be entirely spoilt, its delicious and delicate fat melted, and the gravy lost; of the two it would be preferred underdone, but that is very bad and hardly excusable, when it requires nothing but attention to serve this glorious dish in perfection.

A good haunch of venison weighing from about twenty to twenty-five pounds will take from three to four hours roasting before a good solid fire; trim the haunch by cutting off part of the knuckle and sawing off the chine bone, fold the flap over, then envelope it in a flour and water paste rather stiff, and an inch thick, tie it up in strong paper, four sheets in thickness, place it in your cradle spit so that it will turn quite even, place it at first very close to the fire until the paste is well crusted, pouring a few ladlefuls of hot dripping over occasionally to prevent the paper catching fire, then put it rather further from the fire, which must be quite clear, solid, and have sufficient frontage to throw the same heat on every part of the venison; when it has roasted the above time take it up, remove it from the paste and paper, run a thin skewer into the thickest part to ascertain if done, if it resists the skewer it is not done, and must be tied up and put down again, but if the fire is good that time will sufficiently cook it, glaze the top well, salamander until a little brown, put a frill upon the knuckle, and serve very hot with plenty of plain boiled French beans separate.

Chartreuse de Perdreaux.

Truss two nice partridges with the legs turned inside, stick about ten small pieces of fat bacon two inches in length and the size of a quill through the breasts lengthwise, then cut two nice savoy cabbages in quarters, and boil five minutes, throw them into plenty of cold water; when cold lay them on a sieve, squeeze quite dry with a cloth, season well with pepper and salt, cut out the stalk, and put them into a stewpan, with two onions, three cloves, a bunch of parsley, thyme, and bay-leaves, one carrot, and three quarters of a pound of streaky bacon; cover with a quart of white stock, and let stew an hour or more, till the stock has reduced to a thin glaze; take it off the fire, roast your partridges, take out the skewers and string, bury them in the stewed cabbage whilst hot, and let them remain till wanted; then butter a large plain oval mould, paper it, and again butter the paper; have ready peeled sixty small button onions, which stew in a little white stock and sugar till tender, cut about a hundred pieces of carrots, half an inch in length, and the thickness of a large quill; stew them in the same manner as the onions, have also cut of the same size the same quantity of turnips (do not stew them too much or they would be useless), place a row of onions round the bottom of the mould, then above them a row of carrots, slantwise, but one touching the other, then a row of the turnips, then carrots, proceeding in like manner till you reach the top; drain the cabbage, and squeeze it till it is somewhat firm, put some of it at the bottom of the mould an inch in thickness, and line the sides not quite so thick, put the partridges in the centre with slices of the bacon, finish filling up with the cabbage, place in a stewpan of water over the fire to get hot, but do not let the water get into it; when ready to serve turn out on your dish, and take the paper carefully from it; have ready the following sauce: put the stock from the vegetables and a little of the stock from the cabbage into a stewpan, add a quart of brown sauce, boil to the consistence of demi-glace, add a little sugar, sauce carefully all over, and serve.

Escalopes de Filet de Bœuf à la Reform.

Take out the fillet from beneath a rump of beef, take off all the fat, and cut it into slices (lengthwise) half an inch in thickness, beat them well with the cutlet-bat, which previously dip in water, then cut them into ten or twelve escalopes, the size and shape of fillets of chickens, lay each piece upon the table, season with pepper, salt, and a little chopped eschalots, but two very thin slices of fat bacon to each escalope of beef, trim the bacon to the same size and shape, egg over the escalopes of beef, and stick a piece of the bacon upon each side of them, then egg all over and throw them into a dish of bread-crumbs mixed with chopped lean cooked ham; take them out, beat lightly with your knife, put a little oil in a sauté-pan, place it over a moderate fire, when quite hot put in your escalopes, fry a nice colour, and dress in crown upon a thin border of mashed potatoes, glaze nicely; sauce over with a sauce reforme and serve.

Cotelettes de Mouton à la Reform.

Chop a quarter of a pound of lean cooked ham very fine, and mix it with the same quantity of bread-crumbs, then have ten very nice cotelettes, lay them flat on your table, season lightly with pepper and salt, egg over with a paste-brush, and throw them into the ham and bread-crumbs, then beat them lightly with a knife, put ten spoonfuls of oil in a sauté-pan, place it over the fire, and when quite hot lay in the cotelettes, fry nearly ten minutes (over a moderate fire) of a light brown colour; to ascertain when done, press your knife upon the thick part, if quite done it will feel rather firm; possibly they may not all be done at one time, so take out those that are ready first and lay them on a cloth till the others are done; as they require to be cooked with the gravy in them, dress upon a thin border of mashed potatoes in a crown, with the bones pointing outwards, sauce over with a pint of the sauce reform and serve. If for a large dinner you may possibly be obliged to cook the cotelettes half an hour before, in which case they must be very underdone, and laid in a clean sauté-pan, with two or three spoonfuls of thin glaze; keep them in the hot closet, moistening them occasionally with the glaze (with a paste-brush) until ready to serve; the same remark applies to every description of cotelettes.

Filets de Lièvre sauce reforme.

Procure three good-sized but young hares, when skinned lay them on a table and pass a knife down the back-bone, from the shoulder to the leg, keeping it close to the ribs till you have extracted the fillet, when done lay the fillets on a board the skin side downwards, and with a thin kife cut off the whole of the skin, by pressing your hand upon the fillet and drawing the knife along the thin end to the thick; cut each fillet in halves, beat them lightly, trim them of a nice shape, and lard them neatly, then cover the bottom of a stewpan with thin slices of fat bacon, lay the fillets over, add three onions in slices with a bunch of parsley, a blade of mace, and a couple of cloves, put in a little broth, but not to cover them, place the lid on the stewpan and place them in a moderate oven till tender, glaze and salamander a nice colour, take them out, drain them a minute on a cloth, trim nicely, and dress them in crown on a border of mashed potatoes, and serve with a sauce reforme over, previously placing a thin piece of toasted bread the same size as the fillets between each.

Of the Boar's Head à l'Antique.

Procure a head with as much of the neck attached to it as possible, singe it well, holding it over a charcoal fire, and keeping it moved, then wipe it with a cloth, scrape well with a knife without scratching the skin, and place it on a cloth upon its skull, open it with your knife from one end to the other, and bone it very carefully without piercing the skin, leaving no flesh whatever upon the bones, bone the two necks of the boar, which cut into long fillets two inches square, place the head in a salting-tub, over which put ten pounds of salt, one of brown sugar, ten bay-leaves, half an ounce of peppercorns, a quarter ditto of cloves, six blades of mace, eight minced onions, twenty sprigs of thyme, ten ditto of winter savoury, and two sliced carrots; mix all well together and leave it eight or ten days, (rubbing the head every other day,) until well salted, then take it out, dry it well upon a cloth, lay the head straight before you, skin side downwards, have ready ten pounds of forcemeat (but using the flesh of the wild boar instead of veal,) with which cover the interior of the head an inch in thickness at the thinnest parts, roll the fillets cut from the neck in pieces of the rind, (both salted with the head and dried upon a cloth,) place a layer of them lengthwise in the head, with a long piece of fat bacon half an inch square between each, sprinkle a little chopped eschalots, pepper, salt, and grated nutmeg over, and place here and there about a pound of the best preserved truffles, with one of very green pistachios blanched and skinned, and continue filling with forcemeat and the other ingredients until you have used the whole, finishing by covering forcemeat over; join the two cheeks together with the above in the interior, sew it up with packthread giving it the shape of the head as much as possible and fold it in one or two large thin cloths leaving the ears out and upright; braise as follows: put half a pound of butter in a large braising-pan or stock-pot, over which put fifteen pounds of trimmings of pork or knuckles of veal, eight onions, two carrots, four turnips, eight bay-leaves, a tablespoonful of peppercorns, twelve cloves, ten sprigs of thyme, ten of marjoram, four blades of mace, a bottle of bucellas wine, and four calves' feet, place it upon a sharp fire stirring it occasionally until the bottom is covered with a clearish glaze, then add six gallons of water and a pound of salt, when boiling draw it to the corner of the stove, skim, and put in the head the ears uppermost and let simmer seven or eight hours, perhaps more, according to the size and age of the boar, but the better plan would be to try it with a trussing-needle; if tender it is done; skim the stock, in which leave the head until half cold, when take it out, partly undo the cloths, and tie it again tighter if possible, and press it in a cover or upon a baking sheet with three flat pieces of wood, one at each side with a weight against them, and one upon the top between the ears, on which lace a fourteen pounds weight, let it remain all night until quite cold, when take it out of the cloths, detach the thread it was sewn up with, cut a piece an inch in thickness from behind the ears, (from which part it must be carved in as thin slices as possible,) it will have a marbled appearance, trim the head a little, setting the ears in a proper position, glaze it with a brownish glaze, form the eyes with a little lard and round pieces of truffles, and the tusks with pâté d'office, baking them, have some very fresh tulips and roses, which stick tastefully in the ears and some around, but leaving space to carve, garnish boldly with croutons aspic made from the stock clarified.

Salade de Grouse à la Soyer.

Make a very thin border of fresh butter upon a convenient-sized dish, upon which stand a very elevated border of hard-boiled eggs, (by cutting a piece off the bottoms when quite cold and cutting each one into four lengthwise,) fill the centre with some nice fresh salad, and ornament the eggs with fillets of anchovies, beetroot, gherkins, &c., according to taste; you have previously roasted three grouse rather underdone; when quite cold cut them into neat pieces, that is, into legs, wings, part of the backs, and each breast into six slices, then have ready the following sauce: put two tablespoonfuls of finely chopped eschalots in a basin, with two tablespoonfuls of powdered sugar, the yolks of two eggs, two tablespoonfuls of chopped tarragon and chervil, a saltspoonful of white pepper, and two of salt, with which mix by degrees twelve tablespoonfuls of salad oil and three of Chili vinegar; mix well together and place it upon the ice; when ready to serve whip half a pint of cream rather stiff, which add to the sauce, pour a little over the salad, upon which lay some of the worst pieces of grouse, over which put more sauce, proceeding in like manner to the top, dressing them pyramidically. When it is for the flanc of a large dinner I only use the fillets, roasting four or five grouse instead of three, and when you have dressed three parts of the pieces of grouse upon the salad, build a second row of eggs upon it, having formed a level with the pieces for that purpose, and terminate exactly as the design represents. I must observe that the salad is better adapted for gentlemen than ladies, though if less eschalot were used it might also meet their approbation.*

Gateau Britannique à l'Amiral.

Make a sponge-cake of twenty eggs, have a tin mould in the shape of a vessel, which paper well at the sides, to prevent the mixture running over whilst baking (the mould requires to be eighteen inches in length, six in breadth, and high in proportion); butter and lightly flour the interior of the mould, into which pour the mixture, which bake an hour and a half in a moderate oven (this cake requires to be baked a day or two before using); mask the exterior which chocolate iceing to imitate the colour of a ship, when quite dry partly empty the interior, leaving a piece across in the centre, to fix the mast upon, which you have made of pâte d'office, as also the ladders, rigging, and guns, by rolling pieces of the paste to the thickness required with the hands, cutting them to the

---

* The first time I served a salad of the above description after inventing it was in a dinner which I dressed for some noblemen and gentlemen who had made a wager as to which could send the best dinner, myself or the artiste at a celebrated establishment in Paris, where they had previously dined; my first course being full of novelty, gained the approbation of the whole party, but the salad created such an unexpected effect that I was sent for, and had the honour of sitting at the table for an hour with them and over several rosades of exquisite Laffitte; the salad was christened à la Soyer by General Sir Alexander Duff, who presided over the noble party.

lengths required, and baking them a light colour in a moderate oven; mask the guns with chocolate iceing, made rather darker than for the cake, and form the muzzles with small rings of puff paste, place them judiciously at the sides, as also the mast and rigging at their respective places, place the vessel upon a dish, laying rather upon one side, lay rolls of gelée à la bacchante round, over which lay thin slices of the same to form waves, make the sails of wafer or rice-paper, fix them to the mast as if filled with wind, upon the side the vessel is laying on, have also a flag made of the same material, painted with a little water-colour, which place at the stern; well soak the interior with wine and brandy, mixed with apricot marmalade, just before serving, and when ready fill with a delicate vanilla ice; you have previously formed some ropes of spun sugar, which affix to the rigging at the moment of serving.

This dish has a pleasing effect, and, unlike many ornamental dishes, the whole of it is eatable. It may be rather difficult for many, but with a few trials, aided by the above directions, I flatter myself it may be easily accomplished, but of course a great deal depends upon the taste of the person employed, who, if they could not accomplish one thing, would resort to another, and succeed in making a very handsome dish. Should you have no mould to bake the cake in, bake it in something as near as you can to the size, and afterwards shape it with a knife; and, again, should it be inconvenient to make the green jelly for garnishing, any other description of white clear jelly may be used. The remains and trimmings are very good made into cabinet pudding.

Hure de Sanglier glacé en surprise.

Or mock boar's head; this dish, although more simple than the last, is no less pleasing. Make a sponge-cake of thirty eggs, which bake (in an oval baking-dish or common tin dish-cover) nearly two hours; the cake requires to be ten inches in thickness at one end, and about six at the other (which may be accomplished by tilting the dish slightly upon one end to bake the cake); the next day cut it into the shape of a dressed boar's head with a knife, then carefully take out the interior to within an inch of the surface, in as large pieces as possible, put the pieces back again to keep the cake in its proper shape, turn it over upon the bottom of a large dish, and mask it all over with a chocolate iceing as near as possible to the colour of the real boar's head, form the eyes with white iceing, placing a dried cherry in the centre, and forming the eyelashes with thin fillets of pistachios, make the tusks of gum paste or pâte d'office, and the ears of puff paste by working it a little with the hands, giving them their shape, and baking them upon two round cutters of a corresponding size, fix them with a stiffish paste made of flour and white of eggs, when done, upon the head, and mask them also with chocolate iceing; fix in the tusks, and when well dried and ready to serve empty the interior, which soak with a little brandy, and fill with a lemon-cream ice in which you have introduced four glasses of curaçoa, turn it over upon a silver dish, glaze over with currant jelly, melted and mixed with a little wine, and garnish with gelée au citron made reddish with a little cochineal, to give it the colour of a brown aspic, form some bold design upon the top (between the eyes) with it in croutons, and the remainder chopped and also in croutons around.

Cérito's Sultane Sylphe à la Fille de l'Orage.

Procure a half oval-pointed mould about fifteen inches in height, ten inches by eight in diameter at the bottom, and the size of a five-shilling piece at the top, which bury to the rim in ice with which you have mixed plenty of salt, line the interior with a sheet of white paper, laying it in closely to fit the mould, have ready a pint of cream mixed rather stiffly, with which you have mixed a meringue mixture of three eggs, spread it all over the interior of the mould to about an inch in thickness, place a cover over the mould made to fit tight, over which place some ice, and leave it one hour, when it will be quite frozen, take off the lid, have ready a nice cherry or strawberry cream ice, place a little at the bottom of the mould, upon which lay a few fresh strawberries, then more ice, proceeding thus until quite full, place the cover again over, fixing it tight, bury it in ice and salt, and leave it an hour, or till wanted, when dip it into very lukewarm water, turn it out upon your dish, take off the paper, have ready a silver atelette, upon which you have placed some fine fresh fruit, that is, a peach with a bunch of fine black grapes resting over, and a few red currants or strawberries beneath, which stick into the top, have ready some finely-spun sugar, which twine round lightly like rolls of gauze, not, however, covering the whole of it, and at the moment of serving lay a fine bunch of black grapes upon each side on vine-leaves; have some very light gelée de Dantzic chopped finely, with which garnish round, sprinkling some over the grapes, but not too heavy, and serve as quickly as possible. As soon as it is turned out of the mould you had better set the dish upon the ice and salt you took it from (pouring off all the water) whilst ornamenting, and it would be better to make a border of pâte d'office upon your dish as in the last, but smaller, to prevent it sliding about when carried to table, which would upset the garniture.

Diner Lucullusian à la Sampayo.

I beg to present to my Readers a copy of the Bill-of-fare of the most recherché dinner I ever dressed, which the liberality and epicurean taste of the gentleman who gave it, to a select party of connoiseurs, enabled me to procure; he wishing me to get him a first-rate dinner, and spare no expense in procuring the most novel, luxurious, and rare edibles to be obtained at this extravagant season of the year; I, therefore, much to his satisfaction, placed before him and his guests the following:

"REFORM CLUB.

9 *Mai*, 1846.   *Diner pour* 10 *Personnes.*
Potage à la Comte de Paris.
Do. à la purée d'Asperges.

DEUX POISSONS.

Saumon de Severne   Rougets gratinés
à la Mazarin.   à la Montesquieu.

DEUX RELEVES.

Le Chapon farci de Foie gras à la Nelson.
Saddleback d'Agneau de Maison à la Sévigné.

QUATRE HORS-D'ŒUVRES A LA FRANCAISE.

Les Olives farcies.   Salade d'Anchois historiée.
Thon mariné à l'Italienne.   Sardines à l'Huile de Noisette.

QUATRE ENTREES.

Rissolettes à la Pompadour.

Sauté de Filets de Volaille à l'Ambassadrice.
Petites Croustades de Beurre aux Laitances de
Maquereaux.
Côtelettes de Mouton Galloise à la Réforme.
Turban de Ris de Veau purée de Con-
combres.

Rissolettes à la Pompadour.

DEUX RÔTS.

Les grosses Asperges vertes, sauce à la Crème.

Les Dotrelles aux Feuilles de Vigne.
Le Buisson d'Ecrevisse Pagodatique, au Vin
de Champagne à la Sampayo.

La Gelée de Dantzic
aux Fruits Prin-
taniers.
Les Petits Pois nouveaux
à l'Anglo-Français.
Les grosses Truffes
à l'Essence de Madère.

Les Croquantes
d'Amandes Pralinées aux
Abricots.
Le Miroton de Homard
aux Œufs de Pluviers.
La Crème mousseuse au
Curaçao.

Les grosses Asperges vertes, sauce à la Crème.

DEUX RELEVES.

La Hûre de Sanglier demi-glacée,
garnie de Champignons en surprise.
Les Diablotins au Fromage de Windsor."

I had also proposed the following dish to the party, which was accepted, but which I was unable to obtain from Paris on account of a change in the weather preventing their arrival, the articles being two dozen of ortolans; having already procured twelve of the largest and finest truffles I could obtain, it was my intention to have dug a hole in each, into which I should have placed one of the birds, and covered each with a piece of lamb's or calf's caul, then to have braised them half an hour in good stock made from fowl and veal, with half a pint of Lachryma Christi added; then to have drained them upon a cloth, placed a border of poached forcemeat upon the dish, built the truffles in pyramid, made a purée with the truffle dug from the interior, using the stock reduced to a demi-glace and poured over, roasted the twelve remaining ortolans before a sharp fire, with which I should have garnished the whole round, and served very hot.

(NOTE. The trade people received their orders a week previous to the dinner. The finest mullets I ever saw, as well as the Severn salmon, were obtained at Grove's, in Bond Street; the remainder of the fish was from Jay's, Hungerford Market. At seven o'clock the live Severn salmon was brought to me, it having just arrived direct from Gloucester, and was boiled immediately, being just ten minutes before the dinner was placed upon the table, and was eaten in its greatest possible perfection. The finest of the poultry came from Bailey's, Davis Street, Grosvenor Square, and Townsend's, Charles Street, Haymarket. The foies gras and some very fine fresh French truffles came from Morel's; the hors-d'-œuvres, from Edges and Butler's, Regent Street. The saddleback of lamb came from Newland's, Air Street, Piccadilly, the Welsh mutton from Slater's, and the young green peas and a very expensive dessert came from Solomon's, Covent Garden. My being so minute in mentioning the name of the above tradespeople is not to advertise their fame in their different specialities, as that I believe they have already acquired, but merely to prove the trouble a real gourmet will take to furnish his table, Mr. S. having called many times upon several of them himself, previous to this party taking place, to ascertain what his dinner was to be composed of. The most expensive dishes were the mullets, the salmon, poulardes à la Nelson, and, above all, the crawfish which, when dressed, cost upwards of seven guineas.)

Dialogue Culinaire

Entre LORD M. H. et A. SOYER.

S. Vous avez parfaitement raison, Mylord; le titre de gourmet n'appartient qu'à celui qui mange avec art, avec science, avec ordre, et même avec beaucoup d'ordre.

Lord M. Le gourmand n'est jamais gourmet; l'un mange sans déguster, l'autre déguste en mangeant.

S. L'homme fier et hautain, Mylord, s'occupe de son diner par besoin; l'homme du monde, épicure profond, s'en occupe avec plaisir.

Lord M. Il est certain que l'on ne saurait donner trop d'attention à la rigide exécution et à l'ordre intelligent d'un diner. Le diner étant de chaque jour, de chaque saison, de chaque siècle, est non seulement la seule mode héréditaire, mais aussi l'âme de la sociabilité; lisez l'histoire, et vous y verrez que de tous les temps, et chez tous les peuples, le bien qui s'est fait, et quelquefois le mal, fut toujours précédé ou suivi d'un copieux diner.

S. Rien, n'est plus vrai, Mylord, que de tous les plaisirs de la vie qui nous sont légués en ce monde, celui de la table est le seul auquel les rênes du char de la vie n'échappent qu'à regret; et souvent, en ami fidèle, ne les lâche qu'aux abords du tombeau; tandis que tous les autres s'épanouissent frivolement, comme à la suite d'un beau printemps, et, en nous délaissant, couvrent nos fronts radieux du givre des ans.

Lord M. Il est positif que déguster est une faculté de tout âge; un vieillard de cent six ans, que j'ai beaucoup connu, dégustait parfaitement alors.

S. Nos cent dégustateurs demandent de continuelles études, et réclament, sans cesse, un continuel changement.

Lord M. Le plus bel esprit manquerait d'éloquence s'il négligeait par trop l'ordre de ses repas.

S. C'est ce qui nous prouve, Mylord, que nos plus agréables sensations dépendent non seulement de la nature, mais aussi du soin que nous donnons à notre personne.

Lord M. Oui, car plus l'âme est sensible, plus la dégustation est féconde. Les sensations dégustatives opèrent avec autant d'activité sur le palais que le charme de la mélodie le fait sur l'ouie; par example, l'homme dans un cas de folie, peut bien éprouver le besoin de manger, mais l'action enchanteresse de la dégustation lui est aussi interdite que la raison.

S. Votre argument sur ce point est extrêmement juste, Mylord. N'êtes-vous pas aussi de mon avis, que rien ne dispose mieux l'esprit humain à des transactions amicales, qu'un diner bien conçu et artistement préparé.

Lord M. C'est ce qui m'a toujours fait dire qu'un bon cuisinier est aussi utile qu'un savant conseiller.

S. Je me suis toujours aperçu, Mylord, que le palais le plus fin était le plus difficile à plaire, mais aussi le plus juste à récompenser.

Lord M. Le choix des vins est de haute importance dans l'ordre d'un diner; au vin fin, léger et généreux protège le cuisinier et devient le bienfaiteur du convive.

S. Permettez-moi de vous faire observer, Mylord, qu'une réunion gastronomique sans dames est à mes yeux un parterre sans fleurs, l'océan sans flots, une flotte maritime sans voiles.

Lord M. Certes, de telles réunions sont le berceau des bonnes mœurs et de la jovialité, comme la débauche est le tombeau de la moralité.

REFORM CLUB, MAY 14, 1846.

Soyer, after the first performance of his ballet

Chef to the Poor
The Modern Housewife
A Shilling Cookery for the People

It is hard not to love a man as open-hearted and -handed as Alexis Soyer. He could, what with his salary, his books, his inventions and other sidelines, have been very wealthy. Yet he never was. He gave and lent his money as extravagantly as he did everything else, both to deserving charitable causes and to undeserving private entrepreneurs. Even when plainly cheated, he remained generous and gracious. On one occasion, a French conjuror named Philippe persuaded him to dabble in railway shares, with predictably disastrous results. Soyer lost £1000 and Philippe fled, leaving his debts unpaid. Soyer immediately sent off a most touching letter which conveys, better than anything else could do, the essential goodness of his nature:

'My Dear and Good Philippe,—You are a naughty fellow. You came to see me, not finding me at home, you ought to have written; but believe me, my good friend, notwithstanding the misfortune weighing heavily upon us— more particularly upon me, because I never had a wish to speculate in anything, being satisfied with the produce of my humble talent, whilst, on the other hand, you are a sublime genius, perhaps a little too exalted, leading you to heavenly dreams, but that time has not yet arrived—I hope, however, that we shall have to live and love each other for a long time to come on this earth. N'importe what may happen, be always Philippe; and I swear, on my honour, that Soyer shall always remain Soyer. Do not lose your courage my good friend, you and I are one; together we shall form a colossus, capable, in a short time, to overthrow a thousand adversities, and we shall do it, my devoted and dear friend.

'London is full of people, advertise well, and Christmas will put us on our legs again. Tell me, as a true friend, your tribulations; I shall tell you mine, which are in proportion greater than yours, my situation being all I possess, and even compromised. But no trees are without branches, and one remains which is not yet broken, my celebrated friend: the spring will produce flowers, the fruits of which we shall gather . . .

'Too happy to see, admire, and love you, more than ever, believe me, your most sincere, Soyer.'

Soyer himself lived in surprisingly modest conditions. Unable to bear the loneliness of his married home without Emma, he had moved in with his stepfather-in-law Simonau. The artist had by now completely forgotten his reservations about the chef's suitability as a son-in-law, and the pair had grown very fond of each other. Their rooms were in Leicester Square and, though comfortable enough for two widowers, were far from grand. It was here that they received visitors, and Simonau had his studio.

One element conspicuously absent from the flat was a modern and well-equipped kitchen. Soyer had, in an appendix to *The Gastronomic Regenerator*, described in great detail his 'Kitchen at Home', with the intention of providing a contrast to the magnificence of the Reform kitchens. In imagination he saw it as the perfect model of efficiency and comfort—and imaginary is what it remained. He planned one day to have such a kitchen fitted in the flat, but somehow it never got done. Many readers, however, were intrigued by the idea of this middle-class culinary paradise. One Irishwoman in particular was determined that she should see Soyer's 'Kitchen at Home' for herself, and worked out a stratagem for discovering where the great chef lived. She made an appointment with Simonau to have her portrait painted, and presented herself at the studio, little knowing that it was Soyer's address as well.

The lady's surprise was such that she stood still for a moment, and, forcing a smile on her countenance, said—'Oh, I beg your pardon, sir, for coming at such an unseasonable hour; but living a little distance out of town, I thought that if I had a first sitting this morning, I could transact some other business afterwards, and return home early.'

The artist, who never took portraits unless he had previous notice, said—'I am very sorry, madame; but if you were to give me twenty guineas for a sitting today, you could not have one.'

'Oh, well then, any other day will do quite as well. What is your charge?'

'Twenty guineas, madame.'

'Very well, I then will come this day week; will that suit you?'

'Certainly, madame.'

'Tell me, are all these paintings your work?'

'Oh no, madame, many of these are my pupil's, the late Madame Soyer.'

'Indeed; but how is it that M. Soyer leaves them here? I should say that they would ornament his private residence beautifully.'

'I beg your pardon, madame, but M. Soyer lives here with me.'

'You don't say so?' taking a view all round.

'Yes, I assure you.' The artist, who knew that the time was going fast, and that his broth ought to be on the fire, said—'Excuse me a moment, madame; but I must attend to a little culinary business.'

Off he goes with the mutton, the servant following him with the vegetables, etc.; but, to his surprise, he found the lady at his elbow, in a back-room on the same floor, where the servant slept, and where all the drudgery of cleaning, washing, and cooking was done; in fact, everything was in confusion. The artist, not at all dismayed at the inquisitiveness of the lady, said—

'You see, madame, we are very domesticated; we do everything at home; besides, we foreigners cannot live without good soup and some relishing stews: these are as much the half of our lives, as roast beef and plum-pudding are to the English.'

'Then do you mean that M. Soyer is going to dine with you?'

'Indeed, madame, he does not make it a rule; but I can assure you that he enjoys what I cook, particularly my potage.'

'Do you expect him?'

'No; but he may pop in, for we expect the admirable Mademoiselle Cerito to give her last sitting, and probably he will come.'

The word was hardly out of his mouth before M. Soyer entered. The lady, blushing, and being rather of a prepossessing appearance, soon attracted Soyer's attention, who at once apologized for his intrusion, and said—'I am not aware what is your business with my old friend Simonau; but he is as great an artist in making soup as he is a painter, therefore you are in very good hands.' The lady at once made known her business with M. Simonau, and said that she was really much gratified with the unexpected interview with so great an artist at M. Soyer, and would seize this opportunity to ask permission to see his *kitchen at home*.

M. Soyer, whose presence of mind seldom forsook him, said—'It would afford me great pleasure, madame, to satisfy your curiosity; but my kitchen at home *is out of town*, and, as I am unfortunately a bachelor, I do not see a chance of granting your request.'

M. Simonau, who was listening to the conversation, said—'*Sacresti*, madame, I forgot to tell you we had a country-box.'

However, the lady had her portrait taken, and became one of M. Soyer's subscribers to all his works, but never had the gratification of seeing his *kitchen at home*.

Memoirs of Soyer by Volant & Warren

By the beginning of 1847 Soyer had been at the Reform for a decade. His culinary inventiveness and sublime skills were at their height; he was courted by dukes and princes; his writings and his ebullient exploits had made him a household name. Yet he was restless. A new challenge was needed, and he found it in the streets of London. The Great Reform Bill, the Poor Law Report of 1834 and the repeal of the Corn Laws in 1846 had done little to relieve the poverty and wretchedness of London's working classes. Soyer was already giving private lessons in the making of nourishing and cheap meals for the starving, and now he determined that something should be done on a grander scale. In a letter to the *Times* he outlined a proposal for a model soup kitchen in London, and opened the subscription list with £30 from his own pocket. Furthermore, he drew up plans for a new kind of soup-boiler which might feed upwards of twenty-thousand people.

This was just a start. In Ireland, the plight of the poor was even more grim, due to the potato blight which had ruined the crops of 1845 and 1846. Nearly a million people died over a five-year period. Soyer redoubled his efforts, and in a second, lengthy, letter to the *Times* he gave details of his newly-devised receipts for soup:

'M. SOYER'S KITCHEN AND SOUP FOR THE POOR.

'To the Editor.

'Sir,—In returning my most sincere thanks for the benevolent intentions which prompted you to publish so speedily my letter of the 10th inst., relating to my new kitchen and soup for the poor, in your valuable journal, I beg your insertion of the two following receipts, which, if closely followed, would confer an immediate benefit, not only on the poor, and various charitable institutions, but also on the labouring population of the United Kingdom. I much regret the delay that has taken place since the publication of my former letter, which has unavoidably occurred, the time being consumed in experiments which I have made with various kinds of farinaccous ingredients, produced and imported into this country; and likewise with some of the immense varieties of vegetables, cultivated with so much success in this favoured soil; but which, generally speaking, are not sufficiently appreciated, or used to the greatest advantage by the industrious classes.

'My intention is, with your kind permission, not only to publish the receipt for one kind of soup, but for five or six, the whole, however, being made upon the same principle as the first, to save any confusion in the making, hoping they may prove advantageous, by giving a change in food, which acts as generously on the digestive organs as a change of air does on the convalescent, and likewise to prevent the rise in price of any particular articles; for should the soup be approved of, and become a chief article of consumption for a certain time, such a receipt would be quite useless in some parts of the country where the ingredients could not be obtained; my sincere devotion to this important cause being to take every possible advantage of every kind of nutritious substances, animal and vegetable, and fish, and to convert them, by study and judgment, into a wholesome and cheap aliment for the millions.

'Several hundreds of letters I have already received upon the subject have induced me to give immediate publicity to the two following receipts, which I consider quite correct. Having thus stated my impressions upon this all-important subject, I now give you the result of my first economical study to produce a cheap and wholesome soup:–

'The Receipt for Soup No. 1.

'I first put one ounce of dripping into a sauce-pan (capable of holding two gallons of water), with a quarter of a pound of leg of beef without bones, cut into square pieces about half an inch, and two middle-sized onions, peeled and sliced. I then set the saucepan over a coal fire, and stirred the contents round for a few minutes with a wooden (or iron) spoon until fried lightly brown. I had then ready washed the peeling of two turnips, fifteen green leaves or tops of celery, and the green part of two leeks (the whole of which, I must observe, are always thrown away). Having cut the above vegetables into small pieces, I threw them into the saucepan with the other ingredients, stirring them occasionally over the fire for another ten minutes; then added half a pound of common flour (any farinaceous substance would do), and half a pound of pearl barley, mixing all well together. I then added two gallons of water, seasoned with three ounces of salt, and a quarter of an ounce of brown sugar, stirred occasionally until boiling, and allowed it to simmer very gently for three hours, at the end of which time I found the barley perfectly tender. The above soup has been tasted by numerous noblemen, members of Parliament, and several ladies, who have lately visited my kitchen department, and who have considered it very good and nourishing.

The cost, at full price, was as follows—

Quarter of a pound of leg of beef, at 4*d*. per lb.	1*d*.
Two ounces of dripping-fat, at 4*d*. per lb.	0½
Two onions and other vegetables	1*d*.
Half a pound of flour, seconds, at 1½*d*. per lb.	0¾
Half a pound of pearl barley, at 3*d*. per lb.	1½

Three ounces of salt, with half an ounce of brown sugar 0¼
Fuel 1
Two gallons of water 0

6*d.*

'This soup will keep several days, when made as above described.

'The above expenses make it come to ¾*d.* per quart in London; but, as almost everything can be had at much less cost in the country, the price of this soup will be still more reduced. In that case a little additional meat might be used; and by giving away a small portion of bread or biscuit, better support would be given to the poor at a trifling cost, and no one, it is to be hoped, hereafter, would hear of the dreadful calamity of starvation.

'The Receipt for the Soup No. 2.

'This can be made cheaper, and in less time. Proceed as Receipt No. 1 explains (as regards the fat, meat, onions, and the other vegetables), but add one quart of water upon the whole, which you let boil twenty minutes, stirring now and then to prevent burning; or else, if convenient, set it by the side of the fire, and add one pound of maize, mix well together, and fill the stew-pan with six quarts of water; season as above; let it simmer one hour, skim lightly, and it is then ready for use.

'If a large quantity is to be made—say, 100 gallons—any kind of vessels now in use, such as copper or cast-iron, will do; have ready a spatula, or a piece of board the shape of a cricket-bat, about six inches wide, tapering towards the top as a handle (which must be from one foot and a-half to two feet above the surface of the vessel), to stir with. The fire being well lighted, take 12lb. of solid meat, or 18lb. with the bones (legs or clods of beef, with a portion of cow-heels, are excellent for the purpose; but any kind of edible meat, from beef to doe venison, would do), cut it in pieces about one inch square, put 3½lb. of fat. In case there should be difficulties to procure the fat, put in 1 gallon of water instead; then you have ready 12lb. of onions, lightly peeled and cut in slices, and 24lb. of vegetables of any kind, mixed (such as carrots, parsnips, turnips, leeks, celery, cabbages, savoys, sorel, spinach, mangel-wurzle, Swedes, and Jerusalem artichokes, all cut in a slanting direction, which facilitates greatly the cooking), with the meat in the copper left stewing about one hour, stirring the whole contents until the moisture is nearly gone, which will depend entirely on the fire; then add enough water to cover the whole, which you will let boil ten minutes; then add 25lb. of flour, and mix it well together; add 30lb. of either barley or rice, season with 9lb. of salt, and 3lb. of brown sugar; afterwards fill the copper with water, and boil the whole contents for two hours or more, until the barley or rice is quite tender; the soup is then ready for use.

'In case either the barley or rice did not produce the thickness required (as those ingredients may differ in quality), then add, if too thin, a few pounds of flour or oatmeal, previously mixed with cold water, to make it into a liquid paste, and pour it in when boiling, about twenty minutes before serving it out. But the proper thickness is easily ascertained when the soup hangs lightly on the back of the spatula or ladle.

'One hundred gallons of this soup will cost under £1. Respecting my plan of kitchens for the poor, I am happy to inform you, that my subscription, which is only of a few days' date, has met with the greatest encouragement by benevolent contributors, the list of whom will shortly be published. I have been able, already, to begin one of those kitchens on a small scale, where from 40 to 50 gallons of soup can be easily made, and quickly distributed to 200 or 300 poor, in an ordinary-sized London house. As soon as it is in practice, this simple plan will be made public through the Press; therefore any private application becomes unnecessary, as it would prevent my carrying the plan into effect.

'A correct drawing of my large plan for making and supplying 20,000 persons, is also in a very forward state.

'With high consideration, I have the honour to be, sir, your very obliged and humble servant,

'Reform Club, Feb. 17th.'   'A. Soyer.

The public response was overwhelming. Some praised the chef for his great service to humanity; others complained that his receipts, which recommended unheard-of measures such as the use of vegetable peelings, would produce not 'soup for the poor' but 'poor soup' with no goodness in it. All the same, Soyer was immediately invited by the Government to travel to Dublin and set up his first model soup-kitchen. The experiment was a huge success. Soyer kept an exact record, and was able to show that, in less than five months, the kitchen had supplied over a million meals at an average of 8,750 per day. Furthermore, it had saved the Relief Committee the sum of £7,768—half of their usual costs.

Soyer returned to London in triumph, but public acclaim did not divert him from his cause. He wrote to the *Times* with another appeal. He answered hundreds of begging letters. He badgered his well-heeled friends for subscriptions. He organized an exhibition of Emma's paintings and sketches at the Prince of Wales' Bazaar, under the title of 'Soyer's Philanthropic Gallery'. He published a booklet, *The Poor Man's Regenerator*, in which he amplified his previous receipts for soup and added several others, such as 'Cabbage Stirabout' and 'The Poor Man's Potato Pie', which called for the cheapest of ingredients. For every copy sold, Soyer gave a penny of the proceeds to the poor.

This work was to occupy him, off and on, for the rest of his life. Not that he neglected his other business: he even found time to enter a culinary contest, in which a prize was offered for the 'newest, lightest and most delicate dish' which could be conceived. His five rivals included two of Queen Victoria's principal chefs de cuisine and other notables, but Soyer was more than equal to them, as the *Memoirs* relate:

We well remember his celebrated 'aerial dish,' and the fun connected with it. It was arranged that six of the principal culinary artists should each produce a new dish. Accordingly they all met in the magnificent hotel of Signor Dotesio, at Slough.

Amongst the number present were her Majesty's two principal *chefs-de-cuisine*, the Dowager Baroness Rothschild's, and the head-cook belonging to the establishment, with two others. The table was laid for twelve—six competitors, and six to judge the result of this new trial of skill. The challenge was, that the one that produced the newest, lightest, and most delicate dish, was to be presented with a piece of plate; the judges not to know the authors of the respective dishes until after the degustation and decision. After an excellent course of soup and fish, five dishes were placed upon the table, and four of them met with the greatest approbation from the severe jury; but a general clamour was made for the sixth, when in walked the worthy host, with an elegant dish labelled *'La Croustade Sylphe en surprise à la Cerito,'* and upon the lid being removed by the chairman, to the astonishment of every one present, out flew a beautiful pigeon, which immediately found its way to the terrace, and took its departure for London. The party, however astonished, were not disappointed; for, upon removing a false bottom, an ample supply of *salade de filets de grouse à la Bohèmienne* was discovered, and beneath that some artificial *côtelettes* and mushrooms were sweetly resting on a *crème aux pêches*.

The author of this curious dish made a wager, a few days previous, that he would send part of a dish, of his own composition, from Slough to London, in a manner which for speed should only be exceeded by the electric telegraph; consequently, the moment the dish was placed upon the table, it was announced by telegraph to the parties in London, and in fourteen minutes afterwards they received the principal part of the atmospheric dish, at the spot appointed by the author, with a paper under its wing, upon which was written—'Please to pay the *chef-de-cuisine* of the Reform Club the sum of £50, for my private apartment in his new dish, and make the cheque payable to A. Soyer.'

Now that he had regenerated the cookery of the very rich and the very poor, Soyer turned his attention to the middle classes. In 1849 he completed *The Modern Housewife*, or *Menagère, comprising nearly One Thousand Receipts for the Economic and Judicious Preparation of Every Meal of the Day, and those for The Nursery and Sick Room; with Minute Directions for Family Management in All its Branches.* Having already written a more or less conventional cookery book, he decided to vary proceedings by couching his new work in the form of a correspondence between two married women. Mrs B. ('Hortense') is the model menagère, or housekeeper, who gives most of the advice; Mrs L. ('Eloise') acts as the stooge.

The Modern Housewife was an instantaneous and massive success, surpassing in sales anything that the *Gastronomic Regenerator* had achieved. By 1853 the thirtieth thousand was being printed, and the book remained, until the arrival of Mrs Beeton in 1861, the most valuable companion a young married woman could have. It can still be enjoyed today as an intimately-detailed glimpse into a mid-Victorian bourgeois household, from the coarse shortcomings of a 'plain' cook to the withdrawal of the ladies from the dinner table, so that Mr B. can introduce 'some of his choice Claret or Burgundy in ice coolers'.

Some years later, Soyer completed his triptych of cookery books for all classes by publishing his *Shilling Cookery for the People*. In a disarmingly frank preface, he admits that his first efforts to write for the masses came to nothing, because he soon discovered that he knew nothing about them. 'The only course I had to pursue,' he writes, 'was to visit personally the abodes, and learn the manners of those to whom I was about to address myself, and thereby get acquainted with their wants.' This course was so successful, and Soyer's appreciation of their wants so perceptive, that the *Shilling Cookery* became the most successful of all his books. Sixty thousand copies were sold within six weeks, and by 1867 there were over a quarter of a million in print. Though modest in scale compared to his other two monsters, it once again featured 'Hortense' and 'Eloise', who simplified their prose accordingly.

Selection from
The Modern Housewife (1849)

Introduction

DIALOGUE BETWEEN MRS. B— AND MRS.L—, HER FRIEND AND VISITOR.

Mrs. L. I have now, my dear Mrs. B., been nearly a fortnight at your delightful Villa, and I must say, with all truth, that I never fared better in my life, yet I am considered somewhat of an epicure, as is likewise my husband; but, of course, our means being rather limited, we are obliged to live accordingly.

Mrs. B. Well, so must we; and I assure you that during the first few years of our marriage, our pecuniary resources were but small, but even then I managed my kitchen and housekeeping at so moderate an expense, compared with some of our neighbours, who lived more expensively, but not so well as we did, that, when any of them dined with us, they flattered me with the appellation of the 'Model Housekeeper,' and admired the comforts of our table, but would leave with the impression that I must be the most extravagant of wives. Now, believe me, I have always prided myself, whether having to provide for a ceremonious party, or dining by ourselves, upon having everything properly done and served, that so, if any friends should come in by accident or on business, they were generally well pleased with our humble hospitality, and that without extravagance, as my husband is well convinced; for, when we dine with any acquaintance of ours, he is very eager to persuade them to adopt my system of management; though he is no great judge of what is called the highest style of cookery, yet he does not like to live badly at any time, as he very justly says, it matters not how simple the food,— a chop, steak, or a plain boiled roast joint, but let it be of good quality and properly cooked, and every one who partakes of it will enjoy it.

Mrs. L. Nothing more true!

Mrs. B. But since you talk of limited income and economy, let me relate to you a conversation which occurred a few years ago between Mr. B. and a friend of his, who declared to him that his income would never allow him to live in such luxury, which he called a comfortable extravagance.

'Extravagance!' exclaimed Mr. B., 'if you have a few minutes to spare, I will convince you of the contrary, and prove to you that such an expression is very unjust, if applied to my wife's management. Now, to begin, what sum should you suppose would cover our annual housekeeping expenditure, living as we do, in a style of which you so much approve, but consider so extravagant; there are ten of us in family— viz., myself and wife, three children, two female servants, and three young men employed in my business, and including our usual Christmas party, which of course you know of, (having participated in the last two,) also two separate birth-day parties of twenty persons each, and three juvenile petits-soupers and dances for the children upon their natal anniversaries, besides a friend dropping in occasionally, which is never less than once or twice a week.'—'Well, I do not know,' answered our friend; 'but having nearly the same number to provide for, and in a more humble way, my expenses for housekeeping are never less than £—per annum.'—'Less than what!' exclaimed Mr. B.; 'why, my dear friend, you must be mistaken,' at the same time ringing the bell. 'I wish I were, with all my heart,' was the reply, as the servant entered the room. 'Jane,' said Mr. B., 'ask your mistress to step this way for a few minutes; I wish to look at her housekeeping-book.' But being busy at the time in the kitchen, I sent up a key for him to get it, which happened to be a wrong one; upon discovering the mistake, I sent up the right, with an apology for not coming myself, as I was superintending the cooking of some veal broth, which the doctor had ordered for our poor little Henry, who was ill at the time. 'Well,' said his friend, 'there is a wife for you; I must confess mine can hardly find the way to the kitchen-stairs.' 'Now!' said my husband, opening my desk, and, taking up my book, he showed him the last year's expenditure, which was £—. 'No! no! that is impossible,' replied his friend. 'But,' said Mr. B., 'there it is in black and white.' 'Why, good heavens!' exclaimed the other, 'without giving so many parties, and also two less in family, my expenditure is certainly greater.' To which Mr. B. replied, 'So I should imagine, from the style in which I saw your table provided the few days we were on a visit to your house; therefore I am not in the least astonished. Here, however, is the account for the closing year, just made up to the 28th December, 1848. Let us see what it amounts to, probably to £50 or £60 more.' 'So, so,' replied the other, 'that is an increase.'—'Let it be so,' said Mr. B., 'but you must remember that we are twelve-months older, and as our business increases, so do we increase in our comforts; and this year Mrs. B., with the children had a pretty little house at Ramsgate for two months, which will account for the greater part of it.'

Mrs. L. But, my dear Mrs. B., I am as much astonished as your friend could possibly have been. I should, however, have liked you to explain the matter; but here comes your husband, who will probably initiate me in your culinary secrets.

Good morning, my dear Mr. B., I hope I have the pleasure of seeing you well.

Mr. B. Perfectly so, madam.

Mrs. L. I have been talking to Mrs. B., about her system of housekeeping, who was relating to me a conversation you had with a gentleman, astonished with its economy. I am also surprised, and should like to take a few leaves out of your most excellent book, if you will allow me.

Mr. B. Certainly, my dear madam; in my wife, without flattering her too much, you see almost an accomplished woman, (in hearing such praise, Mrs. B. retired. saying, 'How foolishly you talk, Richard;') she speaks two or three different languages tolerably well, and, as an amateur, is rather proficient in music, but her parents, very wisely considering household knowledge to be of the greatest importance, made her first acquainted with the keys of the store-room before those of the piano; that is the only secret, dear madam; and this is the explanation that I gave to my friend, who thought it a good jest, and one of truth. I told him to do the same by his two daughters, which would not only make them more happy through life, but transmit that happiness to their posterity by setting an example worthy of being followed.

I always say, give me a domesticated wife, and with my industry, I would not change my position for a kingdom; 'Very true, very true,' was my friend's answer, and we then parted.

I have never seen him since, nor his wife, who was probably offended at the economical propositions of her husband; for nothing, you are well aware, is more common than for people to be offended when told the truth respecting themselves; or perhaps she was too advanced in years to think of changing her ideas of housekeeping.

I see, my dear Mrs. L., the Brougham is waiting at the gate to convey you to the railway; allow me to see you safe to the station; you will not have many minutes to spare, for the train will shortly be up.

Thank you, my dear sir, (replied Mrs. L.,) and, in bidding adieu, allow me to express the gratification and delight I have felt during my stay with yourself and your inestimable wife, whose friendship I shall always highly prize.

As she took her seat in the carriage, and departed, a farewell was given from the parlour-window by Mrs. B.

Breakfasts

When we first commenced housekeeping, we were six in family, five of whom breakfasted together, the three young men in the shop, Mr. B—, and myself. The cloth was laid by the servant girl at half past seven precisely; at ten minutes to eight I made tea, and at eight o'clock we were seated. The breakfast, which was composed merely of bread and butter at discretion, fresh watercresses when plentiful, or sometimes boiled eggs; for variation, once a week, coffee; if in the winter, we had toast, which I never suffered the servant to prepare more than five minutes before we were seated, for, if kept longer, the dry toast becomes tough, and the buttered very greasy, and consequently unpalatable, as well as indigestible. Twenty minutes only were allowed for breakfast, after which the table was cleared, the cloth carefully folded and put by for the next morning,—for we kept a separate one for dinner, and imposed the fine of a halfpenny upon any one who should spill either tea or coffee over the cloth by carelessness. Such was always my plan when in business; and you must know as well as myself, it is not only the expense of the washing, but the continual wear and tear of the linen, which make frequent washings so ruinous; but the cloth used always to look clean, and I am confident that not less than five pounds a year were saved on that very trifling matter, washing, and you know we thought as much then of five pounds as we perhaps now do of twenty.

To Make Muffins.

Mix a quart of warm water in which you have dissolved three ounces of good German yeast, with sufficient flour to form a stiff batter, which let remain in a warm place four hours, then stir the mixture down, and break it into pieces, weighing a quarter of a pound each, which mould round with your hands, and put into wooden trays containing a round bed of flour for each; let them remain in a warm place two hours to prove; have your muffin-stove hot; have a round piece of iron, which place on the fire to get hot; set the muffins upon it, and when nicely risen, turn them gently over, baking them upon the stove until sufficiently set, when they are done; they will take about ten minutes baking if the stove is at the proper heat, which is known by a little flour thrown on it becoming brown. Muffins may also be made of brewer's yeast, but then they would require longer proving, and great care must be taken that the yeast is not bitter. The bitterness of the yeast can be removed by putting a hot charcoal or coal cinder in it.

Bacon and Ham for Broiling.

Ham for broiling ought not to be too old or too dry, it would perhaps eat rank. Nothing requires more care than broiling. Either get a slice of ham weighing a quarter of a pound or two ounces, which lay on your gridiron; put it over the fire; it will take perhaps five minutes if the fire is good, and more, of course, if slow; but in that short space of time, turn it three or four times, and it is done. Proceed the same if you want to serve it with poached eggs, but be careful that the eggs be ready at the same time as the bacon or ham, or both would eat badly. If you happen to have a whole ham by you for that purpose only, as is often the case at a farmhouse, begin to cut the slices in a slanting direction, and the same thickness, and proceed to the end of the ham with the remainder. It will prove more profitable to broil with greens, peas, broad beans, &c.

To sauté, put a little butter or good fat in the pan; set it on the fire with the slice in it, sauté very gently, turning very often, and serve on very thin toast.

Black Puddings.

They are in France a regular standing dish for a winter's breakfast, and ought to be more in use in England; but I must observe that I mean the home-made ones, or those made à la Français, because I consider those that are usually sold in almost every shop are too heavy for breakfast; they may pass at dinner-time, though I must confess the flavour is not at all to my liking.

Black Puddings, Broiled.

Make about six or eight incisions through the skin with a knife, slantwise, on each side of the pudding; put it on the gridiron for about eight minutes, over rather a brisk fire; turn it four times in that space of time, and serve broiling hot.

I should recommend those who are fond of black puddings to partake of no other beverage than tea or coffee, as cocoa or chocolate would be a clog to the stomach. In France they partake of white wine for breakfast, which accounts for the great consumption of black pudding. Now really this is a very favourite dish with epicures, but I never recommend it to a delicate stomach.

The Nursery Dinner.

Dear Friend,—Now here I must call your especial attention to the way many people treat this department of domestic comfort, which is often very slight and irregular. Now, for my part, I have made quite a study of it, and could prove that health is always dependent on the state of the digestive organs; and that, if you should improperly treat your stomachs, by over or under supplying their wants, or using them to ill-cooked food, you not only destroy the functionary coating of the stomach, but also impede the development of the intellect. It is, then, as much a science to manage the food of children, as to cater for the palate of the gourmet, and I shall always consider that good food is to the body what education is to the mind.

My plan of managing the nursery meals is as follows:— At eight o'clock in the morning, which was my usual time, I used myself to prepare that glutinous food upon which our ancestors and race were first reared, rather unclassically denominated *Pap*. My method was very simple:

PAP.—Put two ounces of rusk, or tops and bottoms, in a small saucepan, with just sufficient water to moisten them; set the saucepan upon the fire until its contents are thoroughly warm through; pour a little of the water away, if too thin, pressing the rusk with a spoon; then add a teaspoonful of white or brown sugar, and beat the whole with a spoon until quite a pulp; it is then ready for use.

Bread and Milk.

Cut about two ounces of any white bread into small thin slices, and put them into a small basin or a large breakfast cup, in a little saucepan (only used for that purpose) have half a pint of milk; when upon the point of boiling, pour over the bread; cover over the cup five minutes, and it is ready for use.

I much prefer this method to that of boiling the bread and milk together. In first commencing to feed a child upon the above, I always added a little sugar, which I withdrew by degrees, as I do not like to accustom children to too much sweets, as it inclines them when a little older to be always wanting or eating sweet stuff, which often spoils the best set of teeth; and here let me remark, that the finest fortune you can give to your children is health, and as loving mothers, whilst we have them under our control, it is our duty to study their little comforts, and direct their first steps in life in the road to happiness.

Children's Diet for the Day.

Bread and milk for breakfast at eight; the dinner at one, which was composed as follows throughout the week: roast mutton and apple pudding, roast beef and currant pudding, baked apples; boiled mutton with turnips, after which rice or vermicelli pudding; occasionally a little salt beef, with suet dumplings, plain and with currants in them, or pease pudding; or if unwell, a little veal or chicken-broth, or beef-tea (the receipts for which will be found in the series entitled Comforts for Invalids).

When in business, the first three years we could not afford to keep a nursery—in fact, we had no room to spare; the children then used to dine with us at one, but at a side-table with their nurse.

Then they had a little plain meat, cut small in their plates, with potatoes, pieces of bread, and gravy, after which, three times a week, plain rice, bread, or other plain pudding, or rhubarb or apple tart; and, at five o'clock, their bread and milk again, previous to going to bed.

Having here terminated my remarks upon the Nursery, I shall leave this scene of romp and confusion, to walk on tip-toe to the *sick-room door*, and carefully enter, without noise, into the mournful abode of human suffering and captivity, in hopes that, by watching over the diet of its occupants, my small efforts may improve their comforts, and, by proper management, assist in their restoration to health. I shall therefore proceed to give some receipts, entitled *Comforts for Invalids*.

Nothing is to me more painful than to see any food ill-prepared for sick people, whose sense of taste is partially gone; everything ordered by the doctors as food should be cooked in the greatest perfection, especially as all they require is so very simple, and easily done, it is unpardonable to do it badly, although I am sorry to say that this is too often the case, even in many of our first hospitals and other public establishments, where they have provisions in abundance, and of the first quality.

Perhaps you may fancy I am too severe upon this delicate subject, but I can assure you that I have for years been in the habit of visiting some of these institutions for the sick, and can therefore speak with confidence. I have grieved to see it, and often wished that they would follow a system I could lay down, but there are some people who will not change their style, however bad, for a better one, for the world.

Now I must here claim all your intelligence, for pointing out those receipts the accomplishing of which is most plain, and will insure success to those who may try to do them, and cause them to persuade others to follow their example. I therefore inclose the following. Yours, &c.

Hortense.

Comforts for Invalids.

Soyer's New Way of Making Beef Tea.

Cut a pound of solid beef into very small dice, which put into a stewpan, with a small pat of butter, a clove, two button onions, and a salt-spoonful of salt, stir the meat round over the fire for a few minutes, until it produces a thin gravy, then add a quart of water, and let it simmer at the corner of the fire for half an hour, skimming off every particle of fat; when done pass through a sieve. I have always had a great objection to passing broth through a cloth, as it frequently quite spoils its flavour.

The same, if wanted plain, is done by merely omitting the vegetables, salt, and clove: the butter cannot be objectionable, as it is taken out in skimming; pearl-barley, vermicelli, rice, &c., may be served in it if required.

Pure Osmazome, or Essence of Meat.

Take two pounds of the flesh of any animal or bird (the older the better for obtaining the true flavour), as free from sinew as possible, and mince it well; place it in a Florence oil-flask, and cork it; put this in a saucepan filled with cold water, leaving the neck uncovered; place it on the side of the fire until the water arrives at 160° Fahr., at which temperature it must remain for twenty minutes; then remove it, and strain the contents through a tammie, pressing the meat gently with a spoon; should it require to be kept for some time, put the liquor in a basin or cup, which place in the saucepan; subject it to a boiling heat until it is reduced to the consistency of treacle, removing the scum; this, when cold, will become solid, and will keep for any number of years. Osmazome is known under various names in different cookery books, as 'fumet,' 'essence,' &c., and is obtained in a different way, which causes the gelatine to be produced with the osmazome; but by the above plan the gelatine is left in the meat, and the osmazome and the albumen are extracted; the albumen is afterwards removed as the scum.

Eel Broth (very strengthening.)

Take a small eel, which skin as described under fish, and wash well, then cut it into slices, which put into a small saucepan, just covered with water, add a little salt, a few sprigs of parsley, two button onions, and a clove; let it simmer very gently until the eels are tender, when skim off all the fat, pass the broth through a very fine sieve into a cup, it is then ready to serve when required, but a spoonful only should be taken at a time.

A patient is sometimes allowed to take part of the fish, which being so much boiled, constitutes a lighter food than eels are in general; a little melted butter and parsley might be served with them.

Bubble and Squeak.

I am certain you must know, as well as myself, our hereditary dish called bubble and squeak; but, like the preparation of other things, there is a good way and a bad; and, as you prefer the former to the latter, proceed as follows:— Boil a few greens, or a savoy cabbage (which has been previously well washed), in plain water until tender, which then drain quite dry in a colander or sieve, put it upon a trencher, and chop it rather fine with a knife, then for a pound of salt beef you have in slices, put nearly a quarter of a pound of butter into a frying-pan, in which sauté the beef gently but not too dry; when done, keep it hot, put the cabbage in the frying-pan, season with a little salt and pepper, and when hot through, dress it upon a dish, lay the beef over, and serve. Endive or large cabbage-lettuces may be used instead of cabbage, but care must be taken to drain off all the water.

Toast and Water.

Cut a piece of crusty bread, about a quarter of a pound in weight, place it upon a toasting-fork, and hold it about six inches from the fire; turn it often, and keep moving it gently until of a light yellow colour, then place it nearer the fire, and when of a good brown chocolate colour, put it into a jug, and pour three pints of boiling water over; cover the jug until cold, then strain it into a clean jug, and it is ready for use: never leave the toast in it, for in summer it would cause fermentation in a short time. I would almost venture that such toast and water as I have described would keep good a considerable time in bottles.

The idea that bread must be burnt black to make toast and water is quite a popular delusion, for nothing nourishing could come from it; if your house were burnt to ashes, it would be valueless; and the same with burnt bread, which merely makes the water black, but the nutriment of the bread, intended to relieve the chest, has evaporated in smoke by being burnt.

Everyday Recipes.

Preserved Goose for the Farm or Country House.

In case you have more geese in condition and season than what you consume, kill and cut them up into pieces, so that there shall be as little flesh left on the carcase as possible, and bone the leg; rub into each piece with your fingers some salt, in which you have mixed a little saltpetre, put them into an earthen pan, with some thyme. bay-leaf, spice, a clove of chopped garlic, rub them for a couple of days, after which dip each piece in water, and dry on a cloth; when you have chopped fine and melted all the fat you could get from the goose, and scraped a quarter of a pound of fat bacon and melted with it, pass through a sieve into a stewpan, lay the pieces in it, and bake very gently in a slow oven until a stiff piece of straw will go through it, then lay it in a sieve; when nearly cold put it in a bowl or round preserving jar, and press a smaller one on the top, so that it all forms one solid mass, pour the fat over, when cold cover with a piece of bladder, keep it in a cold place, and it will be good for months together, and is excellent for breakfast, luncheon, or supper, having previously extracted the fat. Last winter I kept some for three months quite sweet; having half a one left, I put it by in the above way, bones and all, in a basin, and covered with the fat produced with roasting, and put it in the larder, and it was excellent. Ducks may be served in the same way.

Ducks à l'aubergiste (or Tavern-keepers' fashion.)

Truss one or two ducks with the legs turned inside, put them into a stewpan with a quarter of a pound of butter; place them over a slow fire, turning round occasionally, until they have taken a nice brown colour, add two spoonfuls of flour, mix well with them, add a quart of water, with half a tablespoonful of salt and sugar, let simmer gently until the ducks are done (but adding forty button onions well peeled as soon as it begins to boil), keep hot; peel and cut ten turnips in slices, fry them in a frying-pan in butter, drain upon a cloth, put them into the sauce, and stew until quite tender; dress the ducks upon your dish, skim the fat from the sauce, which has attained a consistency, add some fresh mushrooms, pour round the ducks, and serve.

Ox Heart.

This dish, although not very recherché, is a good family one, and remarkable for its cheapness. Put it into lukewarm water, one hour to disgorge, then wipe it well with a cloth, and stuff the interior with a highly-seasoned veal stuffing, tie it up in paper, and pass a small spit through the sides, set it before a good fire for about two hours to roast, keeping it well basted—being almost deprived of fat, basting is thus required; when done, take off the paper, and serve with any sharp sauce, or a little plain gravy. Two hours would be sufficient to roast a large heart; but if smaller, of course less time in proportion would be required. I have also stuffed a heart with sage and onion, and even ventured the apple sauce: both succeeded admirably, and it can be baked as well as roasted.

I remember, when in business, upon one occasion, having a few friends pop in unexpectedly about luncheon-time upon a Saturday (which is a day I always contrive to keep my larder as short as possible), and having nothing but a heart as a meal to give them, I immediately gave orders to the cook to cut it into slices half an inch thick, dip each piece in flour, and afterwards egg and bread-crumb them, then to put four spoonfuls of oil in the frying-pan, lay part of the pieces in, and sauté of a nice colour, then to keep them hot in a dish, and sauté the remainder; and when all done, to pour off part of the oil, put a teaspoonful of flour in the pan, mixing it with the remaining oil and gravy, then pouring in a gill of water, season with a little pepper and salt, four spoonfuls of the vinegar from piccalilly, and a little of the pickle finely chopped; boil the whole a minute, pour over the heart, and serve very hot. It pleased very much, and they made a hearty meal from it; and I have since had some with a little plain gravy, and broiled bacon; in both instances it was very good.

Fritadella *(twenty receipts in one.)*

Put half a pound of crumb of bread to soak in a pint of cold water, take the same quantity of any kind of roast or boiled meat, with a little fat, chop it up like sausage meat, then put your bread in a clean cloth, press it to extract all the water, put into a stewpan two ounces of butter, a tablespoonful of chopped onions, fry for two minutes, then add the bread; stir with a wooden spoon until rather dry, then add the meat, season with a teaspoonful of salt, half the same of pepper, a little grated nutmeg, the same of lemon peel, stir continually until very hot; then add two eggs, one at a time, well mix together, and pour on a dish to get cold. Then take a piece as big as a small egg, and roll it to the same shape, flatten it a little, egg and bread-crumb over, keeping the shape; do all of it the same way, then put into a sauté-pan a quarter of a pound of lard, or clean fat, or oil; when hot, but not too much so, put in the pieces, and sauté a very nice yellow colour, and serve very hot, plain, on a napkin, or on a border of mashed potatoes, with any sauce or garniture you fancy. These can be made with the remains of any kinds of meat, poultry, game, fish, and even vegetables; hard eggs, or cold mashed potatoes may be introduced in small quantities, and may be fried instead of sautéd, in which case put about two pounds of fat in the frying-pan, and if care is used it will do several times. This is an entirely new and very economical and palatable dish, and fit for all seasons, and if once tried would be often repeated; the only expense attending it is the purchase of a small wire sieve for the bread-crumbs. The reason I call it twenty receipts in one is, that all kinds of food may be used for it, even shrimps, oysters, and lobsters.

Ramifolle.

These are a little more expensive than the fritadella, and worthy the table of a crowned head. The flesh of fowls instead of lamb or veal, with the addition of one or two fat livers cut in dice. Proceed as in the former receipt, using the crumb of French rolls, and one or two truffles cut fine: then make some pancake batter, and sauté two pancakes about one-eighth of an inch thick, cover one with the meat, &c., and lay the other over, and put by until cold; when so, cut them to any shape you like, but if like cutlets add the small bone of fowl of pigeon, or the stalk of a sprig of parsley, egg and breadcrumb them, and saute them in oil or lard of a nice yellow colour, and dish them like cutlets, with any of the sauces or garnitures described for mutton cutlets; or if plain, with fried parsley. They may be made of any kind of meat, fish, or poultry. I have latterly had them sent up to table when we have had a few friends, and they have been very much liked; and, on inquiring the name, I baptized them Ramifolle, without any particular meaning, which name having pleased as much as the dish, therefore let them be called Ramifolles.

They may be made a plainer way with various meats or liver, and spread over one pancake, which roll over, and when cold cut it into three equal lengths, egg, bread-crumb, and sauté as above.

Cutlets a la Victime, or Victimized Cutlets.

Here, *ma belle amie*, is a teriffic title for a receipt; but do not fear it, as the time of the Inquisition is past, and you are not likely to become one in partaking of it. I do not recommend it to you on the score of economy, as it is the tip-top of extravagance, but forward it as a curiosity; and also in case similar circumstances should happen which caused its invention, which I must tell you was done by a culinary artist of Louis XVIII., of France, at the palace of the Tuileries, and first partaken of by that intellectual monarch and gourmet, who, at the end of his stormy reign, through a serious illness, was completely paralysed, and, at the same time, the functionary organs of his digestion were much out of order; being a man of great corpulence, and a great admirer of the festive board, much food was required to satisfy his royal appetite: and the difficulty which his physicians experienced was to supply this want of food in the smallest compass. The head-cook, on being consulted, begged a few hours for reflection before he could give an answer to so important a question, as nothing but mutton entirely deprived of fat was to compose his Majesty's meal. After profound study by the chief and his satellites, a voice was heard from the larder, which was a considerable distance from the kitchen, crying, 'I have found it, I have found it.' It was that of a young man of the name of Alphonse Pottier, who, in saying so, made his appearance in the kitchen with three beautiful mutton cutlets, tastefully trimmed and tied together; he then, with a small skewer, fastened them to a spit, and placed them, to the astonishment of all present, close to the bars of the grate: two of the cutlets soon got brown (observe, not a word was to be said until the trial was made), from brown they soon turned black; every one gazed at each other in astonishment, whilst Pottier, with quite a composed countenance, terminated his scientific experiment, took them off the spit, drew the skewer out, cut the string, threw the two burnt cutlets away, and merely served the middle one, which seems to have received all the nutriment of the other two; it was served and greatly approved of by the physicians, as well as by the gourmet potentate, who, in consequence of two being sacrificed for one, named it, 'Cutlet à la Victime,' and often afterwards used to partake of them when in the enjoyment of health.

Cut three cutlets from the neck of mutton, about half an inch thick, trim one very nicely, free from fat, leave the other two as cut off, put the trimmed one between the two, flatten them together, so that the fat of the outside ones meet over the middle one; tie them together thus, and broil over a very strong fire for ten minutes; remove it from the fire, cut the string, and dish up the middle one only on a very hot dish, with a little salt sprinkled over it. If wanted roasted, proceed as above.

Beefsteak Pudding.

Put a pound of flour upon a dresser, with which mix half a pound of beef suet, very finely chopped, make a hole in the middle, into which put a teaspoonful of salt, and sufficient water to form a rather stiffish paste, mix it well together, using a little more flour to dry it and prevent its sticking; then lightly butter the interior of a round-bottomed pudding basin, roll out two-thirds of the paste to half an inch in thickness, with which line the basin; have ready cut into slices, about the size of the palm of the hand, and a quarter of an inch in thickness, two pounds of rumpsteak, with a little of the fat included; lay them upon a dish, season with two teaspoonfuls of salt and one of black pepper, sprinkle a little flour over, move them about a little until each piece is well covered with flour and seasoning; then lay them within the paste, also putting in whatever seasoning may remain upon the dish, (some add two dozen of oysters, blanched and bearded, which is excellent,) pour a gill of water over, moistening the edges of the paste; then roll out the remainder of the paste to form a lid, which place over, pressing it down with the thumb, then tie the basin in a pudding-cloth, and put into a saucepan containing about a gallon of boiling water, and keep continually boiling for nearly two hours, adding a little more water occasionally, to keep up the quantity; then take it up, untie the cloth, run a sharp-pointed knife into the pudding, and if the meat feels tender it is done (if not, it will require more boiling), turn it over upon your dish, lift the basin carefully from it, and serve, without opening the pudding to add gravy, as many persons do, for a pudding made as above ought to be full of gravy when cut at table.

Bittern, The Common, or Bogbumper
Bitterbum, Butterbump, Miredrum (le Butor)

Bittern (the little) (le Blongios).—Many cooks confound this with the heron, but they are as different as possible, not only in appearance, although of the same species, but in flavour. When fat, about October and November, this bird is exceedingly fine eating; it should be kept for three or four days, then covered with a slice of bacon, and roasted, and served with a sauce.

Starlings, or Stare (l'Etourneau).

These are obtained, at times, in large quantities, by persons resident in the country. When killed, their heads should be immediately pulled off, and as soon as plucked and trussed, put into a little vinegar and water, which will get rid of their bitter taste: cook like Larks.

Cormorants and Herons are unfit to be sent to table; also the Rock Birds, or Penguin species.

Ox-bird, Purre, or Stint (l'Alouette de Mer.)

It is from this bird that the receipt of sea-pie arose; it being a bird of passage, and often surrounding a vessel at sea in thousands; when we get them in London, they have generally been shot, which ought not to have been; but taken in nets and kept alive, and fed like quails, or on bread and milk, hemp-seed and boiled wheat, and two days before they are wanted add sugar, which makes them amazingly fat. When young, their legs are smooth; the contrary when old. In cooking, proceed as for a lark, draw them or not, as may be preferred. With this bird may be classed the following, and cook in the same way:— Knots, Knute, Knout (le Canut); Thrush (Greve); Gambet or Gambetta, by some called the Greenshank; Redshank; Spotted Redshank (Chevalier Rouge); Godwits of all colours very much resemble and equal the flavour of a woodcock—the hens are the best. Dotterels, in spring the most delicious eating; Dotterel-sea or Turnstone, and so fine; Sandpiper or Sanderling, fine in summer; Wheatear, White Tail, or Fallowfinch, good in August and September.

Bustard, Great or Little (l'Outarde, or la petite Outarde).

This is a bird which is now seldom sent to table, its flavour depends much upon the country where it feeds; it would be stuffed and cooked like a turkey.

Blackbirds.

They are eatable when young, and are best at the end of the year; they should be cooked like larks.

Veal and Ham Pies (raised).

The following few dishes will be found extremely useful for breakfasts, luncheons, second course in a dinner party, or for dinner in summer, but above all for supper when you give an evening party.

Having found a great difficulty in raising the crust for a pie with my hands, I purchased for a trifle a tin pie-mould, by the use of which the process is more simple, and the pie retains its shape whilst baking, and secures the gravy, much better.

Well wipe and butter the interior of the mould, then have ready two pounds of pâte à foncé, rather firm than otherwise, two thirds of which roll out to fit the mould, press it evenly over the interior, raising the paste half an inch above the edge of the mould; you have previously prepared six pounds of veal, cut from the fillet, as follows: cut four pounds into pieces an inch square, and as nearly as possible to the length of the pie; with the remainder make some forcemeat; then run eight pieces of fat bacon, each two inches in length, and a quarter of an inch square, through each piece of veal; have also two pounds of lean bacon, cut into pieces of nearly the same size as the veal, then put a quarter of a pound of butter into a frying-pan, and when melted over the fire, lay in the veal and bacon; season rather highly with a teaspoonful of salt, the same of pepper, half that quantity of grated nutmeg, and a tablespoonful each of chopped onion and parsley, sauté the whole a quarter of an hour, occasionally turning the meat, until getting of a nice colour, and the bottom of the pan is covered with a thickish glaze; then line the interior of the pie with some of the forcemeat, to the thickness of half an inch, after which lay three pieces of veal at the bottom with two of the ham, alternately, which cover over with more forcemeat, to about an inch in thickness, then more veal and bacon, with forcemeat again, proceeding thus until full, finishing with the forcemeat, forming a dome about an inch above the edge of the paste, and lay a pat of butter with a bay-leaf at the top, then mould the remainder of the paste into a ball, which roll to the size of the top of the pie, wet the edges with a little egg, lay on the cover, which press down with the thumbs, working the edge up gracefully with the thumb and forefinger, to about an inch above the top of the mould, cutting some of the paste away where too thick, and crimp the extreme edge with a pair of paste nippers; then have ready half a pound of puff paste, which roll to about the thickness of a quarter of an inch, from which cut a piece the size and form of the dome of the pie, upon which place it to form a lid (previously wetting the top with a little water), press it down lightly, egg over with a paste brush, edges as well, make a small hole with a knife at the top, and carve any design upon the puff paste according to fancy; tie a band of buttered paper round the mould, an inch above the pie, put it into a moderate oven to bake about two hours, but to be certain if done, run a pointed knife or trussing needle into the centre, and if it feels tender it is sufficiently baked.

Then take it from the oven, and pour in a gill of strong gravy, in which you have dissolved a little isinglass (especially if in summer); when cold, take it from the mould (which opens at one end by drawing out a pin), and serve upon a napkin, garnished round with parsley. To carve, cut it into slices, the whole breadth of the pie and half an inch in thickness.

Such a pie as above would weigh about four pounds when baked; but should you require a smaller one, diminish the proportions accordingly. If no puff paste, the top might be ornamented with a few leaves from the trimmings of the other paste. I have given you the above receipt very minutely, as the above applies to every description of raised pie, the difference only being its contents.

Young Green Peas.

Young Green Peas! Do not these words sound pleasant to the ear, dearest? I fancy that, by merely raising my eyes from the paper on which I am now writing, I shall see all our garden in buds and blossom; it not only seems to invigorate the sensitive part of one's appetite, but works upon the mind to that point that you may actually fancy you are breathing in a glowing atmosphere, and that the pearly dew is gracefully descending in small globules from heaven, to fix their sparkling eyes on the pinky bloom of myriads of roses. But, alas! how soon this charming illusion has disappeared since I have left for a moment the sight of my paper, to give a peep through the garden-window, where I perceive that though to-day is the 17th of April, the serious and uncheerful Father Winter has once more monopolised those delightful and variegated *nuances* of Nature, by laying out his universal snowy tablecloth over this for the present ephemeral vision which the inviting words green peas had produced upon my senses; no doubt the effect of a good fire in my parlour, where I am now sitting, has had great influence upon me respecting the summery temperature; but as a few weeks longer will realize my wishes, I shall here content myself by giving you the receipt how they ought to be cooked when you can get them.

When they are very young, I like them plain boiled, because their original flavour is so fresh and delicate, that any addition, except a little fresh butter, would be certain to destroy their aroma; I even object to the introduction of green mint, though I do not want to deprive you of it, being only a matter of taste.

Put two quarts of water to boil, with half an ounce of salt, and then place in one pint of peas, boil a full gallop till tender (about ten minutes), put in a colander, drain one minute; lay them, raised in the centre, in a dish, put in them two pats of very fresh butter, and serve.

When older or larger, boil a little longer, add twelve leaves of green mint, which serve with it.

Peas, French Way.

They do not look so inviting, not being so green; but I must say they are excellent as regards flavour. Choose them young and fresh; without both of these qualities they would not cook properly. Put into a saucepan a pint of peas, two ounces of butter, and a pint of water; mix the peas and butter well with your hand, add four button onions, a bouquet of six sprigs of parsley, one ounce of sugar, two saltspoonfuls of salt, and one of pepper, place over a tolerably good fire, moving them often; if getting rather dry, add a wineglassful of water, twenty minutes ought to be enough; when tender, add one ounce of butter, in which you have mixed a teaspoonful of flour, which put in and stir well; make a liaison of the yolk of one egg, a quarter of a gill of cream, which add and stir; take out the parsley and onions, and serve.

Richmond Maids of Honour.

These delicious little cakes, which every inhabitant of London who pays a visit to the most picturesque part of its environs knows so well, derive their name from a period when cookery was not thought to be a degrading occupation for those honoured with that title. It is stated that they originated with the maids of honour of Queen Elizabeth, who had a palace at Richmond. I have a little work now before me, called 'The Queen's Delight,' in which are several receipts invented by the wives of the first nobles of the land, which I think is an excellent example for those housewives who honour this book by their perusal, to imitate. They are made as follows:–

Sift half a pound of dry curd, mix it well with six ounces of good butter, break the yolks of four eggs into another basin, and a glass of brandy; add it to six ounces of powdered lump-sugar, and beat well together one very floury baked potato cold, one ounce of sweet almonds, one ounce of bitter ditto pounded, the grated rind of three lemons, the juice of one, and half a nutmeg grated, mix these well together and add to the curds and butter; stir well up, and proceed as before, filling the tartlet pans.

Entremet Impromptu.

Cut some slices of bread off a half-quartern stale loaf, three quarters of an inch thick, and cut it into lozenges two inches long, put into a deep dish, and place in a stewpan half a pint of milk, which boil with one ounce of sugar and the rind of a small orange; when boiling, pour over the bread, which allow to soak for one minute, take each piece, then drain off the milk, have one egg well beaten, dip each piece of bread into it, and then add some fine bread-crumbs, and fry it in light fat until a golden colour, add pounded sugar over each, and salamander over.

Any kind of preserve, as apricot, marmalade, or currant jelly, strawberry jam, &c., mixed with a little brandy or wine, makes an excellent sauce to be served with this impromptu dish.

Trifles.

Trifles should be made early in the day on which they are wanted; take a stale Savoy cake, cut it in slices of one inch thick, and lay it on the bottom of the dish; lay on that a thin layer of any kind of marmalade, jam, or jelly, have some macaroons and ratafia cakes, and lay on and cover the whole with some sponge cakes. For a dish nine inches in diameter, mix two glasses of sherry, one of brandy, half a one of rum, and the same of noyeau, and pour over, and let it remain until it is well soaked, then pour over about one inch thick of rich custard; put a pint of cream into a bowl, with some sifted sugar, a squeeze of a lemon, and about a tablespoonful of the wine, &c., you have put on the cake, whisk it well up. I use a trifle-blower, which saves some trouble; I also use it for all whipped cream; and as the froth rises remove it with a spoon on to a clean sieve, drain, then place it on the custard until it is high and handsome.

I have occasionally, when being in a hurry, and having no cream by me, proceeded as above, and made the whip with the whites of eggs, and some very white peach or egg-plum marmalade together, until it makes firm froth or whip, which put on the custard; this may also be coloured a nice pink.

Trifles are generally considered unwholesome; I think it is because they are often made too long before they are wanted, and no spirit is used in the cake, the consequence is, the cream turns sour.

The remains of this make an excellent pudding.

ROYAL ST. JAMES'S CAKE.

June 16, 1849.

My Dear Eloise,— Though you did not expect to hear from me again today, after the manuscript I forwarded to you, it is quite an unexpected circumstance that makes me write now, therefore you must know, dear, that, through very great interest, I had this day the honour and pleasure to witness one of the most interesting sights which England alone, at the present time, can boast of. Not to tantalize your womanly curiosity, I shall, without delay, tell you that it was a juvenile entertainment, given by the liberal and indefatigable manager of the St. James's Theatre, Mr. Mitchell, under the roof of which house he had the honour of entertaining the Crown of Great Britain, the blooming buds of the Royal Family, supported by the rising branches of the aristocracy, all with elegant bouquets, and possessing joyful faces, caused by the excellent entertainment the intelligent proprietor provided to gratify their infantine ideas. Nearly three hundred in number seemed to join their happiness with that of the Prince of Wales, Prince Alfred, the Princess Royal, and the Princess Alice, under the superintendence of her Most Gracious Majesty, and their august father, Prince Albert, who, in a homely and happy family manner, seemed, for the time, to have forgotten their mortal grandeur in joining the youthful happiness of those lovely children, who, in time, will be the ornament and pride of England. Knowing, by study, that pleasure and satisfaction of mind, in any state of life, increase or create appetite, especially upon children, on arriving at home, feeling rather tired, I lay down on a couch, and took a short repose; but being full of the pleasing sight I had just witnessed, and my imagination lately so involved with gastronomy, it caused me to dream that, by special order, I was to make a monster cake for the luncheon of those lovely children, which they were to partake of after their terpiscolyridramacomic festivity; to my ephemeral ideas, the cake was made, and the table laid in a vast room, where gradations of chairs and tables were erected in a demi-circle, at the top of which the branches of the royal family were gracefully sitting, and surrounded, according to rank, by the other juveniles; the banqueting-hall seemed to me like the theatre, decorated all over with festoons of natural flowers; the different tables were surcharged with every description of delicacy; fruit, ices, effervescent refreshment of all kinds were provided; every child seemed to be waited on by their noble parents, her Majesty leading them to follow her maternal affection. When grace was invoked, I was appointed to cut and distribute the monster cake, which, to my present recollection, was no less than four feet in height, three wide, and most beautifully ornamented with all kinds of bon-bons, small-fruits, pistaches, &c. Having reached the centre platform, where that supposed chef-d'œuvre of cake was exhibited and gazed at by the widely-opened eyes of the youthful multitude, I was just in the act of raising the knife which was placed there for me to cut it with, when my hand all at once was seized, as if by magic, to prevent me from doing so. After a deep sigh, I awoke, and perceived it was my younger boy Raphael pulling me by the arm, saying, 'Mamma, the dinner is ready!' Though much annoyed with the sudden disappearance of such a fairy scene, I could not find it in my heart to scold his innocent interference with my enchanted illusion; but, as far as recollection serves me from a dream, I perfectly recollect all the delicate ingredients which I supposed I had put in it; therefore, if you want to make a small one, proceed as follows:

CHEF TO THE POOR

St. James's Cake.

Put one pound of very fresh butter in a good-size kitchen basin, and with the right hand work it up well till it forms quite a white cream; then add one pound powdered sugar, mix well, add ten eggs by degrees; put to dry a pound and a quarter of flour, which mix as lightly as possible with it; blanch and cut in slices two ounces of pitachios, two ditto of green preserved angelica, add two liqueur glasses of noyeau, two drops of essence of vanilla; whip a gill and a-half of cream till very thick, mix lightly with a wooden spoon, have a mould made the shape of the drawing, put it in, and send to the baker; it will take about one hour and a quarter to bake; ornament as represented in the subjoined cut:

You will perceive, my dear, that my ideas are more extravagant in my sleep than when awake, but pray consider who was to partake of it.

THE DINNER-TABLE

My Dear Eloise,—I thank you for your kind compliment, but I have always been of opinion that the arrangements and serving of a dinner-table have as much to do with the happiness and pleasure of a party as the viands which are placed upon it; this I had a practical proof of last week. Mr. B. and myself were invited to dine with Mr. D., a city friend, at Balham Hill; I had before met Mrs. D. at an evening party at his partner's, at Hackney, and knew but little of her.

Dinner was served pretty punctually, only half an hour after time. On my entrance in the room my first glance at the table showed me that there was a want of *savoir-faire* in its management; the plate, very abundant and splendid, was of so yellow a cast that it looked as if it were plated, and the cut glass was exceedingly dim. My first surprise was that there were no napkins, the next the soup plates were quite cold, which I have found often the case in other houses; after being served with fish, and waiting until it was cold for the sauce to eat with it, I was rather sceptical how the rest of the dinner would progress. After the first, the second course made its appearance, which was heavy and too abundant; the plain things were well done, but there was only one servant in the room for the whole party of fourteen, and from the strict formality of the table, it would have been a sacrilege to have handed your plate for any vegetables, or anything else you might require. There were four saltcellars, certainly very massive silver ones; at each corner of the table, and a beautiful cruet-frame in the centre; the hot dishes of this course, like the previous one, became cold and tasteless before being eaten, and during the time the servant was serving the champagne all the plates were empty; in fact, it was a good dinner spoilt. The wine drank with less goût than usual, and the long pauses between the courses made the formality appear still greater than it really was, and made you wish for the time to arrive for the cloth to be removed, which was not done, only the slips, a most awkward undertaking for one servant, and should never be practised unless having at least two.

About half an hour after the cloth was removed, and just as the conversation was being thawed from the freezing it received at the dinner-table, Mrs. D. and the ladies withdrew, and for an hour and a half we had to bear the insipid conversation of the drawing-room, the hissing urn on the tea-table bearing a prominent part. Several messages were sent from time to time to the dining-room that coffee was ready; and

51

when at last the gentlemen came, two had had quite wine enough, which caused them to receive sundry angry looks from their wives who were present, and who were glad to get them into their carriages, which were waiting, and right glad indeed was I when ours was announced.

This all happened, my dear Eloise, not from meanness; for if money could have purchased it nothing would have been wanting, but solely from want of *management*; and every one should think before they invite their friends to partake of their hospitality if they know how to entertain them. Money of course will provide delicacies of all kinds, but to know how to dispose of those delicacies to the best advantage, that your friends may appreciate them, is what is sadly wanting in more than one house I visit.

A very excellent remark is made in this week's *Punch* by Mr. Brown, in his Letters to a Young Man about town on the subject of great and little dinners. He says: 'Properly considered, the quality of the dinner is twice blest; it blesses him that gives, and him that takes; a dinner with friendliness is the best of all friendly meetings—a pompous entertainment where no love is, is the least satisfactory.'

Our dinner on which you compliment me so much, we sat down twelve, for although the room and table would accommodate more, yet as my service of plate is for that number, and the arrangements of the kitchen are limited, that is the number I prefer, besides beyond which the conversation becomes partial, which is the bane of a dinner-table. You know we have no regular man-servant, but for these occasions I hire two; and place one on each side the table, and they each have their own side table with a change of everything that is required. The first thing to be looked to is the lights: these ought to be so placed as not to intercept the view of any person at the table, but at the same time they ought to be enough to show everything off to advantage; I prefer removing some of the lights from the table to the sideboard when the cloth is removed, as the light after dinner ought to be more subdued. In laying the cloth, we place it over the baize and remove it after dinner, as Mr. B. says he likes to see the mahogany, for when he asks a City friend to come and put his feet under his mahogany, it looks rather foolish if he never sees it. I have, as you know, my table rather wide, that is, six feet, and I generally place a vase of flowers in the centre, as I think their freshness and odour add greatly to the appearance of the table, and admit a flanc on each side. We prefer the old English plan of taking the top and bottom of the table instead of I and Mr. B. being together at the side.

The cloth being laid with its proper side uppermost, I order a napkin, two knives, two prongs, two tablespoons, and two wine glasses to be placed to each person, a saltcellar between every other, that being a condiment which every one uses, though often wrongly; the cruet-frames and other requisites are kept on the sideboards. I then have the fish and soup served together, the potatoes and sauce on the sideboard; I serving the soup, and Mr. B. the fish, and often a little dish of fried fish, such as smelts, &c., to remove the soups. This gives me an opportunity of seeing that my guests are properly attended to, and also leisure of taking wine with any gentleman who challenges me. During the time this course has been progressing, the cook has had time to dish up the removes nice and hot, and get all close to the door, as I like as little time as possible to intervene in changing the dishes; and these consist generally of variously dressed chickens, which I have before me, as this gives an opportunity for the gentleman on my right to display his gallantry; but, thanks to Soyer's separator, this is an easy task: it also affords me still further leisure to pay attention to my guests. Mr. B., who is a capital carver, either has a saddle or a haunch of mutton, or a quarter of lamb before him, the rest of the dishes consisting of a tongue and entrées. I select those most easy to carve, and also easy for the cook to prepare. This is a period of dinner where a great deal depends upon the attendants; they should know almost by the look what this lady or that gentleman require, and what kind of vegetables to hand them; a first-rate butler should be able to judge by the physiognomy to whom he should offer mint sauce with the lamb, and who prefers cayenne; on their attention and hot plates depends the success of the substantial part of the dinner.

As soon as I see that all are served, and words are few in consequence of the organs which utters them being employed in another way, I give a look to the two servants which they understand, and immediately two reports are heard—they are from two bottles of champagne, opened at the same time by the attendants, who have each a salve with six glasses on it; this takes but a short time to serve, and prepares the palate for the entrées, which generally get praised; indeed, my cook would think something was wrong if two of the dishes did not go down empty. By having the champagne thus, I find it goes much further than if only one bottle was opened at the time, there being sufficient left in the bottles for a gentleman to challenge a lady to take champagne with him. If I have game I remove the top and bottom dishes with them, and make the sweets a separate course, taking care to have *cold plates* for the jelly, and having the liquors handed round when the sweets are on the table; one cheese I place opposite Mr. B., and macaroni opposite myself. Objections have been made to the use of napkins, as being of no service at an English dinner-table, and only a copy of the dirty manners of our neighbours. If we are more cleanly at the table than they are, (which I question), there is no reason why we should not use that which would make us still more so; but Mr. B. is so pleased with the rose water which he has at the court dinners of his company, that he made me a present of those two beautiful dishes which you admired so much. The outside compartment holds rose water, and the inner one a little eau-de-cologne; these are placed on salvers, and passed down each side of the table, the corner of each napkin being dipped into it. They seem to be absolutely required, and I must say they form a delightful adjunct to the dinner-table.

Mr. B.* has also introduced at our table, but *only at Christmas*, another city custom, which the gentlemen seem very much to like,—I cannot say so for the ladies; it is what he calls the loving cup; he has it placed before him when the cheese is put on; and after filling the glass of the lady on each side of him, he rises and drinks to their health and the rest of the company, and then passes it to the gentleman on the left, who in like manner, fills the glass of the lady on his left, rises, drinks to her health and the company, and thus it goes round the table. Your husband, my dear Eloise, thought that the contents were exceedingly good; or, as he expressed it, nectar fit for the gods, and would like to have the receipt—here it is as Mr. B. prepares it:—

LOVING CUP.—The cup holds two quarts: he places in it half a teacupful of capillaire; if he has none he uses dissolved lump sugar, with a few drops of orange-flower water in it, one pint of brown sherry, one bottle of good *Edinburgh* ale, mixing these together, and a minute before placing on the table, adding one bottle of soda water, † stirring it till it froths, he then grates some nutmeg on the froth, and places a piece of toast in it, and sends it to the table with a napkin through the handle of the cup. I must say, since we have had this, it has produced some most interesting conversation as regarded the antiquity of the custom, &c. In addition, Mr. B. bought the cup at a sale, and it is stated to have been drunk out of by Henry the Eighth: this of itself is a subject of conversation, and draws out the talents and conversational powers of our guests, and one in which ladies can join, as there is hardly one of our sex who has not read Miss Strickland's 'Queens of England.' You have often made the remark, that the time always appears short whilst we are at table; this is, no doubt, from the animated conversation which is kept up, for that is the real motive of meeting together, to enjoy the conversation of one another, to gain and impart information, and amuse ourselves with the wit and talent of those around us, and not for the sake of eating and drinking; yet without the assistance of both of these, the most sparkling wit would be as heavy as bad soufflé, and the brightest talent as dull as my looking-glass on a foggy day.

In order to prolong the time, and to enjoy the gentlemen's society as much as possible, I do not have the dessert placed on the table until ten or twenty minutes after the cloth is removed; this gives an opportunity for my guests to admire the beautiful Sevres dessert plates, containing views of different French chateaux; this of course gives a subject for conversation to those who have visited them. In the dessert I generally introduce some new importation, such as bananas, sugar-cane, American lady apples, prickly pears, &c.; these also give a subject for the gentlemen to talk about when the ladies have left, as free trade, colonial policy, &c. About half an hour after the dessert is on the table, and when I see that the conversation is becoming less general, I retire to the drawing-room; the servants then remove the used glass and plates, and Mr. B. introduces some of his choice Claret or Burgundy in ice coolers.

You know, my dear Eloise, I allow very little more than half an hour for us to talk about the last new fashions, or of Mrs. A. and B.'s cap, and the young ones about their partners at the last ball, and other nothings, when the tea and coffee are brought up on salvers; it is always made down stairs, and sent up in cups to the drawing-room, although Mr. B. had a very handsome silver service presented to him just after we were married, for serving as an honorary secretary to some grand masonic festival, yet the milk ewer and sugar basin are all I allow in the room. This does away with the formality of the tea-table and the hissing of the tea-urn; it allows some young gentleman with a Byron collar and a little down under his chin to turn over the pages of a music-book for a young lady at the piano, and take his coffee at the same time; it allows my dear mamma and Mr. P. to make up their whist table, and have their tea whilst playing; or if we make up a quadrille, to have a few turns of a waltz or polka, the coffee is serving during the time; whilst this is going on the hand of the clock advances, and half past ten soon arrives, and with it Mrs. C.'s fly; Dr. D.'s brougham is at the door; the party breaks up, delighted with the evening they have passed in each other's society: and this you see done with trifling management.

* With regard to the wine, that is a matter I leave entirely to Mr. B., but his maxim is, that 'the best is the cheapest.'

† Soyer's nectar, instead of soda water, is an improvement.

Conversation on Household Affairs.

Mrs. L. After all the receipts and information which you have given me, there is one which you have not touched upon yet, which, perhaps, is of more importance than all the rest, it is the management of servants.

Mrs. B. You are right, my dear, it is of great importance, and more so than many of us imagine; as for myself I do not consider that I am a good manager, being perhaps of too forgiving a disposition; but there is one good quality which I possess which makes up for the want of others, that is exactitude; by enforcing this it causes all to know their place, and perform their work.

Mrs. L. But what surprises me is to see everything so well done and clean with so few servants; you seem to have but two maid servants, a cook, a housemaid, and a coachman.

Mrs. B. Yes, that is all, and I generally find that they are enough for the work, unless I have a dinner party, and then of course, as you know, I have extra men; but I will tell you how I pass the day, and then you will be able to judge.

We are what are called early risers, that is, Mr. B. is obliged to leave home every work day at twenty minutes past nine; our breakfast is on the table at half-past eight; the breakfast parlour having previously been got ready, as the servants rise at seven. When we have no visitors, our two selves, the three children, and the governess, form the breakfast circle. The children, in summer time, have a walk before breakfast, but before leaving their room they uncover their beds, and if fine, open the windows, if a wet morning about two inches of the top sash is pulled down. The servants get their breakfast at the same time as we do, as we require hardly any or no waiting upon, everything being ready on the table. In a former letter I told you what was our breakfast some years since when in business, now we have placed on the table some brown bread, rolls, and dry toast; the butter is in a glass butter-dish, and the eggs are brought up when we have sat down to table. The urn is placed on the table, as I make my own tea and coffee; the cocoa is made down stairs.

You will perhaps be surprised when I say that I make the coffee for breakfast myself, but I have done so for some little time past, having found that when made in the kitchen it never came up twice alike, but now we always have it delicious.

In addition to the eggs we often have cold meat, and sometimes Mr. B. has a cutlet or any other nick-nack, which I always cook myself on the breakfast table with my newly-invented Magic lamp-stove.

With this I cook all light things, such as cutlets, poached eggs, ham, bacon, &c., and in many respects it is very convenient.

Mr. B. generally leaves home in the brougham, which is returned in time for me, in case I should be going out; and he returns in a cab or omnibus. Whilst we are at breakfast, I generally consult Mr. B. what he would like for dinner, and if he is likely to invite any friend to dine with him. The fishmonger has previously sent his list and prices of the day. I then write with a pencil on a slip of paper the bill of fare for the nursery dinner, luncheon, should any be required, and our dinner, which I send to the cook. At ten o'clock I go down stairs into the kitchen and larder, when the cook gives me her report, that is, everything that is required for the next twenty-four hours' consumption, including the servants' dinner, which report is filed in the larder and made to tally with the week's list, for I must tell you that the weeks' consumption of all things that will not spoil is had in on the Saturday, on which day the larder is properly scoured out, and everything put again into its proper place, there being bins for all kinds of vegetables, &c. The larder is generally kept locked, the cook and I only having keys, because it is in fact a larder, and not, as in many houses, full of emptiness; this occupies about half an hour, during which time the chambermaids have been attending to the bed-rooms and drawing-room, &c. If I go out or not, I always get my toilet finished by twelve o'clock; I thus have one hour to write notes, or see tradesmen or my dressmaker, and Monday mornings check and pay my tradesmen's accounts, and to dress. If I stop at home I amuse myself by reading, or going to see the children in the nursery, or sometimes go again into the kitchen and assist the cook on some new receipt or preparation, and often have several calls; during the course of the morning the two maids scour out alternately one or two of the rooms, according to size, except on Wednesdays, when one of them is otherwise engaged.

Mr. B. arrives home at twenty minutes to five, and at half-past five we dine; the cloth is laid, and everything prepared as if we had company; it may be a little more trouble to the servants; but when we do have any friends they find it less so; besides it is always uncertain but what Mr. B. may bring somebody home with him, and it prevents slovenly habits; the two maids, with the exception of Wednesdays, are always ready to attend on us. I never allow the coachman to defile our carpets with his stable shoes; all his duties in the house are—the first thing in the morning to clean the knives and forks for the day, for enough are kept out for that purpose, clean the boots and shoes, and those windows the maids cannot easily get at, and assist in the garden if required. Many have made the remark to me, that as you have a male servant why not have him wait at table. I reply that the duties of the stable are incompatible with those of the table, and if he does his duty properly he has enough to do. The servants dine at one—the nursery dinner is at the same hour—and have tea at a quarter to five, by which time the cook has the dinner ready, all but to take it from the fire, and the maids the dining-room ready. After dinner, should we be alone, we have the children and the governess down; if we have company we do not see them; they go to bed at a quarter to eight, and we have tea and coffee at eight; the governess comes and passes the rest of the evening with us; eleven is our usual hour of retiring, before which Mr. B. likes his glass of negus, a biscuit, or a sandwich, which is brought upon a tray.

Selection from
Soyer's Shilling Cookery for the People (1854)

While actively employed, under the authority of government, in a mission to Ireland, in the year of the famine, 1847, it struck me that my services would be more useful to the million than confining them, as I had hitherto done, to the wealthy few. I immediately set to work, but soon found out my error, that I was merely acquainted with the manners and ways of living of the above two classes of society, for whom I had previously catered.

Perceiving that it would be impossible to cure a disease without first arriving at its cause and origin, I found that the only course I had to pursue was to visit personally the abodes, and learn the manners of those to whom I was about to address myself, and thereby get acquainted with their wants.

My readers will easily perceive that, whilst semi-buried in my fashionable culinary sanctorum at the Reform Club, surrounded by the *élite* of society, who daily honoured me with their visits in that lounge of good cheer, I could not gain, through the stone walls of that massive edifice, the slightest knowledge of Cottage life.

Determined to carry out my long thought of project, I cheerfully bade adieu to my wealthy employers, leaving them in a most thriving condition, regretting only my fair visitors; and, like a joyful pilgrim of the olden time, I set forth on my journey, visiting on my route every kind of philanthropic and other useful institution, but more especially the domains of that industrial class, the backbone of every free country— the People,—to whom for the present I bid farewell, leaving them in the hands of *ma chère* Hortense, who will relate to them, with her usual affability, the result of my visits through the United Kingdom.

Introductory Letters.

Dear Eloise,

More than a year has now elapsed since I wrote to you, with a promise that I would send you such receipts as should be of use to the artisan, mechanic, and cottager. The time has, however, passed so quickly, that I was not aware of its hasty flight, until I took up the last edition of our 'Housewife.' But still, dearest, I must say I have not lost any time; for you will find that my letters, which have conveyed my receipts from time to time, have been dated from almost every county in the United Kingdom.

In the course of my peregrinations, I have made a point of visiting the cottages and abodes of the industrious classes generally, and have also closely examined the peculiarities and manners which distinguish each county, as well as the different kinds of labour; and I have viewed with pleasure the exertions made by philanthropic individuals to improve the morals of the labouring class, and render their dwellings more comfortable. But still I have found a great want of knowledge in that one object which produces almost as much comfort as all the rest put together, viz., the means of making the most of that food which the great Architect of the Heavens has so bountifully spread before us on the face of the globe.

Those who visit these humble abodes to inculcate the divine precepts of the Saviour of mankind, do but half the great work, unless they at the same time show how those things which the Almighty has created as food for man can be employed towards his nourishment.

In some of my letters, my dear friend, I think I have sent you a description of some scenes I witnessed in the course of my rambles, especially in Ireland, resulting from a want of knowledge, all of which bears a moral; and what a high feeling of delight and satisfaction it will be to us, should we find that the result of our labour is crowned with success, in ameliorating the conditions of these classes; for believe me, I was right when I stated that the morals of a people greatly depend on their food and wherever the home of an individual, in whatever class of society he may move, is made comfortable and happy, the more moral and religious will that person be.

New Cock-a-Leekie.

Ma chère Amie.—With all due respect to Scotch cookery, I will always give the preference, in the way of soup, to their cock-a-leekie, even before their inimitable hodge-podge. Having a very old friend, from the neighbourhood of Dundee, who used to praise my cock-a-leekie when on a visit to St. John's Wood, I thought I would give him the same treat here, and on looking over my frugal store and garden of Camellia Cottage, I found I had all that was required, barring the bird; but, with a little perseverance and ingenuity, I succeeded in producing a very nice soup, although it wanted the principal ingredient, so that it deceived not only my husband, but my friend from the other side of the Tweed. Here is the receipt:

I bought two pounds of veal cutlet, and cut it into pieces like the flesh from the breast of a fowl, and put them in the pan with a quarter of a pound of butter, the same of lean bacon, three cloves, two good onions sliced, two teaspoonfuls of salt, one of sugar, half a one of pepper, a gill of water; set it on the fire, turn it over until forming a white glaze at the bottom, add to it five pints of water, simmer half an hour, pass through a sieve, save the best pieces of the veal. In the meantime blanch two pounds of leeks, free from the top green part, for ten minutes, in a gallon of water, and drain them; then boil the stock and half the leeks together, till almost in a pulp, then add the other half of the leeks and the meat, also eighteen good fresh French plums; simmer half an hour, and serve.

I must observe that my friend praised it very much for having put in the flesh of the fowl only, as he thought, and not the whole carcase, which is the way they serve it in Scotland; an exceedingly inconvenient way, as everybody expects a piece of the fowl, and you often tear it to pieces in serving.

Simplified Hodge-Podge.

Cut two pounds of fresh scrag of mutton into small pieces, which put into a stewpan, with three quarts of cold water, and a tablespoonful of salt, one ditto of sugar, half a ditto of pepper; set it on the fire; when boiling, place it at the side to simmer for one hour; keep it skimmed; well wash a large carrot, two turnips, two onions, and six small cabbage lettuces; cut them up, and place in the pot, and simmer till done. *A pint* of green peas, if in season, may be added. A carrot grated is an improvement. If in winter, use cabbage instead of lettuce. Serve the meat with it.

CHEF TO THE POOR

The Three-Legged Iron Pot.

Dearest Friend,—You are aware that every cottage throughout the land has a peculiarity in cookery and cooking utensils, which nothing can alter. One of them has a great claim on our gratitude, which neither time nor place can erase. War, famine, epidemic, revolutions, which have from time to time shaken the foundation of mighty empires, has not caused a wrinkle to appear on his noble brow even in this miraculous age of discovery, which has created railways, steam, electricity, photography, and by the last powerful agent we are actually enabled to take the strongest fortifications without bloodshed.

Not even one of the miracles of the nineteenth century has affected his noble position one jot: he is posterity in himself, and no throne ever has been, or ever will be, stronger than his.

In winter, when all nature is desolate, when hoary Frost spreads his white mantle over the myriads of defunct flowers, then this homely king rallies round him his subjects, to entertain, comfort, and feed them, and make them happy, even when nature has almost refused to humanity her powerful service. This mighty monarch, Eloise, is no other than the three-legged iron pot, who has done such good service for so many generations, and will continue to do so if properly treated by his subjects.

So much for his moral virtues; but let us see what he has been doing, and if we can make him do anything more, and that in accordance with the enlightenment of the nineteenth century. You will perhaps say, that it is dangerous to try to make any change in a government so well established. Not at all; my object is not to interfere with his noble position, and deprive him of his rights. On the contrary, I only wish to enrich his kingdom, which I am sure no sensible monarch can object to.

Now for the immortal *Pot-luck*. All these receipts are for one containing two gallons.

Salt Beef.

Put in a piece of six pounds, add four quarts of cold water; boil gently for three hours. One hour before serving, wash clean, and cut the roots away of two cabbages, which cut up in four pieces, and put in the pot with the meat. When done, drain the cabbage, and place round the beef on the dish, and serve. Leave the broth or liquor from the meat on the fire, put in two pounds of split peas, a little pepper and brown sugar; boil slowly till done, and put by, uncovered, for next day, to drink with the cold meat. If more salt and pepper is required, add it: if, on the contrary, it should be too salt, add more water and a pound of potatoes. Or skim-milk may be added, and about one pound of toasted bread, cut into dice, and put in the soup when serving; or half a pound of flour, mixed with a pint of water. Every part of salted beef may be boiled thus, using about four ounces of vegetables to every pound of meat, instead of cabbage. Turnip-tops, brocoli-sprouts, green kale, carrots, turnips, swedes, parsnips, &c. &c., may be used. Suet dumpling may be served with it.

The pieces of beef generally salted are the brisket, edge bone, round, flank, skirt. The ribs, when salted, are very fine, and much more economical than when roasted. This receipt is adopted for a farm-house; but two pounds of beef, and the other things in proportion to be used for a small family. Rice may be used instead of peas.

Salt Pork.

Put four pounds of salt pork, either leg, loin, head, belly, or feet, into the pot with six quarts of water, and one pound of split peas. In one hour add four greens, cut small, or turnip-tops, leeks, parsnips, &c. &c., placed in a net, and boiled in the pot. When done, take them out, and keep warm. Mix half a pound of flour with one pint of water, and put in the pot, and stir it round. Boil for ten minutes, and serve the meat and soup separate, and vegetables round the meat. Pieces of bacon, knuckles of ham, cooked in the same way, are very nice, only they will take rather longer boiling. A teaspoonful of pepper may be added.

You will perceive, my friend, that I have already opened a large field for our old hero, adding in a few lines about twenty new subjects in the shape of receipts to his kingdom.

Rice Panada.

Boil one pound of rice in four quarts of water; add one tablespoonful of powdered sugar, and two tablespoonfuls of salt. Mix with some cold water one pound of flour or oatmeal, so that it forms a thin paste; stir in three teaspoonfuls of curry powder, add all to the rice, boil for twenty minutes, and serve. A quarter of a pound of butter or dripping may be added. *Should it be preferred sweet*, use a quarter of a pound of treacle instead of curry. This will make ten pounds of solid food, and is good either hot or cold.

Peas Panada.

Cut a quarter of a pound of fat bacon, or pork, into small dice; put it in the pot with two onions, sliced, or leeks; fry for ten minutes; keep stirring; then add one and a quarter pound of split peas, two teaspoonfuls of salt, one of sugar, and one gallon of water. Boil till it becomes a purée, or pulp; then add sufficient oatmeal or flour to make it very thick; simmer twenty minutes; keep stirring it, and serve.

Indian meal may be used, but it must be soaked; the husk, which floats, removed, boiled for two hours, and then added to it. If there are no onions, use some sweet herbs.

This may be made sweet by omitting the bacon, and using a quarter of a pound of treacle, and when cold, may be cut to pieces, and given to children as food.

Cheese Stirabout.

Nearly fill the iron pot with water, throw in three tablespoonsful of salt; when boiling, throw in by degrees some Indian meal,—the quantity depends on the quality; on an average, if the water is soft, one pound to every two quarts; that would be four pounds. When well stirred, remove the husk with a spoon, which floats on the top. Then throw in one pound of strong cheese, broken in pieces, or grated. Boil for twenty minutes, and serve. Or, put it on a greasy baking-tin, throw some more cheese on the top, put in the oven for twenty minutes, and serve. Or, allow it to get cold, cut in pieces, and fry.

French Pot au Feu.

(This may also be done in the iron saucepan, stewpan, or baking-pan.)

I cannot expect that this truly national soup of France can be made to perfection, or done with so much care as in that country, therefore I have simplified it, and shall call it *The French Cottage Pot au Feu*, or French Soup.

Put a gallon of water in the pot, put four pounds of the buttock of beef, or shin, or five pounds of the thick part of the leg, three teaspoonfuls of salt, one of pepper, four onions, four leeks cut in pieces, two carrots, and two good-sized turnips, three cloves, one burnt onion, or three spoonfuls of colouring; set it on the fire; when beginning to scum, skim it, and place the pot on one side of the fire. Add now and then a drop of cold water; it will make it clear. Boil four hours. Bread sliced, put into the tureen, and pour the broth with some of the vegetables, over; serve the meat separate, and the remaining vegetables round.

If this simple receipt is well attended to, you will find it a very good soup and bouilli. If you run short of any of the vegetables, make it good with others. If no burnt onions or colouring, the soup will be white, instead of a sherry colour; but still it will be good. In France they always put in half a pound of ox-liver to every four pounds of meat. I am sure they are too good judges, over the water, to spoil their soup; in fact, there the ox-liver costs as much as the meat—sixpence per pound—therefore it is not with a view of saving, but to make it better.

French Ragout of Mutton.

Put in the pot a quarter of a pound of dripping; when hot, peel and cut twenty small turnips, or ten large ones, into pieces the size of a walnut; put them into the fat, and fry until brownish. Take them out, then put into the fat a quarter of a pound of flour; stir round until brown. You have prepared four pounds of scrag of mutton, cut to small pieces; put them in, and stir round; then add enough water to cover the meat; stir until boiling. When the mutton is nearly done, which you will find by trying it with a fork, all the turnips; season with three teaspoonfuls of salt, one of pepper, the same of brown sugar, and a little bit of scraped garlic, if handy. Any part of mutton may be used. Ragout of veal or lamb may be done in this manner.

General Ignorance of the Poor in Cooking.

Ox cheeks may be bought at present, cut from the bone, and very fresh, at about twopence-halfpenny to threepence per pound, in London. It is the most gelatinous food which the ox produces, and contains a large amount of nourishment, as I have already mentioned to you. The only drawback there is to it is the length of time it requires to cook, and the general way in which it is done, being in many cases prejudicial to its use. Frequently on my visits to the abodes of the poor, while in London last winter, I have often seen this article of food completely spoiled. On one occasion, I asked an old lady how she cooked it. 'Sure enough,' said she, 'by fire.' 'But, my dear woman,' I inquired, 'how long do you cook it?' 'Ah!' she replied, 'sometimes as long as an hour, and boiling like the very deuce all the time, till the water will not stand it any longer.' 'And pray,' I asked, 'what do you do with the water?' 'Faith, there is no water left, but only black muck at the bottom of the pot, which I throw away,' was her reply.

When I found she was so ignorant, I asked her if I should come and teach her how to cook, properly, an ox cheek. 'No, faith,' said she, 'I have no money to throw away, not even enough to buy another.' Sanguine as I always am upon my favourite theme, I offered to bring one with me, as a present, the following day, and gave her sixpence to buy some sand to clean her iron pot, which I found done on my arrival the following day; she having also purchased two pennyworth of coals out of the money. I then produced the ox cheek, and put it into the pot with four quarts of cold water, and four teaspoonfuls of salt, and some leaves of celery, which articles were given to her by a neighbouring greengrocer. Her fire was made up, and the pot was placed on it, until boiling, and then removed to the side of it, and skimmed. There I left it, and went round to pay my other visits.

At the end of three hours I returned, and, she having a large basin in the room, I put some crusts of bread in it, and poured the liquid from the pot into it, and the meat I placed on a dish, and sat down with the old dame, serving the soup out into cups with a beer jug, having nothing better, and, to her grat surprise, cut the cheek easily with a very bad knife, it being so tender. After tasting it, and finding it very good, she said she would show her neighbours how to do it. I told her that, if she would do so, I would give her more like receipts, when she exclaimed, 'Bless you, ma'am, do; I will do them as well as you, now I have seen you do it.' In anticipation of sending them to her the next day, I was about to retire, wishing her goodbye. 'Lor', ma'am,' said she, 'you would not go without taking a drop of the "crature." ' To my asontishment, a small bottle was brought out of her pocket, and offered to me. From its strange smell, I was induced to taste it, and I feel confident, if it had been analyzed by the 'Lancet,' it would have proved to be real *blue ruin*, composed, as it was, of a mixture of vitriol, &c.

This opened to me the secret of the emaciated looks of the thousands of the inhabitants of these back alleys, and I could then account for the remainder of my change out of the sixpence. I, however, sent her the following receipts, of course omitting her favourite seasoning—gin.

Having sent her the receipts, as promised, on reconsideration, it occurred to me that the old lady might not be able to read. I was not mistaken, for on calling upon her, I found six elderly matrons and an old man holding council together, and trying to make out the writing. The latter was just sending for his grandson, who, he said, was a scholar, having been three months at a Sunday-school. My arrival set all to rights, at the same time it frightened three of the council away; but I begged the others to stop, and hear the receipts read, which they accordingly did, afterwards giving several copies away.

1st Lesson.—Rub an ox cheek (middle size, or half a large one) with four teaspoonfuls of salt and one of pepper; put it into the iron pot, with four quarts of cold water; set it on the fire to boil; remove it then to the side, and *simmer gently* for three hours after it begins to boil. Skim off the fat, which will do for puddings, and, at the expiration of the time, nearly three quarts of very strong gravy, in addition to the meat properly done and tender, will be found in the pot. A gill of colouring is an improvement to the look of the broth. A head of celery, or some leaves of it, or onions, &c., may be added in boiling. Put the head on a dish, and serve the soup separately, with bread in it.

2nd Lesson.—Or any small quantity of mixed vegetables may be used. They should all be cut into dice, and not peeled, but well cleaned, with the exception of the dried skin of the onion. One pound of rice, at the cost of twopence-halfpenny, when added, is a great improvement; or half-a-pint of split peas, or barley, or a pint of white haricot beans, or a pint of Indian meal soaked the over-night, or a little flour to make the gravy or broth thick. It may be varied in several ways; but the chief point is, when once boiled, simmer slowly till tender, which you may ascertain by piercing it with a fork; if it sticks to it, it is not sufficiently done. Sheep and lamb's head may be done the same way, but will only take one quarter of the time; season accordingly.

This receipt is applicable to all kinds of hard meat.

Good Plain Family Irish Stew.

Take about two pounds of scrag or neck of mutton; divide it into ten pieces, lay them in the pan; cut eight large potatoes and four onions in slices, season with one teaspoonful and a half of pepper, and three of salt; cover all with water; put it into a slow oven for two hours, then stir it all up well, and dish up in deep dishes. If you add a little more water at the commencement, you can take out when half done, a nice cup of broth.

The same simplified.—Put in a pan two pounds of meat as before, which lay at the bottom; cover them with eight whole onions, and these with twelve whole potatoes; season as before; cover over with water, and send to the oven for two hours.

Almost any part of the sheep can be used for Irish stew. A gallon pan is required for this and the preceding receipt.

Ox Tongue, Potted and Braized.

I send you this receipt as a bonne bouche, it being a dish worthy a first-class picnic or the race-course. Take a tongue from the pickle, wash it clean; cut off a part of the rough pieces of the root, put a thick slice of bacon at the bottom of the pan, and over that a pound of lean beefsteak or veal, and then the tongue turned round to fit the pan; have a cow-heel, parboiled and ready boned, place it on the tongue, and cover it with another slice of bacon, and a slice of beef or veal; season with two teaspoonfuls of pepper, a little powdered ginger and cloves, one bay-leaf, one carrot sliced, and two onions sliced; add two wineglassfuls of brandy or sherry, four of old ale, and one quart of water; cover well over, and put in a slow oven for three hours; take off the cover, and put a piece of board with a weight on the top until cold, then the next day turn it out of the pan, which you can do by placing the pan in hot water. But should you wish to use the tongue hot for dinner, take it out, and when done with it, put the remains in and press, as before described. The vegetables may also be pressed in with the meat or served hot round the tongue.

The remains of pickled ox tongues are very nice, intermixed and placed in a pan, and pressed, when they will turn out like collared head. A tongue boiled in plain water will take about two hours.

Ox Tongues, Fresh and Pickled.

Put in the pan, as above, add two carrots, four turnips, four cloves, ten small dumplings, fill the pan with water, add either a little bay-leaf, thyme, or winter savory; stew in an oven for three hours, trim and dish up with vegetables, and dumplings round, making soup of the broth. For fresh ox tongue, proceed as above, adding three teaspoonfuls of salt.

Veal.

Take two pounds of the leg of veal, or meat from the shoulder, or the neck or breast, in fact any part, cut in pieces; season it with one teaspoonful and a half of salt, and a half of pepper, and add a quarter of a pound of bacon cut in slices. To vary the seasoning, use herbs. It will also be very good with some suet pudding, previously boiled in small balls, if you omit either potatoes or stuffing. The pieces of veal should be rolled in flour; add half a pint of water, if with potatoes, and more, if pudding or stuffing; bake one hour and a half, and serve. Mushrooms may be added.

On Roasting.

My Dear Eloise,—My last letter you must have misunderstood, I did not mean that roasting before the fire should be entirely done away with, but that, on the score of economy, it should not be practised in the cottage, but that my new plan of semi-roasting should be followed. I was the more particularly led to these remarks, from having, last Sunday, immediately after church, visited several colliers' cottages belonging to a Mr. Pope, close to this place. My motive for doing so was to see the economy of the cottage, as well as the kind of food they had for dinner. The first I went into had a piece of the belly or flap of beef, just taken down from a dangle, having been roasted. It was lying in the dripping pan, and was a great deal over done; in fact, dried. Noticing, in the course of conversation, that the first was spoiling it still more, I took a plate from the table, and placed it against it, so that it should not burn. The old lady noticed my proceeding, and asked me if I was going to have a bit of dinner with them? 'No, thank you, my dear madam,' replied I. 'Then let me take away the plate, as it will spoil our dinner.' 'How do you make that out?' I asked. 'Well, the fat is not yet half out of the meat, and my Thomas will not eat fat, unless it is dripping in the crust of pies or puddings.' I then perceived that the meat was, in their estimation, a second consideration, and that they paid the price of beef for the fat, paying eightpence per pound for the meat, when they could get the fat at fivepence. There was scarcely any nutriment left in the meat—that which weighed five pounds before roasting, weighing hardly three pounds when done. There were seven to dine off it—the grandmother, the two parents, and four children. There was, besides, a few potatoes galloping on the fire—no other vegetable, and no puddings or sweets for the children, but excellent home-made bread, and not bad small beer. You may now perceive that some little improvement in this style of cookery would be an immense saving to these cottagers, and out of the three shillings and fourpence they paid for the beef, if done in the pan, with a pudding and potatoes under, and the meat not quite so fat, they would have got a good dinner and plenty for the next day.

I visited, immediately after, several other of the cottages, in which I found steaks cooked dry, indeed, some half burnt, chumps of mutton half done, half legs of mutton neither boiled or baked; in one a sheep's head baked, and very nicely done, with potatoes round it, which was very inviting; there was also suet dumplings for the children, with treacle over. This cottage was cleaner than any of the others, and the children were neatly dressed, and about to change their costume, in order to do full justice to the treacle dumplings. In giving those rosy-cheeked urchins a few pence, I retired much gratified by my visit to these antediluvian workmen, who pass one-third of their life in the bowels of the earth.

You will perceive from what I have said, that to the artisan, labourer, and even the small tradesman, the old mode of roasting, which comes to us from Homeric ages and primitive times, is an extravagant and wasteful mode of cooking, and the sooner it is reformed the better. Though it is preferable to meat done in a baker's oven, if well attended to.

But first let me add one more remark on the experience of that day. Returning to the Normanton Hotel to dinner, we had a beautiful dish of greens; and what do you think those greens were? green young nettles, which I had asked the gardener to gather for us the day previous, and in less than half an hour we had a basket full. I picked them with gloves, but he made a grasp at a large quantity, and I found that they did not prick him. He got them as fast as a monkey could get chestnuts out of hot cinders. The cook dressed them, according to my directions, exactly like spinach, and most who ate of them thought they were spinach, only rather too hot of pepper, which is their peculiar nature.

I found that they are known in this part of the country as being good and wholesome in the spring; but because the people can have them for nothing, they will not partake of them; like the watercresses, that rot in every clear stream in the neighbourhood. I intend to make another trial or so on the nettles, which I will forward to you.

Family Steak Pie.

Take and cut two pounds of beef in slices, two pounds of potatoes, a quarter of a pound of onions, season with three teaspoonfuls of salt, one of pepper; mix a well together; put the meat and potatoes into the pie-dish, in alternate layers; add a pint of water; cover over, as above and bake for one hour and a half.

The Artisan's Pie.

Any pieces of meat, but not too fat—four ounces of fat to every pound of meat is enough. Take two pounds of meat cut in slices, season it with three teaspoonfuls of salt, one of pepper, four sliced onions; peel four pounds of potatoes, cut in thick slices, which place in the bottom of the dish, then a layer of potatoes, then the meat; season well; add a pint of water, and bake for two hours.

Poor Man's Potatoe Pie.

Wash and peel six pounds of potatoes, cut them in slices; take half-a-pound of the fat of mutton or beef, or dripping, cut into small dice; season the whole with a teaspoonful of pepper and three of salt; cover with paste, and bake one hour and a half.

A bloater, boned and cut up with the fat, makes a nice change of flavour.

Vegetables.

As I have before remarked, the food of man, in order to give proper nourishment, shoud be often varied; in fact, his health depends upon it, and nature seems to have given him those instruments, the teeth, by which he is enabled to masticate both animal and vegetable food, besides having provided him abundantly with vegetable produce, which seems the balance, in point of health, between that and rich animal food. It is to be regretted that the labouring poor of this country do not partake of more vegetables than they do at present. If we travel over the country, we are surprised to find how small a portion of ground is engaged in horticulture; the consequence is that, excepting near large towns, scarcely a vegetable is to be obtained, and the poor are doomed to live almost entirely on bread and cheese and a small portion of animal food, not even a potatoe is to be had during the winter and spring of the year.

Nettles.

Wash them well, drain, put them into plenty of boiling water with a little salt, boil for twenty minutes, or a little longer, drain them, put them on a board and chop them up, and either serve plain, or put them in the pan with a little salt, pepper, and a bit of butter, or a little fat and gravy from a roast; or add to a pound two teaspoonfuls of flour, a gill of skim milk, a teaspoonful of sugar, and serve with or without poached eggs.

This extraordinary spring production, of which few know the value, is at once pleasing to the sight, easy of digestion, and at a time of the year when greens are not to be obtained, invaluable as a purifier of the blood; the only fault is, as I have told you above, Eloise, they are to be had for nothing; it is a pity that children are not employed to pick them, and sell them in market towns.

Another unused vegetable is mangel wurzel. The young leaf of the mangel wurzel, cleaned and cooked as above, is extremely good.

In all my various visits to cottages during this spring, I have found but one where either of the above vegetables were in use, and that belonging to a gardener, who knew their value.

These nettles are good during five months of the year; for even when large, the tops are tender. They make excellent tea, which is very refreshing and wholesome.

Sweet Docks.

Also a wild vegetable, or weed, are very good when done as follows, using about two-thirds of sweet dock, and one-third of nettles, boiled with a little carbonate of soda. When done, strain them, and to about one pint basin full, add one onion sliced and fried, a sprig of parsley, a little butter, pepper, and salt; put into a stewpan on the fire, stir, and gradually add a handful of oatmeal; when you think the meal has been sufficiently boiled, dish up and serve as a vegetable.

Sweet Puddings.

Plum Pudding.

Pick and stone half a pound of Malaga raisins, wash and dry the same quantity of currants, chop, not too fine, three-quarters of a pound of beef suet, put it in a convenient basin, with six ounces of sugar, two ounces of mixed candied peel sliced, three ounces of flour, three ditto of bread-crumbs, a little grated nutmeg, four eggs, a gill of water, or perhaps a little more, to form a nice consistence; butter a mould, put a piece of white paper over the top and round the sides, tie it in a cloth, boil for four hours in plenty of water; when done, remove the cloth, turn it out of the mould, take the paper off the sides and top, and serve with sweet sauce round; it may also be boiled in a cloth.

The above is only for Christmas. Now for every day.

Put into a basin one pound of flour, one of chopped suet, half a pound of mixed fruit, a little spice, grated lemon-peel, three ounces of sugar, two eggs, half a pint of milk, or enough to make it a proper thickness, tie it in a cloth, boil four hours, turn it out, and serve with melted butter, or sweet sauce; breadcrumbs instead of flour is good, or half of each.

A Series of Economical Puddings,
which can be made either in a mould, basin, tart-dish, or tin cake-pan.

Well butter either, fill lightly with any of the following ingredients:—Either stale buns, muffins, crumpets, pastry, white or brown bread, sliced and buttered, the remains of sponge-cakes, macaroons, ratafias, almond cake, gingerbread, biscuit of any kind, previously soaked. For a change with any of the above, you may intermix with either fresh or dried fruit, or preserves, even plums, grated cocoa nut, &c. When your mould is full of either of the above, put in a basin a quarter teaspoonful of either ginger, a little mixed spice, or cinnamon, if handy, grated orange, lemon, or a few drops of any essence you choose; put in three eggs, which beat well, add three gills of milk for every quarter mould. When the above is well mixed, fill up nearly to the rim. It can be either baked or boiled, or put into a saucepan one-third full of water, with the lid over, and let simmer for about one hour. Pass a knife round the inside of the basin or mould, turn out your pudding, pour over either melted butter with a little sugar, the juice of a lemon or spirit sauce. It ought to be the pride of each cottager's wife to find out a peculiar and cheap mixture, which would entirely depend on the part of the country in which she lives, that would be liked by the family, and give it as a treat every Sunday.

Farm Custard.

Put in a small saucepan the yolks of four eggs, four teaspoonfuls of sugar, the peel of half a lemon, or a quarter of that grated, a grain of salt; mix all well, then add half a pint of milk; set the whole on the fire, stir continually with a wooden spoon till it gets thick and smooth; but do not let it boil, or it will curd; then put it in a basin to cool, stirring now and then; if handy, pass it through a sieve, it gives it a nice appearance, and serve either in glasses or cups, with any fresh or stewed fruit, orange peel, or any essence, brandy, or rum, may be used for flavouring.

When at our friend Lindley's house in Yorkshire, I took a gill of cream, whipped it, and mixed it with the custard when cold. It made it very white and delicate. The custard may be whipped while being made.

You wish to know what I did with the white of the eggs, and perfectly right that you should. Well, I put them in a basin with a very little bit of salt, then with a whisk I beat them till firm and as white as snow, then I add four teaspoonfuls of pounded sugar, mix it well; I put a pint of milk to boil in a very clean *sauté*, or frying-pan, and, with the aid of a spoon, I scoop off the white in the shape of eggs, dropping them in the milk, letting them remain till done, turning them occasionally; take them out, and serve when cold, pouring some of the custard over; the remaining milk was used for puddings.

Even now, Eloise, you do not seem satisfied, so I send you a receipt for a soufflé. It seems to you, no doubt, very simple; let me tell you, however, that it is so only in appearance; the great secret is in properly beating the white of the eggs; therefore, if you fail in your attempt, do not blame me, the details of the receipt being quite accurate.

Egg Pudding, or Omelette Soufflé.

Break four eggs; carefully separate the white from the yolk, put both in different basins; add to the yolk three teaspoonfuls of powdered sugar and one of flour, a little grated orange or lemon peel, or any other flavour you prefer; stir the whole for five minutes, then beat the white of the eggs with a whisk; when firm, mix lightly with the yolk till forming a nice, smooth, light, and rather firm substance; then put it either in a tin pan, cake pan, or a common pan, which can stand the heat of the oven, buttering it well.

If in a tin dish, shape it in pyramids with a knife, put it in a moderate oven from ten to twelve minutes, sugar over and serve. When nearly done, an incision or two with the point of a knife may be made through the thin crust; it will make it lighter. You may also put two ounces of butter in the frying-pan, and when hot put in your mixture, and toss it round three or four times; put it on a dish, bake as above. Ten minutes will do it.

First Class Yorkshire Pudding.

Beat up two eggs in a basin, add to them three good tablespoonfuls of flour, with a pint of milk by degrees, and a little salt; butter the pan, bake half an hour, or bake under the meat, cut it in four, turn it, and when set on both sides it is done. A tin dish one inch and a half deep and eight inches wide, is the most suitable for such proportion.

Second Class.

Put in a basin four tablespoonfuls of flour; add a quarter of a teaspoonful of salt and a little pepper, beat one egg with a pint of milk, pour over on the flour by degrees till smooth, and proceed as above.

Third Class.

If no eggs, chop two ounces of beef suet fine, add a little soda, mix as above, and bake the same. A little chopped parsley, chives, or aromatic herbs, may be introduced in either of the above. These receipts are good with any kind of roasted or baked meat, or poultry. To facilitate the turning, when one side is brown and the pudding well set, cut it into several pieces, turning with a knife or a fork. If preferred served whole, put a plate on the top of the baking tin, turn it over, and slip it back; let it remain in the tin ten minutes longer, and serve either round or separate.

On Salads.

What is more refreshing than salads when your appetite seems to have deserted you, or even after a capacious dinner—the nice, fresh, green, and crisp salad, full of life and health, which seems to invigorate the palate and dispose the masticating powers to a much longer duration. The herbaceous plants which exist fit for food for man, are more numerous than may be imagined, and when we reflect how many of these, for want of knowledge, are allowed to rot and decompose in the fields and gardens, we ought, without loss of time, to make ourselves acquainted with their different natures and forms, and vary our food as the season changes.

Although nature has provided all these different herbs and plants as food for man at various periods of the year, and perhaps at one period more abundant than another, when there are so many ready to assist in purifying and cleansing the blood, yet it would be advisable to grow some at other seasons, in order that the health may be properly nourished.

However, at what period of the year or at what time, these may be partaken of, the following dressing is the one I should always recommend.

In my description of salads, I have advised and described the use of them as plainly dressed, such as they are in many parts of Europe, but perhaps many of our readers will want to know how the sauce is made which is often used with the salad herbs, or such as the Italian count used to make some years since, by which he made a fortune in dressing salads for the tables of the aristocracy. It is as follows:—

Fish Salad.

A very nice and elegant dish may be made with all kinds of cold fish, and some kinds of shell-fish; but the following way of dressing is for a small *Lobster Salad*, and will do for all fish salads: Have the bowl half filled with any kind of salad herb you like, either endive or lettuce, &c. Then break a lobster in two, open the tail, extract the meat in one piece, break the claws, cut the meat of both in small slices, about a quarter of an inch thick, arrange these tastefully on the salad, take out all the soft part from the belly, mix it in a basin with a teaspoonful of salt, half of pepper, four of vinegar, four of oil; stir it well together, and pour on the salad; then cover it with two hard eggs, cut in slices, a few slices of cucumber, and, to vary, a few capers and some fillets of anchovy; stir lightly, and serve.

If for a dinner, ornament it with some flowers of the nasturtium and marigold.

Crab Salad.—*The same as the lobster.*

Remains of cold cod, fried soles, halibut, brill, turbot, sturgeon cut as lobster, plaice, &c., may be used in the same way.

Ma chère Eloise,—In the foregoing receipts you will perceive that I have used each salad herb separate, only mixing them with the condiments or with vegetable fruit. I have a strong objection to the almost diabolical mixture of four or five different sorts of salad in one bowl, and then chopping them as fine as possible; the freshness as well as the flavour of each is destroyed; they agree about as well together as would brandy and soda water mixed with gin and gingerbeer, for each salad herb has its own particular flavour, and the condiments, which are onions, chives, parsley, chervil, tarragon, celery, eschalot, garlic, cucumber, beetroot, &c. &c. are only to give it piquancy like the oil and vinegar, salt, and pepper.

Mustard and cress and water cresses may be considered as a slight condiment, but should be used accordingly. It is remarkable that though the inhabitants of this country were for so many centuries (from the nature of the climate) a salad-eating people, yet they seem the least to know how to season them. Until the introduction of the potato, in 1650, and which was first eaten as a sweetmeat, stewed in sack wine and sugar, the various salads were in common use on the tables in Britain, of which country most of the plants are indigenous.

Relishes.

Herring in Whisky.

Well wash and clean a red herring, wipe it dry and lace it in a pie-dish, having cut off the head, and split it in two up the back; put a gill or two of whisky over the herring, according to size, hold it on one side of the dish, so that it is covered with the spirit, set it alight, and when it goes out the fish is done.

Devilled Bones.

Take the bones of any remaining joint of poultry, which has still some meat on, which cut across slightly, and then make a mixture of mustard, salt, cayenne, and pepper, and one teaspoonful of mushroom ketchup to two of mustard; rub the bones well with this, and broil rather brownish.

Mushrooms, or the Pearl of the Fields.

I here send you, Eloise, a most sumptuous relish. There is one dish which the Devonshire cottager can procure and enjoy better than even the most wealthy person. It is the mushroom. After having plucked them, perhaps on the road home for his breakfast, broiled them over a nice bright fire, seasoned with a little pepper and salt, and a small bit of butter placed inside of them; the flavour is then pure and the aroma beautiful, but by accident I discovered a new and excellent way to cook them. Being in Devonshire, at the end of September, and walking across the fields before breakfast to a small farmhouse, I found three very fine mushrooms, which I thought would be a treat, but on arriving at the house I found it had no oven, a bad gridiron, and a smoky coal fire. Necessity, they say, is the mother of Invention, I immediately applied to our grand and universal mamma, how I should dress my precious mushrooms, when a gentle whisper came to my ear, and the following was the result.

I first cut two good slices of bread, half an inch thick, large enough to cover the bottom of a plate, toasted them, and spread some Devonshire cream over the toast. I removed all the earthy part from the mushroom, and laid them gently on the toast, head downwards, slightly sprinkled them with salt and pepper, and placed in each a little of the clotted cream; I then put a tumbler over each and placed them on a stand before the fire, and kept turning them so as to prevent the glass breaking, and in ten to fifteen minutes the glass was filled with vapour, which is the essence of the mushroom; when it is taken up, do not remove the glass for a few minutes; by which time the vapour will have become condensed and gone into the bread, but when it is, the aroma is so powerful as to pervade the whole apartment.

The sight, when the glass is removed, is most inviting, its whiteness rivals the everlasting snows of Mont Blanc, and the taste is worthy of Lucullus. Vitellius would never have dined without it; Apicius would never have gone to Greece to seek for crawfish; and had he only half the fortune left when he committed suicide, he would have preferred to have left proud Rome and retire to some villa or cottage to enjoy such an enticing dish.

Therefore, modern gourmets, never fancy that you have tasted mushrooms until you have tried this simple and new discovery. Remember the month—the end of September or the beginning of October.

As Devonshire cream is not to be obtained everywhere, use butter, or boil some milk till reduced to cream, with a little salt, pepper, and one clove; when warm put in an ounce of butter, mixed with a little flour, stir round, put the mushroom on the toast with this sauce, cover with a basin, and place in the oven for half an hour. In this way all kinds of mushrooms will be excellent. They may be put into baking pans; cover with a tumbler as above, and bake in oven.

Welsh Rabbit.

Toast a round of bread from a quartern loaf; put about four ounces of cheese into a small saucepan or pipkin with a teaspoonful of mustard, a little pepper and salt, and a wineglass of ale; break the cheese small, set it on the fire, and stir until it is melted, when pour over the toast, and serve quickly.

2nd.—Toast a round of bread, and place on it two pieces of cheese, single Gloucester, a quarter of an inch thick; place it before the fire, and as the cheese melts, spread it over the bread with a knife, also a little cayenne and mustard.

3rd.—Take a penny French roll, cut off a thin slice from one end, and take out some of the crumb and place it in the oven. Melt the cheese as above, and pour it into the roll. It is very good for a journey, or a sportsman, and can be eaten cold.

4th, or Irish Rabbit.—Toast a round of bread; chop up four ounces of cheese, a small piece of butter, one gherkin, some mustard, pepper, and salt, until it is quite a paste; spread it over the toast, and place them in the oven for five minutes, and serve hot.

Mussels

Mussels may be eaten plain. Put a quart of them in a pan, after being well washed, with some onions cut in slices, also a little parsley; put them on a sharp fire for ten minutes, when they will all open; then remove the beard and black part, and eat them plain with some of their juice.

Oysters on Toast.

Open twelve very large oysters, put them in a pan with their liquor, a quarter of a teaspoonful of pepper, a wineglass of milk, two cloves, and a small piece of mace, if handy; boil a few minutes until set, mix one ounce of butter with half an ounce of flour, put it, in small pieces, in the pan, stir round; when near boiling pour over the toast, and serve. A little sugar and the juice of a lemon, is a great improvement.

A Series of New and Cheap Drinks.

Put a gallon of water on to boil, cut up one pound of apples, each one into quarters, put them in the water, and boil them until they can be pulped, pass the liquor through a cullender, boil it up again with half a pound of brown sugar, scum, and bottle for use, taking care not to cork the bottle, and keep in a cool place: the apples may be eaten with sugar.

Another Way.

Bake the apples first, then put them in a gallon pan, add the sugar, and pour boiling water over, let it get cold, pass the liquor as above, and bottle.

Apple Toast and Water.

A piece of bread, slowly toasted till it gets quite black, and added to the above, makes a very nice and refreshing drink for invalids.

Apple Barley Water.

A quarter of a pound of pearl barley instead of toast added to the above, and boil for one hour, is also a very nice drink.

Apple Rice Water.

Half a pound of rice, boiled in the above until in pulp, passed through a cullender, and drunk when cold.

All kinds of fruits may be done the same way.

Figs and French plums are excellent; also raisins.

A little ginger, if approved of, may be used.

For Spring Drink.

Rhubarb, in the same quantities, and done in the same way as apples, adding more sugar, is very cooling.

Also green gooseberries.

Lemonade.

Cut in very thin slices three lemons, put them in a basin, add half a pound of sugar, either white or brown; bruise altogether, add a gallon of water, and stir well. It is then ready.

For Summer Drink.

One pound of red currants, bruised with some raspberry, half a pound of sugar added to a gallon of cold water, well stirred, allowed to settle, and bottled.

Mulberry.

The same, adding a little lemon-peel.

A little cream of tartar or citric acid added to these renders them more cooling in summer and spring.

Soyer's New Christmas Receipts.

Soyer's New Christmas Pudding.

You are right, dearest Hortense, this is by far the most delicate and best plum-pudding I ever tasted, without being, at the same time, too rich; the combination of ingredients is perfect, and although there is hardly any difference in the materials used in this to an ordinary plum-pudding, it tasted to me like one made of entirely new ingredients, and I consider it a great acquisition to this, the hundredth thousand of our Shilling Cookery.

This receipt, if closely followed, would, at this festive season of the year, save tons of fruit and other expensive ingredients, which are partly wasted for want of knowing how to turn them to the best advantage.

Carefully prepare the following previous to mixing the pudding:—

Christmas Pudding.

Four ounces of stoned raisins, four ounces of sultanas, half-a-pound of well-cleaned currants, half-a-pound of beef suet chopped fine, two ounces of powdered white sugar, two ounces of flour, half-a-pound of bread crumbs, twelve bitter almonds blanched chopped small, half a nutmeg grated, two ounces of candied citron, the peel of half a small lemon chopped fine. When all is prepared separately, put in a basin, break over four eggs, and add half a gill of brandy. Mix these all well the evening before wanted, cover over till the morning, then add half a gill of milk, and well stir your pudding; slightly butter a cloth, sprinkle a little flour over, put it in a basin, pour in the mixture, tie your cloth in the usual way, not too tight; put in half a gallon of boiling water, adding a little more now and then to keep it to half a gallon, let simmer two hours and thirty minutes, turn out of cloth, and serve on a hot dish.

After which, when at the dining-room door, pour round a gill of either brandy or rum, which set on fire with a piece of paper; place the dish on the table, let burn half a minute, and pour the following sauce over from the saucer. Cut seven or eight slices from the pudding crossways, or according to number, when help, and serve very hot.

The sauce I prefer with it is as follows: Make half-a-pint of melted butter, or ordinary plain melted butter, rather thick, add to it two teaspoonfuls of sugar, a small glassful of noyeau, the juice of half a lemon, and a pat of butter; stir quick, pour over your pudding when very hot, or serve separate in a sauce-boat.

You beg of me a simplified receipt of my Christmas pudding. You cannot expect that it will be as good as the above; and if I consent to give it you, it is upon the sensible remark that you make to me on this subject, that though it cannot be expected to be as good as the above, yet in its way it will far excel thousands of puddings with richer ingredients, which are made at this festive season of the year for want of judgment in the proportion.

The above Pudding simplifed.

Stone half a pound of common raisins, wash and clean half a pound of currants, half a pound of beef suet chopped fine, two ounces of brown sugar, three ounces of flour, three eggs, half a pound of bread crumbs, half a gill of rum, and a gill of milk. Mix all well the night previous, put in a cloth as above, boil three hours, and serve. Pour over melted butter in which you have put one tablespoonful of sugar and the juice of half a lemon, if handy.

How to vary and improve the Pudding at a trifling expense.

The addition of a little mixed spice or pounded cinnamon, lemon, or orange peel, chopped fine, or a drop or two of any essence, a couple of sharp apples cut in dice, and a few dates or French prunes. Cut the same, using only half the raisins or currants.

New Christmas Dish.

A most delicious and cheap dish, easily made.—Buy sixpenny worth of light sponge-cake and raspberry rolls, which cut across in slices about half-an-inch thick; lay them on a small dish in a circle, one lying half over the other; put in an oven for ten minutes, add in a small stew-pan two tablespoonsful of currant-jelly, two glasses of sherry, put on the fire, and when boiling pour over and serve.

Pancake à la De la Pole.

Break four fresh eggs, separate the yolk from the white, which put in two different basins, add to the yoke two tablespoonsful of white pounded sugar, half a one of flour, half the rind of either an orange or lemon, chopped very fine, or a drop of any good essence; beat the whole together, and then with a whisk whip the white of the eggs as you would for a sponge-cake: This requires some practice. When hard and white as snow, mix lightly with the yolk, then have ready a very clean frying-pan, which put on a slow fire, add an ounce of butter, when melted put in two tablespoonsful of the batter, let it fry half a minute, then toss it up on the other side, as a pancake, turn it on a dish, use all the batter thus, and when done put them one on the other. Sugar over, bake ten minutes, and serve. While paying a visit in Devonshire, where I invented this dish, I introduced a gill of cream, previously whipped, which made it very delicate. Ordinary cream may be used instead.

How to make Mincemeat.

Chop fine one pound of beef suet, four ounces of lean beef previously roasted, half a pound of apples, four ounces of raisins previously stoned; the above articles must be chopped separately; put them all in a basin, add to it two ounces of candied lemon and orange peel and citron; cut these small, then put in a quarter ounce of mixed spice, four ounces of sugar, mix the whole well together, add in the juice of a lemon, a quarter of a pint of brandy, stir it, put it in a jar, and use when required. Stewed tripe (cold) may be used instead of beef, and half an ounce of bitter almonds and lemon peel. The above, if made one week before Christmas, will answer every purpose, as I wholly object to fermentation. Line your patty-pan with puff-paste, egg over, sugar, and bake.

Royal Christmas Fare.

The mince-meat as made at Windsor Castle every year, the ingredients being mixed one month before wanted, is as follows: 240 lbs. of raisins, 400 lbs. of currants, 200 lbs. of lump sugar, 3 lbs. of cinnamon, 3 lbs. of nutmeg, 3 lbs. of cloves, 3 lbs. of ground allspice, 2 lbs. of ginger, 300 lbs. of beef, 350 lbs. of suet, 24 bushels of apples, 240 lemons, 30 lbs. of cedret, 72 bottles of brandy, 3 lbs. of mace, 60 lbs. of lemon-peel, and 60 lbs. of orange-peel.

New Style of Mince Pies.

Have ready some mince-pie pans, take some firm butter, cover the inside of each pan with it to the depth of an eighth of an inch, lay on this half an inch of bread crumb, let it all be of the same depth, then fill your pans with stewed apples, as above, till quite full, then lay on some more bread crumbs, on which put a small piece of butter, and bake for half an hour in an oven, then turn out on a dish. They will be found excellent. You may use any kind of small baking-dish.

Goose Stuffing.

For a middling sized bird, peel and cut in two, crossways, four large-sized onions, weighing altogether about one pound; slice these rather fine, chop them up with some green sage, or buise with both hands some dry; then put in a black pot or pan two ounces of butter, lard, or dripping; add in the chopped onions, two teaspoonsful of sage if green, three if dry, one of salt, one of brown sugar, half one of pepper. Set this on a slow fire, letting it stew for fifteen to twenty minutes; then with a spoon stuff your bird while the onions are quite hot. This may be done in winter a few days before it is put to the spit, as it imparts to the goose a nice savoury flavour.

How to Vary the Stuffing.

Four tablespoonsful of bread crumb may be added, or two of broken biscuit, or four of chopped apples, or four of rice, or four of cold boiled potatoes, or a little chopped lemon, or a little herbs of almost any kind, or chopped boiled beetroot.

Chef to All Nations
The Pantropheon

Early in 1850 a dreadful rumour rang round the corridors of the Reform Club. The great Soyer had resigned! We will never be sure quite what brought this about. The official reason was that he had objected to a proposed change in the club rules which would allow non-members into the coffee room every day. He considered that this would turn the place into a 'regular restaurant' and that the resulting increase in work for the kitchen staff would lead inevitably to lower standards. There is something unconvincing here. Soyer was certainly adamant about the high quality of the food from his kitchens, but was this proposal really a just cause for leaving? Several other reasons suggest themselves. Perhaps the club committee had become irritated at the large amount of time which their chef was devoting to outside causes, such as soup kitchens and art exhibitions. Perhaps they resented the way he seemed to hog the limelight. Perhaps Soyer himself felt that, culinarily, he had done all he could for the Reform and needed a change.

Whatever the truth of the matter, he left his beloved kitchens in Pall Mall in May of that year. Any regrets he may have had were swept rapidly aside by the flood of good wishes, invitations, propositions and suggestions which followed. He should conduct a Gastronomic Pleasure Party to Paris, said one; he should take over the running of a chain of London restaurants, said another; he should undertake only the grandest of city banquets, said another; he should establish a College of Domestic Economy, said a fourth. The most sensible (if least glamorous) advice was given by a Mr T.P—, 'a high authority in law', who suggested that he should 'take a house and give therein, without any clap-trap, show, or external demonstration, the best dinners that a man could get in London.' Needless to say, Soyer—a lover of clap-trap, show and external demonstration—took no notice of the estimable Mr T.P—. As his biographers resignedly remark: 'the course followed by M. Soyer afterwards, proves that, even then, this good advice was of very little use, if any.'

The fact is that Soyer was not a taker of advice. He had to lead, and all his enterprises had, if possible, to be conceived by him alone. So first of all he set out on a tour of the provinces to promote his latest invention, The Magic Stove. Strictly speaking, this was not entirely his own brainchild:

One day the Chevalier Lemolt brought with him a small stove, not above six inches in diameter, heated by spirits of wine, ingeniously contrived. M. Soyer at once perceived the importance of this little apparatus, and, very shortly afterwards, it was brought out, with valuable improvements, as 'Soyer's Magic Stove,' to which was added the 'Camp Kitchen.' The noise it created all over the country was something extraordinary: his office, No. 5, Charing Cross, was crowded from morning till night by the aristocracy—particularly at the hour named for the great *chef's* own attendance to cook, with his wonderful dexterity, *les côtelettes sauce tomate, filets de volaille à la maitre d'hôtel, foie de veau au jambon, œufs au miroir,* and his famous *rognons de moutons aux fines herbes*; all cooked on the drawing-room table, and as quickly demolished by the company present, accompanied with claret, champagne, Soyer's nectar, etc., etc.

The sale of the Magic Stove was so rapid, that it was difficult to supply the orders; but through the exertion of Messrs. Gardner, the famous lamp manufacturers, of Charing Cross, and M. Soyer's great exertion in the provinces, in less than fifteen months between £5000 and £6000 worth of stoves were sold, leaving an enormous profit, but which unfortunately did not enter into Soyer's pocket.

Memoirs of Soyer by Volant & Warren

Another profitable line—at least in terms of prestige—was Soyer's sauces. The first of these appeared in 1848: one for the gentlemen, and one for the ladies. With their elegantly bulbous bottles and their curvaceous labelling they were immediately popular, even being reviewed in glowing terms in the press. The *Sun* called Soyer 'the Great Napoleon of Gastronomy'; the *Morning Post* described the sauce as 'so perfect that "it would create a soul under the ribs of death" '. Soyer's Relish did even better, whilst Soyer's Nectar, composed 'of the most delicious fruits, mingled with the scientific dash of a master-hand', inspired not only delirious newspaper articles, but several poems. One of these is after the style of Flann O'Brien's 'Hymn to Porter'.*

> 'When I arise in feverish pain,
> And feel a giddiness of brain,
> What brings back my health again?
>   Soyer's Nectar.
>
> Walking in the cool parterre,
> Fête champêtre, or fancy fair,
> What regales the debonair?
>   Soyer's Nectar.'

Such were the materials which might have made the newly freelance Soyer a wealthy man. Of course, they did not. The receipts for the sauces and Relish were sold to a Mr Crosse and a Mr Blackwell (the Relish was still being manufactured in the 1920s), and his share in the Nectar went in 1850 for a mere £800.

After the Reform Club, Soyer could only direct his ambitions in one course—upwards. His projects began to grow increasingly extravagant. In June 1850, he waas invited to prepare a fête champêtre for the nobility and gentry in honour of two French playwrights, Scribe and Halévy, who had

---

*'When things go wrong and will not come right,
Though you do the best you can,
When life looks black at the hour of night—
A PINT OF PLAIN IS YOUR ONLY MAN' etc.
At Swim-Two-Birds

adapted Shakespeare's *Tempest* for Her Majesty's Theatre. Soyer responded with a magnificent spread, which included one of his now customary tours-de-force, named Croustade Shakespearienne à la Halévy-Scribe. This was a replica of the wrecked 'Tempesta', complete with jelly and spun-sugar waves, chartreuses de pêches in imitation of the cargo, and flotsam of grapes, apricots and peaches.

Exactly a month later, he was organizing an even vaster dinner, for one thousand people, for the Royal Agricultural Society at Exeter Castle. It was a challenge on a scale which he had never faced before but, as Volant and Warren shrewdly point out: 'Everything of importance undertaken by M. Soyer was always for him a stimulant; and as he was ever fond of doing things as nobody else did, to add to his reputation, he did not forget that this was an opportunity to distinguish himself. He was not a man to consider whether he would keep within the bounds of his contract—gain or loss did not enter into his head, so long as the committee were satisfied that the preparations made were on such a scale that the guests would not only have plenty for their money, but that all would be done in a superior style.'

Grandeur and plenty were two of Soyer's most obvious hallmarks, and the committee were not to be disappointed. He roasted an entire ox, weighing 500 lb, in the castle yard, as well as providing copious amounts of ribs or beef, roast lamb, veal galantine, ham, pressed beef, beef à la Garrick, chicken, venison pies, pies à la Soyer, salads, tarts, potatoes and special Exeter puddings. There was enough left over from this suitably yeoman blow-out to furnish a feast for seven hundred poor people of the city next day.

In October, the incandescent Soyer outdid himself once again, at a grand civic banquet given by the Lord Mayor of York and the other provincial mayors to Prince Albert and the Lord Mayor of London. He was given carte blanche, and was able to indulge his delight in pomp and splendour to the utmost. Here is the staggering bill of fare:

Grand Civic Banquet given to His Royal Highness Prince Albert
and the Lord Mayor of London, by the Lord Mayor of York and the
Worshipful Mayors of the United Kingdom, in the Guildhall of the ancient
and loyal City of York, October 25, 1850.

TRENTE-DEUX POTAGES.

Quatre Potages à la Victoria.	Huit Potages à la Tortue transparente.
Quatre idem à la Prince of Wales.	Seize idem à la Moderne.

TRENTE-DEUX POISSONS.

Huit Turbots à la Mazarin.	Huit Filets de Merlans à la Crême.
Huit Truits Saumonées à la Marinière.	Huit Crimp Cod aux Huitres.

THE SELECTED SOYER

TRENTE-DEUX RELEVES.

Six Chapons à la Nelson.
Six Saddlebacks de Mouton Gallois.
Quatre Aloyaux de Bœuf au Raifort.

Six Hanches de Venaison.
Six quartiers d'Agneau de Maison à la
    Sévigné.
Quatre Dindonneaux en Diadème.

TRENTE-DEUX FLANCS.

Huit Jambons à la York.
Huit Poulardes à la Russe.
Huit Timballes de Riz à la Royale.
Huit Pâtés chauds à la Westphalien.

QUARANTE-HUIT ENTREES.

Huit Sautés de Faisans au Fumet de Gibier aux Truffes.
Huit de Côtelettes de Mouton à la Vicomtesse.
Huit de Blancs de Volaille à la Palestine.
Huit de Ris de Veau à la Palestine.
Huit de Rissolettes de Volaille à la Pompadour.
Huit de Salmi de Gibier à la Chasseur.

Second Course.

QUARANTE RÔTIS.

Huit de Perdreaux aux feuilles de Céleri.
Huit de Faisans bardés au Cresson.
Six de Canetons au jus d'Oranges.
Six de Grouses à l'Ecossais.
Six de Levrauts au jus de Groseilles.
Six de Bécasses et Bécassines au jus.

CENT ENTREMETS.

Dix Chartreuses de Pêches.
Dix Gelées de Fraises Françaises à la Fontainebleau.
Dix Salades de Grouses à la Soyer.
Dix Galantines Aspiqués à la Volière.
Dix Petits Macédoines de fruit cristalisé.
Dix Mirotons de Homard aux Olives.
Dix Crevettes au Vin de Champagne.
Dix Gâteaux Crèmant à la Duke of York.
Dix Crèmes transparentes au Kirschwasser,
Dix Tartlettes Pralinés aux Cerises de Montmorency.

VINGT RELEVES.

Dix paniers de Fruits Glacés à la Lady Mayoress.
Dix Jambons en Suprise à l'Ananas.

Céleri à la Crème.	Side Table.	Céleri à la Crème.
Choux fleurs au Beurre.	Vegetables.	Choux fleurs au Beurre.
Haricots verts.		Sea Kale.
Choux de Bruxelles.		Choux de Bruxelles.

Grand Dessert floréal à la Watteau.

Besides this elaborate bill of fare, the Lord Mayor's royal table had to be provided with a separate supply of the most *recherché* dishes, consisting of the following:—

The Lord Mayor's Table.

TROIS POTAGES.

Un Potage à la Victoria.
Un idem   Tortue à l'Anglaise.
Un idem   Transparente.

TROIS POISSONS.

Le Turbot à la Mazarin.
Les Mulets blancs à l'Italienne. Les Truites Saumonées à la
Les Truites Saumonées à la Marinière.

TROIS RELEVES.

L'Extravagance Culinaire à l'Alderman.
Les Chapons à la Nelson.
Le Quartier d'Agneau de Maison à la Sévigné.

TROIS FLANCS.

La Timballe de Riz à la Royale.
Le Jambon à la York.
Les Canetons Canaris Macédoine de Légumes.

QUATRE ENTREES.

Le Sauté de Faisans au Fumet de Gibier.
Les Blancs de Volailles à la York Minster.
Côtelettes de Mouton à la Réforme.
Les Riz de Veau à la Palestine.

Second Course.

TROIS RÔTIS.

Les Perdrix aux feuilles de Céleri.
Le Paon à l'Anglaise.
Les Bécasses et Bécassines au jus.

TROIS RELEVES

Le Jambon en Surprise à la Soyer.
La Hure de Sanglier à l'Allemande.
Le Rocher de Fruits Glacés à la Lady Mayoress.

HUIT ENTREMETS.

La Galantine d'Oisons à la Volière.
La Gelée de Fraises Françaises à la Fontainebleau.
La Salade de Grouse à la Soyer.
La Crème de la Grande Bretagne.
Les Mirotons de Homards aux Olives.
Les petits Gâteaux Crèmant à la Duke of York.

La Chartreuse de Fruits au Pêches.
La Crème de la Cité de Londres.

The climax of the banquet was the arrival of L'Extravagance Culinaire à l'Alderman', otherwise known as 'the one-hundred-guinea dish':

We cannot omit giving, as one of M. Soyer's extraordinary conceptions, the most conspicuous dish of the whole, and which excited the greatest curiosity when placed on the table; a dish that could never have been produced, but for the vast number of articles obtained for the whole banquet. This was the one-hundred-guinea dish, laughed at as an impossibility, owing to its not being understood; but easily explained by the undermentioned bill of cost:—

5 Turtle's heads, part of fins, and green fat		*costing*	£34	0	0
24 Capons, the small *noix* from each side of the middle of the back only used, being the most delicate parts of every bird		*costing*	8	8	0
18 Turkeys, the same		*costing*	8	12	0
18 Poulardes, the same		*costing*	5	17	0
16 Fowls, the same		*costing*	2	8	0
10 Grouse		*costing*	2	5	0
20 Pheasants, *noix* only		*costing*	3	0	0
45 Partridges, the same		*costing*	3	7	0
6 Plovers, whole		*costing*	0	9	0
40 Woodcocks, the same		*costing*	8	0	0
3 dozen Quails, whole		*costing*	3	0	0
100 Snipes, *noix* only		*costing*	5	0	0
3 doz. Pigeons, *noix* only		*costing*	0	14	0
6 doz. Larks, stuffed		*costing*	0	15	0
Ortolans from Belgium		*costing*	5	0	0
The *garniture*, consisting of Cockscombs, Truffles, Mushrooms, Crawfish, Olives, American Asparagus, *Croustades*, Sweetbreads, *Quenelles de Volaille*, Green Mangoes, and a new Sauce		*costing*	14	10	0
			£105	5	0

The way M. Soyer accounted for the extravagance of this dish is as follows, viz., that if an epicure was to order this dish only, he would be obliged to provide the whole of the above-mentioned articles.

As usual on such great occasions, the *chef* invited all who had lent him their assistance to a supper; and thus ended the festival which must form an epoch in the annals of the ancient city of York.

Memoirs of Soyer by Volant & Warren

While Soyer was in York, 'his head full of a multitude of fancies', a suggestion was made to him which was ambitious even by his own standards. All

London was in a ferment of preparations for the Great Exhibition of 1851: why should not Soyer open his own restaurant near the new Crystal Palace to feed the hordes of visitors? The chef fastened onto this with delight. A friend put up the money, and a lease was taken on Gore House, a long low building set amid gracious walled gardens. Carpenters, scene-painters, plumbers, glaziers, gardeners, upholsterers, carvers and gilders were hired; plans were drawn up which were spectacular enough to satisfy Soyer's wildest cravings for ostentation. A catalogue was published, bursting with Soyeresque hyperbole:

'When, like the phoenix, it has arisen fresh and revivified; when its halls once more glitter with light, and its chambers re-echo with the voices of the noble and the talented; when all its former glories are called into new and even more glorious life, by the enchanter's wand of Alexis Soyer.

And his, moreover, is an enchanter's wand which, like that of Merlin, will triumph over geographical limits, and laugh the restrictions of space to scorn. From all quarters of the globe, civilized or uncivilized, will his visitors come—the doors of the Symposium will be thrown open to universal humanity. The lightning-winged locomotive, the heavy vetturino, the clumsier diligence, the steamboat, the caique, the junk, and the felucca, will bring their myriad visitors to the gates of Gore House. Cosmopolitan customs should demand cosmopolitan cookery; and it is by no means an exaggerated expectation, we think, to imagine within the walls of the Symposium grave and lively Frenchmen, expatiating over their potages and fricandeaux; phlegmatic Turks, discussing pillaf and hachis; mercurial Persians, enjoying their sherbet; sententious Spaniards, luxuriating over olla podrida; wide-awake Americans, consuming johnny-cakes and canvas-backed ducks; pigtailed Chinese, devouring their favourite stewed dog; metaphysical Germans, washing down prodigious quantities of sauerkraut with ocean of rheinwein; swarthy Russians, up to their eyes in caviair; Cossacks, calling for more train oil; Tartars, swallowing quarts of mare's milk; and New Zealanders—no, not New Zealanders, for who could form any idea of the horror and dismay which would be caused by some ebony-skinned and boomeranged chieftain demanding 'baked young woman' for two, and a 'cold boiled missionary' to follow?'

Memoirs of Soyer by Volant & Warren

The Gastronomic Symposium of All Nations, as it was modestly called, was far, far, more than an eating house. Gore House was splendid enough to begin with, but Soyer transformed it into something fantastical. Here is the programme, which was printed on satin paper, the edges delicately tinted green and scalloped:

'Soyer's Universal Symposium,

Gore House, Kensington.

Season Tickets.
Single Ticket, ... One Guinea.

THE SELECTED SOYER

Double Ticket,   .   .   .   One and a-Half Guineas.
Family Ticket, admitting Five,   .   Three Guineas.
None of which are transferable.

To be had at Mr. Mitchell's Royal Library, Bond Street;
Sams' Library, St. James's Street;
and all the principal Libraries and Music Sellers.

'The tickets will admit to all parts of this monstre and unique establishment, which is capable of providing Dinners and Refreshments of every description for five or six thousand persons daily, the charges for which will not preclude persons of every station from partaking of the hospitality of the *Maison Soyer*. Amongst the numerous attractions of this extraordinary Mansion and Grounds (which enclose the famous and park-like Prè D'Orsay), are—

'Le Vestibule de la Fille de l'Orage—The Hall of Architectural Wonders—The Blessington Temple of the Muses—The Temple of Danæ, or the Shower of Gems—The Transatlantic Passage—La Forèt Péruvienne, or the Night of Stars—The Grand Staircase, containing the Macédoine of all Nations, being a Demisemitragimimicomigrotesquepanofunniosymposiorama, or 'Such a Getting up Stairs' to the Great Exhibition of 1851, Painted in Fresco by Mr. George Augustus Sala—The Gallic Pavilion, or l'Avenue des Amours—The Temple of Phœbus—The Glittering Rocaille of Eternal Show—The Bower of Ariadne—The Door of the Dungeon of Mystery—The Boudoir de la Vallière, or the Doriana— L'Oeil de Bœuf, or Flora's Retreat—The Celestial Hall of Golden Lilies—The Grand Banqueting Bridge, al Fresco—The Washington Refreshment Room, for the dispensation of every sort of American Beverage—Soyer's Colossal Offering to Amphitrite—Cupid's Delight—The Impenetrable Grotto of Ondine—Hebe's Mistake, or the Enchanted Fountain—The Aerial Orchestra—The Baronial Hall, containing the late Madame Soyer's celebrated Pictures, and the complete Gallery of Eminent Characters by Count D'Orsay, munificiently presented to M. Soyer by J. Mitchell, Esq., of Bond Street—Gigantic Encampment of all Nations, with Monster Tablecloth, 307 feet long, of British manufacture—Picnic Tents—Magic Cookery, by Soyer's original Liliputian Kitchen—Marble Statues and Fountains—Bacchanalian Vases—Emerald Pyramids of Morning Dew—Gipsy Dell—And Statuettes à la Watteau, etc.

'Subscribers will be permitted to view, from 12 till 2 o'clock, the Symposium Kitchen, in which no less than 600 Joints can be cooked with ease in the course of the day.'

Memoirs of Soyer by Volant & Warren

The Hall of Architectural Wonders contained murals of a myriad of famous buildings, from the Leaning Tower of Pisa and the Mosque of St Sophia to the Porcelain Tower of Nanking and Eddystone Lighthouse. The Transatlantic Ante-chamber had walls decorated ('prettily') with the Stars and Stripes. In The Shower of Gems, tears of embossed gold and silver cascaded down the walls from a ceiling of perforated arabesque, and the windows opened onto a verandah and a Venetian bridge. La Grotte des neiges Eternelles boasted icicles, ice-encrusted mirrors and a stuffed Arctic fox. The Celestial Hall of

84

the Golden Lilies contained carvings of Chinese monsters, 'grotesque coloured cartoons', and a Chinese hexagonal lantern. The centrepiece, in Soyer's eyes (though not those of Sala, who painted it, and thought it 'hideous rubbish'), was the Grand Staircase, bearing a monstrous mural called 'The Grande Macédoine of All Nations'. Here it is, described by Volant and Warren.

The Grand Macédoine, being a 'comigrotesquepanofanofanifoolishiorama, or such a getting up stairs to the Great Exhibition of 1851.' Some sixty or seventy feet of the walls of the staircase—three stories, in fact—were decorated with an incongruous medley of grotesque and monstrous-headed figures, painted, or rather sketched, in a species of fresco, on a tinted ground, and rushing up stairs as fast as ever their limbs would carry them. Some walked, some rode, or tried to ride, on animals which decidedly never entered into Buffon's system of zoology, and which Cuvier would be puzzled to describe, and M. Soyer as much puzzled to cook. Hippogriffs, griffins, dragons, giraffes, elephants, hippopotami, rhinosceri, mastodons, the megatherium, crocodiles, camels, butterflies, cats, rats, mice, whales, scorpions, dromedaries, and other quadrupeds, bipeds, unipeds, sinepeds, and centipeds appeared in this galaxy of pictorial monstrosities. Of the characters, as the playbills says, many were portraits; we had the ghost of Billy Pitt and his opponent Fox; then came Brougham, Thackeray, Wellington, Napoleon, Ali Baba, Abd-el-Kader, Thiers, Guizot, Joinville, Dickens, Mark Lemon, Horace Mayhew, George Cruikshank, Jullien, Prospére, Balfe, Jerrold, Chatterton, Anderson (the wizard), 'grave' Dr. Walker, Bunn, Maddox, Dumas, Victor Hugo, Disraeli, Cobden, Minerva, and Mr. Toole (the toast-master). These, with Indian chiefs, Exquimaux, dogs, with protected and unprotected females, and a host of others, parts of which were invisible to the naked eye, represented in garbs as grotesque, and picturesque positions as uncommon, as can well be imagined, were rushing and tearing past. The artist to whom these comic cartoons were due (Mr. George Sala) inscribed his name on a tombstone, which, considering its situation on the wall, would seem to indicate a probability of his being partial to the system of *intramural interments*. We may add that the pictorial monstrosities alluded to were all marching under an ample azure verandah, and over a platform of crimson cloth. They were illumined in their nocturnal progress by beautiful lamps in the Etruscan style.

Memoirs of Soyer by Volant & Warren

Only a year after he had left the Reform Club forever, Soyer flung open the doors of the most extravagant of all his ventures. He was not to be disappointed. Every day the house and gardens were thronged with an average of one thousand visitors. Most of them ate the half-crown dinners in what was optimistically described as the Baronial Hall; the more rich and genteel customers had their meals privately cooked. Afterwards, they would stroll about the grounds, where Soyer's frenetic imagination had ordered further entertainment. A band played national anthems; a group of Serenaders had been imported from Ethiopia; theatricals were performed; fortunes were told: balloons ascended; games of various kinds were organized. A huge visitors' book, bound in Morocco leather and blocked in gold leaf, bore the names of a breathtaking variety of celebrities—noblemen and ladies, actors and ballerinas, writers and politicians, clowns and boxers. And around it all darted Soyer himself, ecstatically adding further frills to his gaudy enterprise.

Such hectic glory could not last. The whole scheme had been dreamed up in haste and put into operation with little regard for practical difficulties, such as budgetting and management. Tentative attempts were made to reform the running of the Symposium by imposing stricter economies and setting up a committee, but Soyer was not the man to canter when he could continue galloping. He foresaw the Symposium becoming a permanent establishment by outlasting the Great Exhibition and metamorphosing into part-music hall, part culinary college.

The end was sudden and dramatic, with a breath of Whitehall farce to it. In order to continue running, the Symposium committee had to renew their licence to sell drinks. The presiding magistrate chose to make his inspection on an unusually boisterous evening, when he was confronted by what must have appeared to be a riot of debauchery. The bars were heaving, several bands competed with each other, and both grounds and house thronged with merrymakers. One can almost see the Justice's eyebrows shooting up. He had, he said, never been a witness to such disgraceful dissipation in his life. Knowing that the licence would now be refused, Soyer immediately shut down Gore House, paid off the creditors and turned his back on the project which had absorbed so much of his energies.

He still, of course, had plenty to occupy him. There were soup kitchens to run and fund-raising balls to organize; there were new relishes to mix and kitchen aids to invent. Above all, there were books to write. *The Gastronomic Regenerator* was now in its eighth edition, and *The Modern Housewife* had reached its thirtieth thousand. Now Soyer had the (comparative) leisure to fulfil a long-held amibition and write an exhaustive history of food and cookery. By 1853 he had completed *The Pantropheon, or the History of Food and its Preparation in Ancient Times*, probably the most extraordinary of all his works. As well as being enormous fun to read, it is the result of a staggering amount of research among classical authors, a fact proudly attested to by the Table of References, which takes up thirty pages. The book seems somehow to be a fittingly grand postscript to the episode of the Gastronomic Symposium of all Nations.

Selection from
The Pantropheon (1853).

Thanks to the impressions received in boyhood, Rome and Athens always present themselves to our minds accompanied by the din of arms, shouts of victory, or the clamours of plebeians crowded round the popular tribune. 'And yet,' said we, 'nations, like individuals, have two modes of existence distinctly marked—one intellectual and moral, the other sensual and physical; and both continue to interest through the lapse of ages.'

What, for instance, calls forth our sympathies more surely than to follow from the cradle that city of Romulus—at first so weak, so obscure, and so despised—through its prodigious developments, until, having become the sovereign mistress of the world, it seems, like Alexander, to lament that the limits of the globe restrict within so narrow a compass its ungovernable ardour for conquest, its insatiable thirst of *opima spolia* and tyrannical oppression. In like manner, a mighty river, accounted as nothing at its source, where a child can step across, receives in its meandrous descent the tribute of waters, which roll on with increasing violence, and rush at last from their too narrow bed to inundate distant plains, and spread desolation and terror.

History has not failed to record, one by one, the battles, victories, and defeats of nations which no longer exist; it has described their public life,—their life in open air,—the tumultuous assemblies of the forum,—the fury of the populace,—the revolts of the camps,—the barbarous spectacles of those amphitheatres, where the whole pagan universe engaged in bloody conflict, where gladiators were condemned to slaughter one another for the pastime of the over-pampered inhabitants of the Eternal City—sanguinary spectacles, which often consigned twenty or thirty thousand men to the jaws of death in the space of thirty days!

But, after all, neither heroes, soldiers, nor people, can be always at war; they cannot be incessantly at daggers drawn on account of some open-air election; the applause bestowed on a skilful and courageous *bestiarius* is not eternal; captives may be poignarded in the Circus by way of amusement, but only for a time. Independently of all these things, there is the home, the fire-side, the prose of life, if you will; nay, let us say it at once, the business of life—eating and drinking.

It is to that we have devoted our vigils, and, in order to arrive at our aim, we have given an historical sketch of the vegetable and animal alimentation of man from the earliest ages; therefore it will be easily understood why we have taken the liberty of saying to the austere Jew, the voluptuous Athenian, the obsequious or vain-glorious senator of imperial Rome, and even to the fantastical, prodigal, and cruel Cæsars: 'Tell me what thou eatest, and I will tell thee who thou art.'

Frumenta.

Do not be alarmed, fair readers, at the Latin noun which heads this chapter; tolerate it in consideration of our promise seldom to solicit a like favour. It meant, among the Latins, all the plants which produce ears of corn, the seeds of which can be converted into flour. Clearly there never was a more innocent expression.

Barley seems to claim the first place among cereals of the second order; the Greeks looked upon it as the happy symbol of fertility, and the ancient inhabitants of Italy gave it a name *(hordeum)* which, perhaps, recalled to their mind the use mankind made of it before wheat was known *(exordium)*.

The Jews had a great esteem for barley, and sacred history generally assimilates it to wheat, when the fruits of the earth are mentioned. Thus a beloved spot produces both these plants: Shobi offered to David wheat and barley; and Solomon promises twenty thousand sacks of wheat and as much barley to the workmen charged with cutting down the cedars of Lebanon.

The Greeks and Romans did not carry their love for this grain so far as the Hebrews. In Rome it was the food of the flocks and cowards. In Lacedæmon and at Athens the gladiators and common people had no other aliment; they made it into barley-gruel *(alphiton)*, the composition of which was very simple, and would not probably tempt a modern Lucullus. Here is the recipe of this ancient and national dish:—

Dry, near the fire or in the oven, twenty pounds of barley flour, then parch it. Add three pounds of linseed meal, half a pound of coriander the end of that time squeeze out all the water, and place the paste in another vessel; reduce it to the consistence of thick lees, pass it through a piece of new linen, and repeat this last operation; dry it in the sun, and then boil it in milk.

As regards the exact seasoning of this exquisite Roman dish, it is your own genius which must inspire you with the proportions.

Let us not omit to notice the *Erupmon* of the Greeks, the *Irion* of the Latins, the *Indian Wheat* of the moderns. This plant produces a wholesome and easily digestible food; it was well known in Italy in the time of Pliny, at which period the peasants used to make a crisp sort of heavy bread, probably somewhat similar to that which is till used in the south of France.

Since the famine of 1847 great attention has been paid to this flour; much was imported into England from America, where it is used in domestic economy; when green, its milky pulp is an excellent food: the various advantages of this flour, however, are not sufficiently developed to give all the benefit of its goodness to the world; habit and prejudice assist materially to prevent its being generally employed.

The Romans also ate it as hasty-pudding, parched or roasted, with a little salt. A writer equally remarkable for his elegant and easy style, as well as for the justness of his observations, informs us that, in our days, the Indian inhabitants of the unfruitful plains of Marwar never dress Indian corn in any other way.

Such are the principal *graminea* which the ancients thought worthy of their attention, or allowed to appear on their tables, with more or less honour according to the degree of esteem in which they were held. It is probable that the cooks in the great gastronomic period of Rome and Athens, who knew so well the capricious nature of their masters' palates, had to borrow from magiric chemistry, then so flourishing, some wonderful means of giving to various kinds of cereals a culinary value they now no longer possess—what might we not expect from a Thimbron, a Mithoecus, a Soterides? This latter performed a feat which does him too much honour to be unnoticed here.

The King of Bithynia, Nicomedes, was taken with a strong, invincible, and imperious longing which admitted of no delay; he ordered his cook, Soterides, to be sent for, and commanded him to prepare instantly a dish of loaches. 'Loaches, Sire!' cried the skilful, yet terrified cook; 'by all the gods, protectors of the kingdom, where can I procure these fish at this late hour of the night?' Kings ill brook resistance to their will. Nicomedes was not celebrated for patience when pressed by hunger. 'Give me loaches, I say,' replied he, with a hollow and terrible voice 'or else—' and his clear, fearful, pantomimic expression made the unfortunate cook understand too well that he must either obey or immediately deliver up his head to the provost of the palace. The alternative was embarrassing; nevertheless, Soterides thought how to get out of the scrape. He shut himself up in his laboratory, peeled some long radishes, and with extraordinary address gave them the form of the fatal fish, seasoning them with oil, salt, black pepper, and doubtless several other ingredients, the secret of which the illustrious *chef* has not handed down to posterity. Then, holding in his hand a dish of irreproachable-looking fried fish, he boldly presented himself before the prince, who was walking up and down with hasty strides awaiting his arrival. The King of the Bithynians ate up the whole, and the next day he condescended to inform his court that he never had loaches served he so much liked. This digression, which the reader will kindly pardon, sufficiently shows to what height the art of ancient cookery was carried, and of which this work will furnish new and abundant proofs.

The cereals having had so much of our attention, we have now to consider those grains or seeds which serve as the bases or necessary adjuncts to different dishes.

Vegetables.

All nations have sown vegetables, and judged them worthy of their particular attention; sometimes they have even confounded many of these plants with the cereals, because they were concerted into flour and bread, especially in time of famine.

After the Deluge, when God made a covenant with Noah he said, with respect to the food of man:— 'Even as the green herb have I given you all things;' and, subsequently to that epoch, the holy writers frequently demonstrate, in their simple and interesting style, the various uses which the Hebrews made of vegetables. Esau, pressed by hunger, sold his birth-right to Jacob for a dish of lentils.

Among the presents which David received from Shobi, were beans, lentils, and parched pulse.

The four Hebrew children were fed with vegetables, at the court of Nebuchadnezzar, King of Babylon. It is sufficient, we think, to indicate these passages, without uselessly increasing the number.

The heroes of Homer, those men covered with iron and brass, whose terrible blows dealt death and desolation, reposed after their exploits, partaking of a dish of beans or a plate of peas. Happy simplicity of the Homeric ages! Patrocles peeled onions! Achilles washed cabbages! and the wise Ulysses roasted, with his own hands, a sirloin of beef!

One day the son of Thetis received under his tent a deputation sent by the Greeks, to entreat him to be friends with Agamemnon. The young hero, who could only be accused of a little pride and passion, invited these worthy personages to dinner, and with the assistance of his friend, gave them a magnificent banquet, in which vegetables occupied a most conspicuous place.

Sixteen Greek authors have devoted their vigils to profound researches concerning the qualities of these useful plants; their works have not been transmitted to us, but their names are to be found inscribed in the gastronomic treasure which Athenæus—that grammarian, philosopher, and epicurean—has bequeathed to the meditations of posterity.

But it is principally with the Romans that this interesting branch of the magiric art flourished. They have told us that this great family of herbs took the name of vegetables *(legumina)*, because they were chosen and picked by the hand; and their most celbrated horticulturists have prided themselves on the preparation of the ground to which they were confided, on the attention which they claimed, and on the Hygeian virtues which experience attributed to them. Heathen theology, too, consecrated several of them to the solemnities of their religion, and some nations even considered them worthy of their homage and the fumes of incense.

Apicius, that profound culinary chemist, who nobly expended immense treasures in inventing new dishes, and who killed himself because the remainder of his fortune was not sufficient for him (though to another it would have seemed magnificent)— Apicius shows us what he believed to be the most suitable manner of preserving vegetables. 'Choose them,' he says, 'before they are perfectly ripe, put them in a vessel coated with pitch, and cover it hermetically.'

The reader will decide for himself between this process and those which science has since discovered.

The capitulars (or statutes) of Charlemagne enter, on the subject of vegetables, into some instructive details. They inform us that lettuces, cresses, endive, parsley, chervil, carrots, leeks, turnips, onions, garlic, scallions, and eschalots, were nowhere to be found, except in the emperor's kitchen-gardens. Charlemagne had all those vegetables sold, and derived from them a very considerable revenue.

Anderson makes an observation (under the date 1548), which deserves to be noticed here, were it only on account of its singularity. 'The English,' says he, 'cultivated scarcely any vegetable before the last two centuries. At the commence-ment of the reign of Henry VIII, neither salad, nor carrots, nor cabbages, nor radishes, nor any other comestibles of a like nature, were grown in any part of the kingdom; they came from Holland and Flanders.'

According to the author of a project, printed in London in 1723, in 8vo., 'for the relief of the poor, and the payment of old debts, without the creation of new taxes,' Queen Catherine herself could not procure a salad for her dinner. The king was obliged to send over to Holland for a gardener to cultivate those pot-herbs, with which England is, perhaps, better furnished now than any other country in Europe.

Anderson asserts (1660) that cauliflowers were not known in England until about the time of the Restoration. And, lastly, the author of the 'State of England,' printed in 1768, remarks that asparagus and artichokes were only introduced a few years antecedent to that date.

Dried Vegetables.

Beans.

This innocent vegetable, which with us certainly awakens no lugubrious thoughts, was formerly consecrated to the dead. It was offered in sacrifices to the infernal gods, and its mysterious virtues evoked by night, spirits, and shadows. The Flamen of Jupiter could not eat it, and he was forbidden to touch a bean, or even to pronounce its name; for the fatal plant contains a little black spot, which is no other than a noxious character—a type of death.

Pythagoras and his followers carefully avoided this dismal food, in the fear of submitting a father, sister, or beloved wife to the danger of a cruel mastication; for who knew where wandering souls might rest during the course of their numerous transmigrations.

Grave writers say the cause of this abstinence is, that beans are difficult of digestion; that they stupify those who make use of them as food; and that hens who eat them cease to lay eggs. What more shall we say? Hippocrates, wise as he certainly was, had some of these strange fears, and he trembled for his patients when beans were in blossom.

In spite of such ridiculous prejudices, this plant had numerous and enlightened defenders. When green, it was served on tables renowned for delicacies; and, when fully ripe, it frequently replaced both wheat and other corn. One of the festivals of Apollo—the *Pyanepsia*—owed its origin and pomp to the bean. This vegetable then obtained pre-eminence over all that were boiled in the saucepan, and offered to the God of Day and the Fine Arts. Is it possible to imagine a more brilliant rehabilitation?

If we are to believe Isidorus, this plant was the first culinary vegetable of which man made use; he was, therefore, bound to preserve a grateful remembrance of it.

King David did not deem it unworthy of him, and the Prophet Ezekiel was commanded to mix it with the different grains of which he made his bread.

We possess few certain indications proving the different culinary combinations to which beans gave rise among the ancients. All we know is, that they ate them boiled, perhaps with bacon; raw, with salt, we should imagine; or fried with fat, butter, or oil.

Two kinds especially attracted the attention of true connnoisseurs of that class of *gourmets* elect, whose palate is ever testing, and whose sure taste detects and appreciates shades, of almost imperceptible tenuity—first, the bean of Egypt, recommended for its rich, nutritious, and wholesome pulp; this bean was also cultivated in Syria and Cilicia: and secondly, the Greek bean, which passed at Rome for a most delicious dish. Certain gastronomists, however, preferred another vegetable of which we are going to speak.

Ever since the middle ages the bean has played a very important part in the famous 'Twelfth-night cake,' almost all over Europe. The ephemeral royalty it bestowed was often sung by the poets, and consecrated in chronicles. Thomas Randolph informs us that Lady Flemyng was queen of the bean in 1563. Some days after the Duke of Guise was assassinated by Poltrot. History has its puerilities as well as its great tragedies.

The Spaniards had also their Twelfth-night cake. When John, Duke of Braganza, had obtained the crown of Portugal (1640), Philip IV of Spain informed Count Olivares of the event, and added, as if it were a consolation for the loss of a kingdom, that this new sovereign was nothing more than a 'king of the bean.' Philip was mistaken.

These cakes were made in former days nearly in the same manner that we make them now. Sometimes they contained honey, flour, ginger, and pepper. One portion was for God, another for the Holy Virgin, and three others for the Magi; that is to say, they gave all these portions to the poor.

In England the cake was often full of raisins, among which one bean and one pea were introduced.

'Cut the cake,' says Meliboeus to Nisa; 'who hath the beane shal be kinge; and where the peaze is, shal be queene.'

'At the present day the bean is one of the vegetables most cultivated in Egypt and Italy. At Naples, as in Egypt, they are eaten raw when young, and the large ones cooked and grilled in the oven. They are publicly sold already cooked.'—Leman.

Haricots.

It is well known that Alexander the Great was fond of travelling, and that he was generally accompanied in his peregrinations by a certain number of soldiers, who occasionally took for him, on his route, cities, provinces, and sometimes kingdoms. It happened, one day, that as the Macedonian prince—worthy pupil of Aristotle—was herbalizing in India, his eyes fell upon a field of haricots, which appeared to him very inviting. It was the first time that he had seen this plant, and he immediately ordered his cook to prepare a dish of them—we do not know with what sauce; but he thought them good, and, thanks to this great conqeuror, Europe was enriched with a new vegetable.

Virgil was doubtless ignorant of this noble origin, when he decried haricots severely, by qualifying them so disgracefully. It is true that the lower classes of people, who were very fond of them, did great injury to their reputation; for things the most exquisite soon lose their value when they fall within the reach of the vulgar. It is thus with a pleasing melody—when given up to the barbarous and melancholy street organs it ceases to charm the ears of drawing-room fashionables. The same again with a plaintive ballad—it loses its attraction the moment a street Orpheus begins to murder it with his Stentorian bawl.

Let it not be thought, however, that the plant of which we speak was exclusively reserved for the vulgar appetite. Oh, no! the Greeks and Latins had too much good taste for that. The former allowed it a distinguished place on their tables, together with figs, and other side dishes. They only required that haricots should be young, tender, and green.

In Rome they were preserved with vinegar and garum; and, prepared in this manner, they excited the appetites of the guests at the beginning of the repast. Moreover, it was admitted that this vegetable was much more wholesome than beans, that the stomach was less fatigued by it, and that persons of delicate constitutions might partake of it without fear. Certain amateurs even pretended that no vegetable was to be compared to haricots; but others differed from them on this point; and the latter, right or wrong, pronounced in favour of peas.

Lentils.

The Egyptians, whose ideas were sometimes most eccentric, imagined it was sufficient to feed children with lentils to enlighten their minds, open their hearts, and render them cheerful. That people, therefore, consumed an immense quantity of this vegetable, which from infancy had been their principal food.

The Greeks also highly esteemed this aliment, and their ancient philosophers regaled themselves with lentils. Zeno would not trust to any one the cooking of them; it is true that the stoics had for their maxim: 'A wise man acts always with reason, and prepares his lentils himself.' We must confess that the great wit of these words escapes us, although we are willing to believe there is some in them.

However it may be, lentils were abundant in Greece and in the East; and many persons, otherwise very sensible, maintained, with the most serious countenance in the world, that they softened the temper and disposed the mind to study.

It is hardly necessary to observe that this plant was well known to the Hebrews. The red pottage of lentils for which Esau sold his birthright, the present of Shobi to David, the victory of Shammah in the field of lentils, and, lastly, the bread of Ezekial, sufficiently prove that the Jews numbered this vegetable as one of those in ordinary use among them.

The Romans had not the same esteem for it as the nations we have mentioned. According to them, the moisture in lentils could only cause heaviness to the mind, and render men reserved, indolent, and lazy. The name of this vegetable pretty well shows, they said, the bad effect it produces. Lentil derives its origin from the word *lentus* (slow), *'lens a lente.'*

And, as if enough had not been alleged to disgrace this unfortunate plant, and to give the finish to the ill-fame it had acquired, it was placed amongst funereal and ill-omened foods. Thus Marcus Crassus, waging war against the Parthians, was convinced that his army would be defeated, because his corn was exhausted, and his men were obliged to have recourse to lentils.

How was it possible to resist such attacks! The humble plant gave way in spite of the few flattering words of the poetic Virgil, and the assurance of Pliny that this food produced two uncommon virtues—mildness and moderation.

Kitchen Garden.

The art of gardening, which may be called the luxury of agriculture, was known at the most remote periods. In the same inclosure was to be found the kitchen garden, orchard, and flower garden, at a short distance from the habitation of the rich. Royal hands did not disdain to embellish those spots which afforded a pleasing retreat, solitude, and repose.

Thus Attalus resigned the cares of his crown to cultivate his little garden, and sow in it the seeds of his favourite plant.

Babylon, the renowned city of antiquity, was celebrated amongst other wonders for her gardens suspended in the air; they were partly in existence sixteen centuries after their erection, and astonished Alexander the Great by the sublime grandeur of their prodigious boldness and the rare beauty of their workmanship.

Homer has left as the description of Alcinous's garden, from which can be traced the birth of the art of gardening; its luxury consisted in the order and symmetry of its form, in the richness of its soil, the fertility of the trees, and in the two fountains which ornamented it. It was not so with the Romans. Those conquerors of the world displayed every where pomp and ostentation: Lucullus, Crassus, Pompey, and Cæsar, filled their gardens with the riches of Asia and the spoils of the universe.

The serious horticulturist, who wanted a garden for enjoyment, and not for show, carefully laboured, to see it bring forth fine fruits and excellent vegetables. Water was properly distributed for irrigation by means of aqueducts of tiles, wood, or lead pipes, and everywhere the plants received the necessary moisture; and clever experienced gardeners were constantly occupied in improvements suggested by an attentive and skilful master.

The kitchen garden of the ancients contained mostly the vegetables, herbs, and roots, of which we still make use; but they also cultivated certain other kinds, which modern cookery has either put aside or rarely employs. We shall describe all those which appear most worthy of notice.

Asparagus.

'Quiconque ne voit guère n'a guère à dire aussi.' But travellers, those daring pioneers

of science, have sometimes, in their travels, the strange good fortune to behold wonders invisible to other eyes. Thus some skilful explorators of Africa saw, about the middle of the second century of the Christian era, in Getulia, asparagus of excellent quality and of very beautiful growth, being no less than twelve feet high! It is needless to add that the Libyan vendors rarely sold them in bundles. But these veridical travellers, on quitting the plain to ascend the mountains, found something still more wonderful; the land there seemed to suit these plants still better, for they acquired the height of twenty cubits. After this, what shall we say of our European asparagus, so shrivelled and diminutive in comparison with that of Getulia?

The Greeks, not having any better, contented themselves with the ordinary sort, such as we have at the present day. They considered it very useful in the treatment of internal diseases. Diphilus, who was very fond of it, regrets that this vegetable should be so hurtful to the sight: is it because we eat asparagus that spectacles have become necessary at nearly all periods of life?

The Romans cultivated this plan with extreme care, and obtained the most extraordinary results. At Ravenna, they raised asparagus each stem of which weighed three pounds.

Then, as in our days, they were allowed but a short time to boil; hence the favourite expression of Augustus, who, to intimate his wish that any affair might be concluded without delay, was accustomed to say: 'Let that be done quicker than you would cook asparagus.'

The cooks of Rome had a method which appears to have been subsequently too much neglected; they chose the finest heads of asparagus, and dried them. When wanted for the table, they put them into hot water, and then boiled them a few minutes. Thanks to this simple process the plant swelled considerably, and passed as being very tender and fine flavoured.

The Apicii, Luculli, and other connoisseurs of renown, had this vegetable brought from the environs of Nesis, a city of Campania.

It is asserted that Asia is its native soil, and that it was originally brought to us from that part of the world. Nevertheless, wild asparagus grows naturally in certain sandy soils, as, for instance, in the islands of the Rhône and the Loire.

'When it is found impossible to eat all the asparagus you have cut, and which has arrived at a convenient maturity, place them by the thick ends in a vessel containing about two inches of water; or else, bury them half-way up in fresh sand. By means of these precautions asparagus may be preserved several days.'—Parmentier.

Gourd.

This vegetable, which the wise *gourmet* is too discreet to despise, and to which the whimsical fancy of Roman gardeners gave the most grotesque forms, appears to be the very image of those soft and easy dispositions who yield to and obey every one, and whose unintelligent mildness is only repaid with sarcasm or disdain. Observe this creeping vegetable, left free to grow to its full size, which would sometimes attain the length of nine feet, and which the will of man was able to reduce to the slender and tortuous shape of a hideous dragon. When hardly ripe, it was cut and served on the tables of the most dainty, where it was eaten with vinegar and mustard, or seasoned with fine herbs: and whilst the ungrateful guests savoured the stomachic and nourishing flesh of the gourd, they did not cease to amuse themselves at the expense of its round and almost empty body—the proverbial image of a head not over well-provided with brains.

To the present day even, more than one popular joke continues to pursue this plant, although its culinary qualities are appreciated as formerly.

We are indebted to India for the seed of the gourd, which the Greeks designated, according to the species, by the names of Indian and common gourd. The latter kind was either boiled or roasted; the former was generally boiled in water. Antioch furnished the finest specimens to the markets of Athens.

The ancients were acquainted with the manner of preserving this vegetable in such a state of freshness as to enable them to eat it with pleasure in the month of January: the method is as follows,—the gourds were cut in pieces of a moderate size; these pieces, strung like beads, where first dried in the open air, and then smoked; when winter arrived, each piece was well washed before putting it into the stewpan, with the various culinary herbs which the season produced; to this was added endive, curled cabbage, and dried mushrooms. The rest of the operation is easily understood. The Romans prepared this vegetable in different ways: a few of the principal ones will suffice.

1st. Boil the gourd in water, squeeze it out carefully, place it in a saucepan, and mix some pepper, a little cummin seed, rue, gravy, vinegar, and a small quantity of wine, reduced to one-half by boiling. Let the whole stew, and then sprinkle it lightly with pepper, and serve.

2nd. Boil and carefully squeeze them to extract the water, then put the gourds into a saucepan with vinegar and gravy: when it begins to simmer, thicken with fine flour, sprinkle lightly with pepper, and serve.

3rd. Throw some salt on the gourd after it has been boiled, and the water pressed out of it; put it into a saucepan, with a mixture of pepper, cummin seed, coriander, green mint, and the root of benzoin; add some vinegar; then chop some dates and almonds; a little later, more vinegar, honey, gravy, sun-made wine, and oil; sprinkle lightly with pepper, and serve.

4th. Put into a stewpan a fowl, with a gourd; add some apricots, truffles, pepper, cummin, sylphium, mint, parsley, coriander, penny-royal, and calamint; moisten with wine, gravy, oil, vinegar, and honey.

These four recipes are sufficient to prove that this vegetable stood very high in the estimation of the Romans.

Artichoke.

A young and unfortunate beauty had the ill-luck to displease a vindictive and irascible god, who instantly metamorphosed her into an artichoke. This poor girl's name was Cinara. Although she had become a bitter plant she preserved this sweet name, which the moderns have strangely modified. Our readers, who eat artichokes with so much indifference, will, perhaps, sometimes lament this poor victim of a blind resentment.

This plant was well known to the ancients; the hilly regions of Greece, Asia, and Egypt were covered with it; but the inhabitants made no use of it as an aliment, and it remained uncultivated.

It would be rather difficult to trace the precise period when it was first introduced into Italy. All we know is, that it grew there more than half a century before the Christian era, in the time of Dioscorides, who mentioned it. It appears, nevertheless, that hardly any one troubled himself about artichokes, or their esculent qualities, up to that time; but the wealthy, about a century after, began to appreciate them, and Pliny, in one of his jesting whims, reproaches the rich with having deprived the lower classes and *asses* of a food which nature seemed to have destined for them.

This vegetable was then very dear, for it did not succeed, and was subsequently given up. It was so far forgotten that in the year 1473 it appeared as a novelty at Venice; and towards the year 1465 it was brought from Naples to Florence, whence it passed into France in the sixteenth century.

Galen looked upon the artichoke as a bad fool. Columella sung its praise in his verses; he recommended it to the disciples of Bacchus, and forbid the use of it to those who were anxious to preserve a sweet and pure voice.

This plant, whatever may be in other respects its estimable qualities, does not please every one equally well; its bitterness and unpleasant odour keep it at a distance from numerous palates—perhaps because too many allow themselves to be prejudiced by deceitful appearances. Here are two very ingenious methods by means of which a trial might be made to overcome, or lessen, the defects it undoubtedly has, and which we can but deplore:—

Artichokes will become mild by taking care to steep the seed in a mixture of honey and milk. They will then exhale the most agreeable perfume, particularly when this seed has passed three days in the juice of bay leaves, lilies, or roses.

Having quoted the authority, we give the recipe for what it is worth.

Until the result of this experiment is known, artichokes may be eaten raw, with a seasoning of hard eggs chopped in very small pieces, garum, and oil.

If you prefer a sharper sauce, mix well some green mint with rue, Greek fennel, and coriander; add, afterwards, some pepper, alisander, honey, garum, and oil. They are also eaten boiled, with cummin, pepper, gravy, and oil.

'It is well known under what form artichokes, either raw or cooked, appear on our tables. The best way to preserve them is to half cook them, separate the leaves from the fur, and preserve the fleshy part, called *the bottom*, and throw them, still warm, in cold water, to make them firm. That operation is called *blanchir*. They are laid afterwards on hurdles, and put four different times in the oven, as soon as the bread is taken out. They become then very thin, hard, and transparent, like horn, and return to their original form in hot water. They must be kept free from damp.'— Parmentier.

Onions.

Whoever wishes to preserve his health must eat every morning, before breakfast, young onions, with honey. Such a treat is assuredly not very tempting; besides, this rather strong vegetable leaves after it a most unpleasant perfume, which long reminds us of its presence; wherefore this recipe has not met with favour, and, indeed, it is much to be doubted whether it will ever become fashionable.

Alexander the Great found the onion in Egypt, where the Hebrews had learned to like it. He brought it into Greece, where it was given as food to the troops, whose martial ardour it was thought to excite.

Pliny assures us that Gaul produced a small kind, which the Romans called Gallic onions, and which they thought more delicate than those of Italy. At any rate, it was a dish given up to plebeians and the poor. Horace opposed to it fish—the luxurious nourishment of rich and dainty Romans. In spite of this reprobation on the part of the elegant poet, Apicius does not fear to introduce the plant in his *Olus*

Molle, a kind of *Julienne*, not devoid of merit.

Take onions, rather dry, and mix pepper, alisander, and winter-savory, to season a variety of vegetables previously boiled in water and nitre, the which, when very fine, thicken with cullis, oil, and wine.

Leeks.

This vegetable—a powerful divinity, dreaded among the Egyptians, and a food bewailed by the Israelites in their journey through the Desert—cured the Greeks of numerous diseases, which in our days it is to be feared would resist its medicinal properties. Everything changes in this sublunary world, and the leek no doubt follows the common law.

The authors of a compilation rather indigestible at times, but often very curious, assert that this vegetable attains an extraordinary size, by putting as many of the seeds as one can take up with three fingers into a piece of linen, which is then to be tied-up, covered with manure, and watered with care. All these seeds—so they say—will at last form themselves into one single seed, which will produce a monstrous leek.

This process, which is revealed to us by the geoponics, would have had an enthusiastic reception from those fervent pagans who vied in zeal with each other, to see who could offer Latona, on the day of the Theoxenias, the most magnificent leek.

The mother of Apollo received this plant with pleasure, although presented to her quite raw; but she would probably have preferred it dressed in the following manner:—

Take leeks, the mildest it is possible to procure; boil them in water and oil, with a handful of salt, and put them into a dish, with gravy, oil, and wine.

Or, cover the leeks with young cabbage leaves; cook them under the hot embers, and season afterwards as above.

Horse-Radish.

'By Apollo!' cried, mournfully, a philanthropic and gastronomic Greek, 'one must be completely mad to buy horse-radish, when fish can be found in the market.' So thought the philosopher Amphis. And at Rome, as in Greece, this reviled and despised root hardly found a place on the table of the poor, when anything else could be had.

There were several serious causes for this fatal proscription: this plant was found to be bitter, stringy, and of difficult digestion; it was looked upon as a very common food; the lowest class alone dared to feed upon it; the opulent were therefore compelled to exclude it from the number of their dishes. And again, certain strange customs, authorised by the Roman law, contributed greatly to make the horse-radish an object of horror and detestation; so true it is, that the manner in which objects are associated with our ideas determines almost invariably our love or hatred for them.

Nevertheless, all the species of this vegetable (and there were five in number, distinctly mentioned by Theophrastus) ought not to have been condemned so severely. The Corinthian, the Leiothasian, the Cleonian, the Amorean, and the Bœotian, were so many distinct and separate species, each of which possessed its own peculiar property and quality. The last-named, with its large and silky leaves, was tender, and had a sweet, agreeable taste. The others, not so good, perhaps, were wholesome and nourishing, and their natural bitterness never failed to disappear, when the seeds were allowed to soak for some time in sweet or raisin wine before they were sown.

Shall we now mention the properties the horse-radish possessed, and which ought to have been sufficient to establish its reputation, if prejudice were not both deaf and blind?

Take, fasting, some pieces of this beneficent and despised root, and the most inveterate poisons will be changed for you into inoffensive drinks.

Would you have the power to handle and play with those dangerous reptiles whose active venom causes a speedy and sure death? Wash your hands in the juice of horse-radish.

Do you seek an efficacious remedy for the numerous evils which besiege us unceasingly? Take horse-radish,—nothing but horse-radish.

It is true that this incomparable root attacks the enamel of the teeth, and, indeed, soon spoils them; but why should we be so particular when so many marvellous properties are in question?

As to its culinary preparation, Apicius recommends us to serve mixed with pepper and garum.

Garlic.

Garlic was known in the most remote ages. It was a god in Egypt. The Greeks held it in horror. It was part of their military food—here came the proverb, 'Eat neither garlic nor beans;' that is to say, abstain from war and law. There was a belief that this plant excited the courage of warriors; therefore, it was given to cocks to incite them to fight. The Greek and Roman sailors made as great a use of it as soldiers, and an ample provision was always made when they set out on any maritime expedition. It was a prevailing opinion that the effects of foul air were neutralized by garlic; and it was, no doubt, that idea which made reapers and peasants use it so lavishly.

However, the taste for this vegetable was not always confined to the people, in the southern countries of Europe; it gained, at times, to high regions of the court. It is reported that, in 1368, Alphonso, King of Castile, who had an extreme repugnance to garlic, instituted an order of knighthood; and one of the statutes was, that any knight who had eaten of this plant, could not appear before the sovereign for at least one month.

The priests of Cybele interdicted the entry of the temple of the goddess to persons who had made use of garlic. Stilphon, troubling himself very little about this interdiction, fell asleep on the steps of the altar. The mother of the gods appeared to him in his dream, and reproached him with the little respect his breath disclosed for her. 'If you wish me to abstain from garlic,' replied Stilphon, 'give me some thing else to eat.'

The ancients, great lovers of the marvellous, believed that this despised vegetable possessed a sovereign virtue against the greater number of diseases, and that it was easy to deprive it of its penetrating odour by sowing and gathering it when the moon was below the horizon.

The Greek and Roman cooks used it but very seldom, and it was only employed as a second or third-rate ingredient in some preparations of Apicius which we shall hereafter mention.

'Garlic is called the physic of the peasantry, especially in warm countries, where it is eaten before going to work, in order to guarantee them from the pernicious effects of foul air. It would be too long were we to relate all that has been written in favour of this vegetable; let it suffice to say that it is employed in numerous pharmaceutical preparations, and among others in vinegar, celebrated by the name of *aromatic vinegar.'*—Bosc.

Parsley.

Hercules, the conqueror of the Nemæan lion, crowned himself with parsley; a rather modest adornment for so great a hero, when others, for exploits much less worthy, were decked with laurels. A similar crown became, subsequently, the prize of the Nemæan and Isthmian Games.

Anacreon, that amiable and frivolous poet, who consecrated all his moments to pleasure, celebrates parsley as the emblem of joy and festivity; and Horace, a philosophic sensualist of the same stamp, commanded his banqueting hall to be ornamented with roses and parsley.

Perhaps it was thought that the strong, penetrating odour of parsley possessed the property of exciting the brain to agreeable imaginations; if so, it explains the fact of its being worn by guests, placed round their heads.

Fable has made it the food of Juno's coursers. In battle, the warriors of Homer fed their chargers with it; and Melancholy, taking it for the symbol of mourning, admitted it at the dismal repasts of obsequies.

Let us seek to discover in this plant qualities less poetic and less brilliant, but, assuredly, more real and positive. In the first place:—

Wash some parsley with the roots adhering; dry it well in the sun; boil it in water, and leave it awhile on one side; then put into a saucepan some garlic and leeks, which must boil together a long time, and very slowly, until reduced to two-thirds—that done, pound some pepper, mix it with gravy and a little honey, strain the water in which the parsley was boiled, and pour it over the parsley and the whole of the other ingredients. Put the stewpan once more on the fire, and serve.

The following recipe is much less complicated and more expecditious:—

Boil the parsley in water, with nitre; press out all the water; cut it very fine, then mix, with care, some pepper, alisander, marjoram and onions; add some wine, gravy, and oil; stew the whole, with the parsley, in an earthen pot or stewpan.

If the illustrious pupil of Chiron, the warlike Achilles, had known the culinary properties of parsley as well as he knew its medicinal virtues, he no doubt would have been less prodigal with it for his horses; and the conquerors of Troy would have comforted themselves, during the tediousness of a long siege, by cooking this aromatic plant, and enjoying a new dish.

Parsley, according to some writers, was of Egyptian origin; but it is not known who brought it into Sardinia, where it was found by the Carthaginians, who afterwards made it known to the inhabitants of Marseilles.

Water-Cresses.

The water-cress, the sight alone of which made the learned Scaliger shudder with terror, is supposed to be a native of Crete. It was, doubtless, the cresses of Alen (Suabia), which are cultivated in our gardens, and not those commonly found in brooks and springs.

The Persians were in the habit of eating them with bread: they made, in this manner, so delicious a meal, that the splendour of a Syracusan table would not have tempted them. This is one of those examples of sobriety which may be admired, but are seldom followed.

Plutarch did not share the opinion of the Persians, but scornfully ranked cresses amongst the lowest aliments of the people. Nevertheless, the Romans, as well as the Greeks, granted to this cruciform plant a host of beneficent qualities, and among others, a singularly refreshing property. Refreshing! to say the truth, it refreshes much in the same way that mustard and pepper do. Boiled in goat's milk, it cured thoracic affections; introduced into the ears, it relieved the toothache; and finally, persons who made it their habitual food found their wits sharpened and their intelligence more active and ingenious.

Plants Used in Seasoning.

We will point out, as briefly as possible, those plants mostly used in the kitchens of the ancients to heighten the flavour of their dishes, or to give them a particular taste, according as the dish or fancy might require it. In them especially lies the secret of those *irritamenta gule*, or excitements of the palate, which Apicius brought so much into fashion.

Poppy.

The seed of this plant was offered, fried, at the beginning of the second course, and eaten with honey. Sometimes it was sprinkled on the crust of a kind of household bread, covered with white of eggs. Some of it was also put into the panada, or pap, intended for children—perhaps to make them sleep the sooner.

Sesame.

This seed was used in nearly the same manner as the poppy, and it occupied a distinguished rank among the numerous dainties served at dessert. Certain round and light cakes were covered with this seed. The Romans brought sesame from Egypt.

Rocket.

Persons about to undergo the punishment of the whip were recommended to swallow a cup of wine, in which rocket had been steeped. It was asserted that this draught rendered pain supportable. And again, that this plant, taken with honey, removed the freckles which sometimes appear on the face.

Whatever may be the degree of credence accorded to these two recipes, this vegetable enjoyed some reputation among the ancients, who mixed the wild and the garden rocket together, so as to temper the heat of the one by the coldness of the other.

Dill.

This plant, which, according to the ancients, weakened the eyes, was much renowned for its exquisite odour, and its stomachic qualities. A much-admired perfume was made from it; it produced an agreeable sort of wine or liqueur; and a small number of choice dishes, for the enjoyment of connoisseurs, owed to it the reputation they had acquired.

Anise-Seed.

The production of an umbelliferous plant, which grows wild in Egypt, in Syria, and other eastern countries. Pliny recommends it to be taken in the morning, with honey and myrrh in wine: and Pythagoras attributes to it eminent Hygeian properties, whether eaten raw or cooked.

Hyssop.

The Greeks, the Romans—and before them, the nations of the east—believed that hyssop renews and purifies the blood. This plant, mixed with an equal quantity of salt, formed a remedy much extolled by Columella. It was crushed with oil to make a liniment, used as a remedy for cutaneous eruptions. An excellent liqueur was obtained from it, known under the name of hyssop wine; and lastly, this plant was used in a number of dishes, which it rendered more wholesome and refreshing.

Pennyroyal.

The ancients entwined their wine cups with pennyroyal, and made crowns of it, which were placed on their heads during their repasts, by the aid of which they hoped to escape the troublesome consequences of too copious libations. On leaving the table, a small quantity of this plant was taken, to facilitate digestion.

Pennyroyal occupied, also, an important place in high gastronomic combinations.

Rue.

The territory of Myra, a city of Lycia, produced excellent rue. Mithridates looked upon this vegetable as a powerful counter-poison; and the inhabitants of Heraclea, suspicious—and with reason—of the villany of their tyrant, Clearchus, never stirred from their dwellings without having previously eaten plentifully of rue. This plant cured also the ear-ache; and to all these advantages, it joined that of being welcomed with honour on all festive occasions.

Mint.

There was formerly—no matter where or when—a beautiful young girl, who was changed into this plant through the jealous vengeance of Proserpine. Thus transformed, she excited the appetite of the guests, and awakened their slumbering gaiety. Mint prevented milk from curdling, even when rennet was put into it.

Capers.

Young buds of the caper tree, a shrub—native of Asia, where the species are in great varieties. It was but little thought of at the tables of the higher classes, and therefore was left to the people.

The buds of the caper are gathered, and thrown into barrels filled with vinegar, to which a little salt is added; then, by means of several large sieves made of a copper plate, rather hollow, and pierced with holes of different sizes, the different qualities are separated, and classed under different numbers. The vinegar is renewed, and the capers are replaced in the barrel, ready for exportation.

Fruits.

Apple Tree.

A very ancient tradition—for it is six thousand years old—represents the apple as being, from the beginning of the world, the inauspicious fruit to which may be traced all the miseries of mankind. We crave permission to defend it from this accusation, merely by these few words, 'That it is nowhere written.'

The holy books rarely speak of the apple tree. If we are not mistaken, it is only mentioned in five passages of the sacred writings, and at periods very distant from the first offence of man. Therefore, nothing indicates aversion or contempt on the part of the inspired writers for this tree, which on one occasion serves even as a graceful term of comparison; from which it might be concluded that the inhabitants of the east thought as much of it as other nations.

There is one (and perhaps only one) example of a singular and excessive repugnance to apples. It is said that Uladislas, King of Poland, no sooner perceived them than he became so confused and terrified that he immediately fled. It certainly required very little to disturb this poor prince!

Greece produced very beautiful apple trees, and their fruit was so excellent, that it was the favourite dessert of Philip of Macedon, and of his son, Alexander the Great, who caused them to be served at all their meals. Probably they were obtained purposely for them from the island of Euboea, which enjoyed an extraordinary reputation for apples.

The Athenian legislator—the wise Solon—almost succeeded in throwing discredit on this aliment, so much liked by his fellow-citizens, by a sumptuary law which he thought it necessary to establish.

The inhabitants of Attica were fond of good living; and when one of them took a wife he spared no expense to give splendour to the nuptial banquet—a very excusable pride on such an occasion. Solon was in the habit of interfering rather too much in the affairs of others. Every one has his failing, and this was *his*: he imagined that his fellow citizens fared too sumptuously on their wedding day; and, in order to curtail an expense contrary to his ideas of economy, he ordered that the bridegroom should be content with a single apple, while his guests were regaling themselves at his expense. Who would believe it? This law was religiously observed by the Greeks, and the Persians thought it so original that they, in their turn, adopted it.

The Latins gave a favourable reception to the apple tree, and cultivated it with care. Eminent citizens of Rome did not disdain to give their names and patronage to different kinds procured by themselves, or which they had improved in their orchards. The Manlian apples were so called after Manlius; the Claudian after Claudius, their patron; the Appian owed their name to Appius. Some others preserved that of their native country: such were the Sidonians, the Greeks, and the Epirotes.

After the conquest of Gaul, the Romans introduced all these fruits; and as the climate was more favourable to apple trees than that of Italy, they soon multiplied to a surprising extent. France ought to be grateful to those proud warriors for a present that enriched that province of the empire, and which perhaps still contributes to its prosperity.

Lemon Tree.

Among the richest productions of Media, Virgil mentions a tree, to whose fruit he attributes the greatest virtues against all poisons. The description he gives of it seems to belong to the lemon tree. However this may be, its origin, and even its identity, have given rise to the most animated disputations.

Many have asserted that Juba, King of Mauritania (50 years B.C.), spoke of the lemon tree, and that he looked upon it as being very ancient. They add, that the Lybians gave to its fruit the name of 'Hesperide apples,' that Hercules stole, and which, on account of their colour, were called 'golden apples' by the Greeks, who were indebted to that hero for their introduction.

Others maintain that no one has spoken of them before Theophrastus, who called them 'Median apples,' after the place of their origin; and that consequently those persons were wrong who confounded them with the apples taken from the garden of the Hesperides.

These difficulties will probably disappear, if we remember that the ancients have given to the lemon tree various names which belong to other trees. The truth is, that the Athenians received it from the Persians, who were neighbours of the Medes, and from Attica it spread all over Greece.

Lemons were only known to the Romans at a very late period, and at first were used only to keep the moths from their garments. The acidity of this fruit was unpleasant to them, and Apicius makes no use of it: those who wish to satisfy their curiosity on the subject may read the remarks of Lister, the celebrated physician of Queen Anne, and editor of the works of this famous gourmet.

In the time of Pliny, the lemon was hardly known otherwise than as an excellent counter-poison.

Fifty years after that, Palladius reared the plants which he had received from Media, and at last this tree was slowly naturalized in the south of Europe.

A considerable number of anecdotes have been told of the antivenomous properties of the lemon. Athenaeus speaks of two men who did not feel pain from the bite of dangerous serpents, because they had previously eaten of this fruit. Either this story is false, or men and things have strangely altered.

Apicius preserves lemons by putting each of them into a separate vessel, which is hermetically sealed with plaster, and afterwards suspended from the ceiling.

In another place we shall speak of the tables and beds made of the lemon tree, so fashionable amongst the Romans, and for which they spent prodigious sums.

One thing remains to be noticed; and that is, that preserved lemon peel was considered as one of the best digestives, and that doctors recommend it to weak and delicate persons.

CHEF TO ALL NATIONS

Orange Tree.

If confidence is to be placed in some authors, the native land of the orange tree would appear to be the gardens of the Hesperides, so remarkable in mythologic ages, and it was found also in Western Africa, Mauritania, and the Fortunate Islands; to which they add those mountains of Atlas so little known in a botanical point of view, notwithstanding the daring excursions of several learned men.

According to other observers, it originally came from the southern countries of China, from the islands of the Indian Archipelago, or even from that portion of the globe called Oceania.

One incontestable fact is, that writers of antiquity were completely ignorant of the existence of this superb tree. Had they known it, its majestic height, the dark green of its foliage, the suavity of its flowers, its fruit, so fine, bright, and so flattering to the taste, could not have failed to inspire them with brilliant pages. Theophrastus, and the Latin geoponics, never would have neglected to speak of the luxury and fecundity it displays, even in the season of hoary frost. Besides, the name of *Portughan*, which is given to the orange by the Arabs—a name foreign to their language, but which is again heard among the Italians, Spaniards, and even in the southern provinces of France—is it not an indication that the introduction of this tree has some connection with the Portuguese voyages to India, particularly those of Juan de Castro in the year 1520?

It is the Portuguese who have planted the orange tree in the Canaries, at Madeira, where it was supposed to be indigenous on account of the vigorous vegetation it there displays: it is the Portuguese who have introduced this tree into all countries washed by the Mediterranean: and it is still the Portuguese who have furnished the parent suckers, whence the Spaniards have been enabled to form their immense groves in Andalusia and Algarvia.

From the foregoing recital we may conclude that the grand poliphagic triumvirate of antiquity—Archestratus, Vitellius, and Apicius—never tasted this fruit, which heaven reserved for the appreciation of modern times. Blessed shades! if, attracted sometimes by the exquisite vapours of our stoves, you should wander again round those succulent dishes which a more experienced chemistry enables us to elaborate: if fruitless gastronomic reminiscences should lead you into the delightful retreat of some one of your disciples, who by his enlightened skill is there preparing the treasures of the dessert: oh! turn away your eyes from those enticing fruits which display their golden rays, and rise in pyramids upon a porcelain pedestal. Here are oranges, the nectar and ambrosia of the Olympian ages, which you doubtless regret, and we have again discovered. These wonders of sweetness existed perhaps in China, but you knew it not, for China did not become a Roman province. But console yourselves, giants of cookery! we have not yet attained the high pinnacle of your art; your wild boar *à la Troyenne*, your peacocks' brains, and your phenicopters' tongues, secure for you a triumph which posterity will dispute in vain!

The orange known under the name of 'Portugal orange' comes from China. Not more than two centuries ago the Portuguese brought thence the first scion, which has multiplied so prodigiously that we now see entire forests of orange trees in Portugal.

It appears to have been the custom formerly, in England, to make new-year's presents of oranges stuck full with cloves. We read in one of Ben Jonson's pieces, the 'Christmas Masque,' 'He has an orange and rosemary, but not a clove to stick in it.'

At the present day we can dispense with this embellishment.

The first orange tree cultivated in the centre of France was to be seen a few years ago at Fontainebleau. It was called *Le Connétable* (the Constable), because it had belonged to the Connétable de Bourbon, and had been confiscated, together with all property belonging to that prince, after his revolt against his sovereign.

Fig Tree.

Antiquity, sacred and profane, has not left us, on any other tree, facts so clear and certain as upon the fig tree; it is the only tree of Eden of which the sacred books have preserved to us any mention. In the East there were immense plantations of it; Egypt had some also; and the land of Canaan produced figs, which enabled Moses to judge of its fertility.

The Scriptures, in order to give us an idea of the happiness and tranquility the Jews enjoyed under the reign of Solomon, tell us that, 'in Judea and Israel all dwelt safely, every man under his vine and under his fig tree.'

And the fruit of this tree was no doubt very dear to the Hebrews, since Rubshakeh, the general of the Assyrian army, thought to seduce them from their obedience to Hezekiah, King of Judea, by saying to them: 'Come out to me, and then eat ye every man of his own vine, and every one of his fig tree.'

Thus the trade carried on with figs in Jerusalem had become so considerable and active, that Esdras was obliged to interdict it on the Sabbath day. It appears that figs were arranged in small masses, to which they give the form of loaves or cakes, either round or square, which were sold nearly in the same way as at the present day.

From the East the fig tree passed into Greece, then into Italy, Gaul, Spain, and throughout Europe.

The Athenians pretended that this tree was native of their soil, and this people never wanted mythologic facts to support their assertions; they imagined, and would have others believe, that the grateful Ceres rewarded the Athenian, Phytalus, for his hospitality by giving him a fig tree, which served for all the plantations of Attica.

Whatever may be the way it came to them, they received it with transports of joy; it was planted with great pomp in the centre of the public square of Athens: from that time this spot was sacred to them.

Ere long the fame of the figs of Attica spread far and wide: they were the best in Greece; and the magistrates strictly prohibited their exportation. This law was afterwards modified, that is, the exportation of figs was allowed on payment of a very heavy duty.

They then appointed inspectors, whose duty it was to discover contraventions, and report them: thence arose the name of Sycophant, taken by those informers—a vile and dispised set of men, whose denunciations were often false, and with whom the infamous authors of a base calumny were eventually assimilated.

In Greece every one feasted on figs: it was a sort of regular gastronomic *furore*, which knew no bounds, and the wise Plato himself ceased to be a philosopher when presented with a basket of that fruit. As an aliment it was considered so wholesome and strengthening, that on the first introduction of them they constituted the food of the athletæ, whose patron, Hercules, had also fed on them in his youth.

The superiority of the Greek figs was so generally acknowledged that the kings of Persia even had a predilection for them: dried ones were served on the tables of these ostentatious princes.

The Romans believed, according to an antique tradition, that their first princes,

Romulus and Remus, were found under a fig tree on the shore of the Tiber; they therefore rendered signal honours to this tree when it was brought into Italy: they planted it in the Forum; and it was under its shade that a sacrifice was offered every year to the shepherdess who had suckled their founder.

It may, nevertheless, be affirmed, that no one before Cato had noticed the fig tree, which probably appeared in Rome at the same period as the peach, apricot, and other trees of Asia. Sixty years afterwards Varro speaks of it as a novelty from beyond sea, and points out to us that its various species have retained the names of the countries whence they came.

Those varieties were so numerous, that Pliny counts no less than twenty-nine of them, and the designation of the greater part recalled to mind the illustrious families who had taken them under their patronage.

The people of the north, especially the moderns, cannot well explain the extraordinary infatuation of the ancient southern nations for the fruit of the fig tree. Perhaps we ought to look for the reason in the nourishing, fresh, and sweet qualities of its pulp, and in the numerous plantations of those trees, which sometimes furnished an agreeable food to entire armies, when other provisions failed. That of Philip of Macedon owed its preservation to the figs brought to it by the Magnesians. A long time before, David received with joy, from the hands of Abigail, two hundred baskets of dried figs, for himself and his exhausted men.

More than once the far-famed reputation of some beautiful plantations of fig trees brought long and disastrous wars on an entire country, as steel attracts lightning. Xerxes left Persia, and rushed on Attica, to take possession of those delicious figs, whose renown only had crossed his territory: and it was partly to eat the figs of Rome that the Gauls waged war against Italy: thank Heaven we have now more respect for our neighbours' fig trees.

The best things in the world have had their detractors, and the fig is not an exception. Philotimus and Diphilus looked upon it as bad food; Galen was unwell after partaking of figs, and he recommends us to mix almonds with them; Hippocrates himself thought them indigestible, and advised to drink plentifully after eating them.

All these great men may have been right, but the Greeks, their contemporaries, acted as if they were wrong: happily we are not called upon to decide between them.

Figs were commonly served on aristocratic tables with salt, pepper, vinegar, and some aromatics; they were eaten fresh, or dried in the oven, or on hurdles in the sun.

Mulberry Tree.

The ancient mulberry tree was considered the wisest and most prudent of trees, because it took care, they said, not to let the smallest of its buds come to light before the cold had entirely disappeared, not to return. Then, however, it hastened to repair lost time, and a single night was sufficient to see it display its beautiful flowers, which the next morning brightly opened at the rising of Aurora.

The voluptuous Romans, reposing late on their soft couches the day after the fatigues of a banquet worthy of Vitellius, did not trouble themselves much about this interesting phenomenon, which occurred, if Pliny does not mistake, in the gardens of their villas. But they knew that mulberries agree with the stomach, that they afford hardly any nourishment, and easily digest: therefore, no sooner had they opened their heavy eyelids than an Egyptian boy—attentive living bell—at a sign disappeared, and quickly returned, bearing a small crystal vase, filled with mulberry juice and wine reduced by boiling. This beneficent fruit preserved in this mixture all its sweet flavour, and enabled the rich patrician to await until evening the hour for new excesses.

It is quite evident that this luscious fruit was a native of Canaan, for the high road by which the tribes of Israel went up to the feasts at Jerusalem lay through the valley of *Baka*, or Mulberry Tree; and the whole tract of country from Ekron to Gaza abounded in these trees.

Shell Fruit.

Almond Tree.

This tree, whose fruit was called at one time 'Greek Nut,' and, at another, 'Thasian Nut,' is a native of Paphlagonia, according to Hermippus. The nations of the east thought much of almonds, and Jacob found them worthy of appearing among the presents he designed for Joseph. The almond tree of Naxos supplied the markets of Athens. The Romans, in their turn, sought them, and believed, like the physician spoken of by Plutarch, that it was only necessary to eat five or six almonds to acquire the ability of drinking astonishingly.

Besides, this fruit had not always so mean a destination: the disciples of Apicius made of it one of the most delicate of dishes. Here it is, as taught to them by their master:—

Take almonds that have been pounded in a mortar, and mix them with honey, pepper, garum, milk, eggs, and a little oil; submit the whole to the action of a slow fire.

The ancients were acquainted with the oil of almonds, of which they made nearly the same use as we do ourselves; but they possessed, in addition, an infallible means of augmenting the fertility of the almond tree. It was very simple:— A hole was made in the tree, a stone was introduced into it, and, thanks to the virtue of this new manure, the branches soon bent under the weight of almonds.

The good almonds come from Barbary and the south of France. When young, they are preserved like green apricots. They are eaten at table, fresh or dry; in comfits, pastry, &c.: they are also used to make orgeat and refreshing emulsions. The oil extracted from almonds, even bitter ones, is very sweet; it is best extracted cold, by pressure. The pulp is employed, under the name of almond paste, for several purposes, one of which is to render the skin soft and flexible.

Walnut Tree.

Asia, the cradle of most fruit trees, gave birth also to the walnut tree. It is believed to be a native of Persia, and its pleasing foliage already adorned, in Biblical times, the orchards of the east. One of the most ancient of the sacred books informs us that it was known to the Jews, and it may be inferred from a passage in the Song of Solomon that they possessed numerous plantations of this tree.

Among the Persians, walnuts were not lavished on the first comer, as with us; the sovereign reserved them for his dessert, and the people were obliged to abstain from them. But perhaps it may be said that, however fond this prince may have been of walnuts, he could not eat all that were produced in his states. The objection is embarrassing, we own, and chroniclers are silent on this point. But let us suppose that this generous potentate distributed to his favourites the walnuts from which his satiated appetite was compelled to abstain; and, indeed, we find that a king of Persia sent some to the Greeks, who called them 'Royal Persian nuts,' in gratitude and remembrance of the august gift.

They did still better; the king of Olympus had a great liking for this fruit, so they hastened to consecrate it to him, and the 'nuts of Jupiter' were cultivated with honour in the whole of Greece.

Italy received the walnut tree from Attica, and, by degrees, the conquerors of the world introduced it to the different countries of Europe.

The Romans, imitators of the piety of the Greeks, placed this tree also under the protection of the most powerful of their gods. One of their most whimsical customs, perhaps, owed its origin to this consecration, which will serve to explain it:—

After the wedding feast the bridegroom stewed in the nuptial chamber, at night, several baskets of walnuts; which children hastened to pick up. This was, they said, a kind of offering to Jupiter, and thus he was entreated to grant his supreme patronage to the husband, and to adorn the wife with the virtues of Juno. The god could not have failed to smile at this part of the request of blind mortals, and it is asserted that, at times, he condescended not to grant it.

Others have given a different interpretation. According to them, the walnut, being covered with a double envelope when fresh, became a presage of abundance and prosperity.

It would be too tedious to relate all the singular opinions to which this ceremony gave rise. The most reasonable appears to be that adopted by certain commentators:— Walnuts, say they, served as playthings for children, and, by throwing them on the ground the day of his wedding, the bridegroom made it understood that he and his companion renounced the frivolities of youth, henceforth to devote themselves to the serious exigencies of a family.

This fruit was considered astringent, stomachic, and proper to facilitate digestion. It was made into preserve, and eaten in small quantity, mixed with figs. In this manner paralysis of the tongue was avoided—an effect to which it was believed those who partook of them to excess were exposed. Green walnuts were much esteemed; they were served at dessert, notwithstanding the opinion of Heraclides, of Tarentum, who looked upon them as a stimulant to the appetite, and advised a trial of them at the beginning of a repast.

When Pompey had made himself master of the palace of Mithridates, he had search made everywhere for the recipe of the famous antidote against poison used by that king. At length it was found; it was very simple: however, we offer it to the curious:—

Pound, with care, two walnuts, two dried figs, twenty leaves of rue, and a grain of salt. Swallow this mixture—precipitate it by the assistance of a little wine, and you have nothing to fear from the most active poison for the space of twenty-four hours.

Animal Food.

Heathen authors, guided by the lights of reason, some gleams of tradition, and perhaps not absolutely strangers to the writings of Moses, agree pretty well on the diet of the Golden Age; that age of innocence, acorns, and happiness, when everywhere were seen streams of milk, and nectar, and honey, flowing from the hollow oaks and other trees of the forests.

But when the question is to point out the time at which the use of animal food was introduced, ideas become clouded, and highly intelligent minds, bewildered by the obscurity which envelops the subject, have frequently appealed to absurd legends and ridiculous fables, invoking the the aid of their false and contested authority.

Xenocrates pretends that Triptolemus forbad the Athenians to eat animals. Man must, then, have been still frugivorous for four centuries after the Deluge.

This opinion found contradictors, who maintained that man contented himself with fruit only because fire was wanting to cook meat; but Prometheus came, and taught him how to draw the useful element from the flint which concealed it, and was the first to venture on the sacrifice of an ox. This happened in the year of the world 2412.

All this is a mistake, say other and very sensible writers; here is the truth on the difficult point: The goddess Ceres had sown a field, and the wheat came up as desired, when a pig entered, tumbled about, and caused considerable damage, which so irritated the lady that she punished him with death. Now, as a pig is good for nothing except to eat, this one was eaten; and from that day, so fatal to the swinish race, mankind learnt to appreciate the flesh of animals.

At the same time, Bacchus killed a goat he found nibbling at the tendrils of his darling vines; and Hyberbius, son of Mars, and a slasher, like his father, amused himself by killing another, in order to become familiar thus early with scenes of combat. These goats were roasted; and as experience had as yet furnished no rule of comparison, and formed no taste—that exquisite sentiment of the beautiful in the plastic arts, and of the good in the culinary science—it was decided that this dish was very tolerable.

Hitherto the bovine race had only lost one individual: its sad destiny began in the year 1506, before our era, under the reign of the fourth king of Athens, Erichtonius, on a day of great solemnity, when an ox, pressed probably by hunger, came near the altar, and devoured one of the sacred cakes with heathen piety had dedicated to Jupiter. The zealous Diomus rushed forward, and pierced the heart of the sacrilegious quadruped.

It might be supposed that the anger of the god was immediately appeased; but no! the terrible Jupiter knitted his brows; Olympus was in great agitation; and pestilence came, and spread its ravages amongst the Athenians.

'All did not die, but all were struck;' and, to propitiate the implacable scourge, they thought of nothing better than to institute the Buphonic Feast, which happily re-established their health, and which they continued to celebrate every year. They sacrificed an ox, offered a piece to Jupiter, and the faithful divided the rest among themselves.

At Tyre, in Phœnicia, meat was consumed on the altar, but the gods had the profit of it, and nobody else. Some fruit and a few vegetables were sufficient for the frugality of people enjoying innocent and primitive customs. But it happened, in the time of Pygmalion, that a young sacrificer having perceived that a piece of the victim had fallen, hastened to pick it up and replace it carefully on the fire of the altar. In the performance of this operation he burned his fingers, and instantly put them into his mouth, to lessen the pain. As he could not help tasting the fat with which they were covered, the greedy young man experienced a new sensation, which tempted him to swallow a mouthful—then a second—a portion of the victim was eaten; he put another piece under his cloak, and, with his wife, made the finest supper in his life. All went on very well until the prince, being informed of this profanation, loaded them with reproaches, and condemned both to the punishment of death.

Gluttony, however, is rash: other sacrificers ate—at first in secret—of this forbidden food; then they were imitated; and, at last, by degrees meat passed from the altar of the gods, who did not taste it, to the tables of mortals, who feasted upon it. People may or may not believe this anecdote, which informs us in so satisfactory a manner of the epoch at which man, from being frugivorous, became carnivorous; but one thing is certain, that in the time of Homer (there is only eighty years between him and Pygmalion), the flesh of animals was then much in fashion, for we read of his giving to his heroes, as their principal food, a whole hog, three years old, and oxen roasted—not even jointed.

Some ideologists and dreamers have risen against the use of meat; their declamations, often very eloquent, have been read; but, from Pythagoras, a sublime and honest enthusiast, down to the whimsical J. J. Rousseau—who, by-the-by, was very fond of mutton chops and *boeuf à la mode*, although he exclaimed against the cruelty of mankind, whose hands were stained with the blood of animals—no nation has yet determined to adopt the partriarchal diet of the first ages of the world.

Plutarch was a vegetarian; and we possess one of his treatises, in which he endeavours to prove that flesh is not the natural food of man. As a conclusive answer—meat was eaten. So, when an ancient philosopher one day denied the movement of matter, a person reduced him to silence by walking.

But, if animal diet has, from time to time, met with a small number of detractors, what an immense crowd of apologists and adepts has it not also found! It would signify nothing to name individuals; let us point out whole nations. Who is not acquainted with the delicacy and luxury of the Assyrians and Persians? Who is not aware that the genius of the Greeks improved the culinary art, and that their cooks were famous in history? What of the Syracusans, whose dainty and curious ideas passed as a proverb; and of the Athenians, who were so passionately fond of the pleasures of the table; or of Naples, Tarentum, and Sybaris, so celebrated for their good cheer? The Romans surpassed even these refinements and sumptuous repasts: theirs is the honour of the pontiffs' feasts, the excesses of Capreæ, the profusions of Vitellius, of Galba, Nero, and Caligula. They have the honour of the banquet of Geta, which lasted three days, and ended by exhausting the alphabetic list of all the dishes that the universe could supply.

May heaven preserve us from imitating such prodigies of intemperance and gluttonous folly; but let us, at least, be allowed to use with moderation the good that Providence has granted us, and which it has not forbidden us to make agreeable and savoury. The inhabitants of the air, earth, and water, entered within our domains, as well as the fruits of the fields, on the day when the Creator condescended to say to his creature:

'Every moving thing that liveth shall be meat for you; even as the green herb have I given you all things.'

Animals.

The Pig.

If intelligence, strength, or graceful beauty of form were to decide what rank this numerous class of animals—which has contributed its quota to the triumphs of the culinary art—should occupy on our tables, the pig, with its vile and stupid ugliness, its depraved habits, and its waddling obesity, would be banished for ever from the farm-yard and larder in every civilised nation of the world.

But, in refusing to it brilliant external qualities, Nature, by a wise compensation, has conferred on it others much more solid; and this quadruped, so despised during its life-time, does not fail after its death to conciliate the constant favour of rich and poor—of the man indifferent to the attractions of good cheer, and of the Sybarite, ever attentive to enlarge its domain.

Pliny, the naturalist, places the pig one degree below the scale of beings. Apicius, the cook, gives it a marked preference over all meats which passed through his skilful hands. From this, it will easily be understood that the pig presents itself first in this survey of the animal diet of those nations who have transmitted to us an account of their gastrophagic exertions.

History shows us this animal variously appreciated by different countries. Certain people consecrated it, when living, to their divinities most in vogue; others honoured its image—a symbol, they thought, of the quiet happiness of states; a small number abhorred it, and the greater part found it excellent eating.

The inhabitants of Cyprus abstained from it, in order to offer it to Venus. The Cretans loaded it with acorns and all the comforts of life, because Jupier was first suckled by a sow in their island. The Egyptian priests never allowed a ham to grace their feasts; they fled at the sight of pigs, unclean beings, whose presence alone defiled them, although respected by the whole nation on account of the services they rendered in turning up the earth, and covering the seeds thrown upon it.

The law of Moses forbad the Jews to eat this quadruped, or to touch it after its death, and more than once they exposed themselves to the most frightful torments rather than be defiled by this proscribed viand.

Tradition, again, strengthened their religious dread, by interdicting the faithful from even pronouncing the name of this animal, from looking at it, or selling it to foreign nations.

The fear of the frightful malady to which the pig was subject in Palestine, was, perhaps, the cause of this prohibition. Has not a Jewish doctor observed, that if ten measures of leprosy were to fall in the world, this unhappy animal would take nine parts for his share. However, some theologians of that nation believe that the Messiah whom they expect will allow them the use of this now odious food.

Like the Jews, the Phœnicians and Indians did not eat pork. The followers of Islamism also abstained from it, in consequence of a law of the Koran, which Mahomet borrowed from Moses.

The Greeks and Romans had very different ideas. They knew that their gods showed a particular predilection for those altars on which bacon or swine's flesh smoked; they therefore offered this meat in sacrifice to the Earth, the Lares, to Ceres; and many a time a medal struck at Rome perpetuated the remembrance of this solemnity, in honour of the goddess of harvest.

The pig, emblem of fecundity with these two nations, became, on the banners of Italy, a sign of pardon and piece. Kings and princes immolated two on their wedding-day; and nations subdued by the Roman arms prostrated themselves before the standard, whose image promised them the clemency of their conquerors.

The re-establishment of the succulent quadruped would have been complete, if the cynical carelessness of its rather inelegant habits had not caused it to become a symbol of debauchery and profligacy of manners.

Hitherto the pig has only figured in a point of view purely historical; we have not sought to weaken its faults, nor have we made mention of the qualities attributed to it—for example, that of discovering truffles. Nevertheless, we ought not to lose sight of the fact, that this animal has not passed entirely without renown through the centuries which divide us from the earliest ages of the world. We shall now speak of its flesh, its exquisite flavour, and the place it occupied in feasts: there it reigned with honour; there we must follow it, with all that antiquity has possessed of celebrated man in the science of degustation and good living.

Nature has created the pig for a man's palate; he is good only to be eaten; and life appears to have been given to him merely as a sort of salt to prevent his corrupting. It is true that he possesses only a vulgar and purely animal substance; but how good is this substance, and how high does it deserve to be placed on account of its delicacy and flavour?

Such is the praise of which a physician and two philosophers have thought it worthy.

The pig furnishes a strong and somewhat heavy kind of food; wherefore wrestlers were recommended to eat much of it, and Galen advised it to persons who worked hard, or used violent exercise.

But it was not necessary to recommend to the Greeks a meat of which they were so fond. Look over the long work of Athenæus—he everywhere extols it, everywhere speaks of it with fresh complacency, and in pompous terms.

An Athenian, renowned as a man of taste and for the refined elegance of his table, would have thought his reputation lost had he not offered to his guests fat *andouilles*, sausages, pigs' feet, and pork cutlets; above all, he was careful not to forget salted and smoked hams—the honour of the banquet, and the delight of the human race.

The Macedonian, Caranus, invited twenty of his best friends to his wedding, and gave them a feast, of which gastrophagic annals have preserved the remembrance. Each guest received from his munificence a flagon and crown of silver, a crown of gold, and vases of the same precious metal. What shall we say of the dishes displayed at this meeting of learned epicureans? Composed by the art of the most skilful cooks, struck with admiration, they ate and relished, whilst unexpected wonders unceasingly solicited their fatigued, yet not satiated, appetites; when at last appeared an immense silver dish, on which was displayed an entire roasted hog, whose vast sides concealed a multitude of quails and other small birds, *tétines de truie*, relishing yolks of eggs, oysters, and a host of shell fish, prepared with that scientific regard for gastric energy which considerably increases its power.

Macedonia possessed a particular species of pig, greatly envied by the rest of Greece. Certain individuals of this giant race acquired enormous proportions, and King Eumenes used to give as much as sixty-four pounds sterling for one of these animals, provided it measured four feet seven inches in height, and as much in length.

It will be easily understood that the cooks vied with each other, to see who could form unheard-of combinations with the succulent pieces which these enormous pigs furnished. They disguised the taste and form in a thousand different ways, and the most experienced palate was always the dupe of these exquisite deceptions. Thus Titius Quintus, a clever amateur, being enraptured with the number and astonishing variety of dishes which his host caused to be served, at Chalies in Etolia, what was his surprise when the amiable Amphytrion smilingly told him that he had eaten nothing but pork!

Rome, be it observed, knew how to follow the example of Greece; and, in the hands of its skilful cooks, the flesh of this heavy animal was often transformed into delicate fish, ducks, turtle doves, or capons.

But the masterpiece of these great artists—the *ne plus ultra* of their fertile imagination—was the hog *à la Troyenne*, so named because from the depth of its inside issued battalions of thrushes, myriads of ortolans, and fig-peckers (becaficoes) —an ingenious image of those armed cohorts inclosed in the horse of Troy. Everywhere the sumptuous dish is cited, but nothing is said of the manner in which it was prepared. The curious will perhaps be thankful to find that this omission is here repaired:—

The animal is artistically bled under the shoulder. When all the blood has flowed, the intestines are drawn out by the throat, and washed for a long time with wine, taking care to pass it through them. The pig is then hung up by the feet, and washed also with wine. An excellent gravy must be prepared beforehand, with meat hashed small and well peppered, with which you stuff the intestines, and then force them back into their place by the throat. Pour in at the same time a great quantity of gravy, and fill the animal with small game. Half of the pig is afterwards covered with a thick paste of barley meal, wine, and oil. It is then put into a portable oven, on a small metal table, where it is roasted by a slow fire. When the skin has assumed a fine colour it is withdrawn, and boiled on the other side; the paste covering is then entirely removed, and the pig *à la Troyenne* may be served. The Romans reared a great number of these animals, and also procured many from foreign countries, especially from Arcadia, which produced some of extraordinary size. Varro relates that in this part of the Peloponnesus he was shown a pig so fat that it was impossible for the animal to make the least movement; and that a mouse had settled on its back with her young family, softly ensconced in the fat, where they fed at the expense of the careless animal.

Rome adopted, with a kind of gastronomic rage, the preparations and *ragoûts* celebrated in Greece. The Trojan pig never failed to appear on tables renowned for their luxury; and sucking pigs were eaten in such profusion, that the censors were obliged to interdict their use. Alexander Severus renewed this prohibition. The large pigs stuffed with game (an expensive delicacy of patrician tables) also called forth new sumptuary laws, which only provoked disdain, and which fashion soon rendered obsolete.

We hardly dare mention a strange dish, in great request among the rich and luxurious, who alone could procure it. The first preparation consisted in stifling the young before they were littered. Thank Heaven, this culinary atrocity could not survive an epoch without parallel, perhaps, in the history of human follies, by we know not what refinement of incredible gluttony, of frightful depravity, and atrocious cruelty, which, together, prepared the downfall of the Roman colossus.

Besides this disgusting dish, much was thought at Rome, as well as at Athens, of pig's head, spare-rib, hams, and bacon. Seven other parts occupied the second rank—these were the ears, feet, foreloin, fillet, cheek, intestines, and blood.

The Ox.

A profound sentiment of gratitude has been often the cause of rendering to the ox extraordinary honours, which no animal, perhaps, ever shared with him. The Egyptians considered this quadruped as the emblem of agriculture, and of all that serves to support existence; and incense smoked on its altars at Memphis and Heliopolis.

The Phœnicians religiously abstained from its flesh, and the Phrygians punished with death whosoever dared to slay the labouring ox.

In Greece, during the heroic ages, an ox was the reward adjudged to the conquering wrestlers and pugilists; a horse was the prize of racing or the quoits.

At a later period the Athenians decreed that their coins should bear the image of this useful quadruped; and though they then offered it to their gods, the ceremonies even of the sacrifice testified the repugnance felt at shedding its blood.

The sacrificer fled with the greatest speed after he had struck it; he was followed, and, to avoid being arrested, he threw away the axe he had used, and accused it of causing the death of the innocent ox. The axe was then seized and tried; some one defended it, and alleged that it was less guilty than the grinder who had sharpened the blade. The latter cast the odium of the crime on the grinding stone, so that the trial was never ended, and the pretended offence remained unpunished.

For a long time the greater part of the ancients considered it a sin to eat the flesh of the ox, the companion of the agriculturist, whose patient vigour hollows the furrow which is to be the means of his support. But the bad example of Proserpine, who prepared one for Hercules, caused these scruples, one by one, to be hushed, the solemn prohibition of the legislator of Athens forgotten; and, in spite of the obstinate resistance of the Pythagorians and the disciples of Empedocles, every one declared in favour of the doctrines of Zeno and Epicurus.

Moreover, it is certain that the heroes of Homer were not so scrupulous: Menelaus offered roast-beef to Telemachus; Agamemnon also presented some to the wise Nestor; and an ox, roasted whole, frequently appeased the robust appetite of the illustrious chiefs of Greece.

If we go back to centuries still more remote, and of which a venerable historian has preserved us an account, we find herds of oxen were possessed by the great patriarchal families. Abraham cooked a calf and served it to the three angels, in the valley of Mamre; and the flesh of this animal, whither ox or heifer, was evidently much in use in the primitive ages, since no particular proscription exempts them from those beings having life and motion, and which are to serve us as food. As to Moses, far from interdicting it to the Israelites, he places the ox in the first rank of pure animals, whose flesh was allowed them.

The oracle of ancient medicine, Hippocrates, praises the flesh of the ox, in which he recognises the most nutritious qualities, but nevertheless he believes it to be heavy and indigestible.

Of what material, then, must have been the stomach of Theagenes, of Thasos— he, who devoured a whole bull in one day.

To be sure, the same exploit is attributed to Milo of Crotona, whose ordinary meal consisted of eighteen pounds of meat, as much bread, and fifteen pints of wine. These formidable polyphagists could, without much expense, indulge their fabulous appetites; for, in the time of Demosthenes, 354 B.C., an ox of the first quality cost only eighty drachmas, or about two pounds, eleven shillings, and eightpence.

The ox was so precious among the Romans, that mention is made of a certain citizen accused before the people and condemned, because he had killed one of his oxen to satisfy the fancy of a young libertine, who told him he had never eaten any tripe. He was banished, as if he had killed his farmer.

The Brahmin women think to obtain abundance of milk and butter by invoking one particular cow,—the darling cow of the king of heaven; the type, mother, and patroness of all cows. The entire species are treated with the greatest deference; they have lavished upon them every expression of gratitude, and one day of each year is set apart as a solemn festival consecrated to their worship.

Some centuries ago the large pieces of meat were boiled first, and then roasted. Roasted meat was always served with sauce. Animals roasted whole were generally filled with an aromatic stuffing. Sage was the common seasoning for geese, and sucking-pigs were stuffed with chestnuts. Some minutes before these were taken from the spit, they were covered with bread crumbs; and appeared on the table enveloped in a crust composed of bread, sugar, orange juice, and rose water.

Boeuf Gras. — There is a very old custom in the whole of France, and which consists in leading throughout the streets, in the provincial towns, on Shrove Tuesday, a fatted ox, ornamented with flowers and ribbons. This ceremony is considered as a commemorative emblem of the fecundity of the earth. In Paris, the ox chosen for the same purpose has generally obtained beforehand the prize awarded by the Agricultural Society. The horns of the animals are gilded; he is afterwards decorated in a sumptuous manner, and led through the principal thoroughfares of that city, on Shrove Sunday, Monday, and Tuesday, to the Palace of the Tuileries, the ministerial residences, the Hôtel-de-Ville, and the foreign embassies. Troops of butchers, dressed in appropriate fancy costumes, both on horseback and on foot, are preceded by bands of music; and the heathen divinities, drawn by eight horses in a richly gilt triumphal car, form one of the most splendid and grotesque pageants of modern times.

The Lamb.

Formerly, sworn examiners of the clouds, skilful in discovering the storms they concealed, announced to the inhabitants of the country the hail by which their crops were threatened, and every one immediately offered a sacrifice to the inimical cloud, in order that it might carry ruin and desolation elsewhere. The most devout sacrificed a lamb; the luke-warm worshippers a fowl; some even contented themselves with pricking their finger with a pin, and throwing towards heaven the drops of blood which came out. The cloud, it is said, satisfied with these pious offerings, soon disappeared never to return.

The lamb, an oblation pure and agreeable in the sight of the gods, reconciled the earth with Olympus. In Egypt, the inhabitants of Sais and Thebes offered it to their divinities. Minerva and Juno also were pleased to see its flesh smoking on the altars which Greece and Italy raised to them.

These practices, no doubt, were an obscure imitation of the religious rites which Moses prescribed to his people, and which heathen nations adopted in their turn, one from the other.

The Hebrew law forbad the killing the Paschal lamb before it was weaned, and also the cooking of it in its mother's milk. It was to be eaten roasted, with unleavened bread, lettuces, mustard, or bitter herbs: whatever might remain was to be burnt with fire. It was not to be boiled, nor a bone of it broken. It must be chosen of that year, a male, and without fault or blemish.

Many passages of the sacred writings allow us to appreciate the pastoral riches of the first nations of the East; and an idea may be formed of the number of their flocks, when we are told that Jacob gave the children of Hamor a hundred sheep for the price of a field; and that the King of Israel received a hundred thousand every year from the King of Moab, his tributary, and a like number of rams, covered with their fleece.

The delicate flesh of the lamb was the ornament of the tables of the voluptuous inhabitants of Sion and Samaria. The prophet Amos reproaches them with this luxury, and threatens them with the Divine anger on that account. The Greeks carried their love for this meat to such a height, that the magistrates of Athens were obliged to forbid the eating of lamb which had not been shorn. This restriction did not prevent the epicures of Attica from buying one of these animals every day, which cost them ten drachmas (6s. 5d.), and the head of which, prepared with art, heightened the beauty of the first course. Rome and Italy imitated Greece, and the flocks of the fertile Campania hardly sufficed for the exigencies of the capital of the world, especially towards the end of autumn, a period of which lambs afforded, according to the Romans, a more highly flavoured and wholesome meat than in the spring.

Blount informs us of a very ancient and rather strange custom. He says:—

'At Kidlington, in Oxfordshire, the custom is, that on Monday after Whitson week, there is a fat, live lamb provided, and the maids of the town, having their thumbs tied behind them, run after it, and she that with her mouth takes and holds the lamb is declared *Lady of the Lamb*, which, being dressed, with the skin hanging on, is carried on a long pole before the Lady and her companions to the Green, attended with music, and a morisco dance of men and another of women, when the rest of the day is spent in dancing, mirth, and merry glee. The next day the lamb is part baked, boiled, and roast, for the Lady's feast, where she sits majestically at the upper end of the table, and her companions with her, with music and other attendants, which ends the solemnity.

The Kid.

The kid was one of the most delicate dishes of the Hebrews: Rebecca prepared some for Isaac, in order to dispose him to give his blessing to Jacob. Moses ordered that, for the Feast of Passover, a lamb or a kid should be slain. Samson carried a kid to his young wife when he wished to be reconciled to her. The brother of the prodigal son complains to his father that he has never given him a kid to make merry with his friends.

The Egyptians, who represented their god Pan with the face and legs of a goat, abstained religiously from killing a kid or eating its flesh. Their veneration for this animal went so far, in some countries, that goat-keepers appeared in their eyes invested with an august and sacred character. The Greeks did not judge it convenient to adopt these strange ideas, although on other points their theology was sufficiently ridiculous. The kid was considered one of the most dainty dishes in state banquets; it was served whole, on a silver basin, to each of the guests at the wedding of the Macedonian, Caranus.

The Ass.

The ass was an impure animal, according to the law of Moses, whose flesh was forbidden because it did not ruminate. However, at the siege of Samaria, the Jews were compelled to eat it for want of other food. The famine was such, that the head of an ass was sold for eighty pieces of silver.

The Roman peasants thought the flesh of the young ass had a very agreeable taste, and regaled themselves with it at their rustic festivals. The celebrated Mecænas one day tasted of this dish at the house of one of his free slaves; he spoke of it with much praise, caused it to be served on his own table, and even succeeded in introducing it on those of the great and rich, who gave up the onager, or wild ass, which they had hitherto preferred, to humour this illustrious favourite. But this new gastronomic conquest had only a short vogue; and was forgotten after the death of Mecænas. Galen tells us that the cooks of Alexandria thought much of the ass, whose flesh, he says, much resembles that of the stag. Still, this great physician disapproves of the use of this food, which he considers unsuited to mankind.

It is asserted, even at the present day, that the flesh of the young ass is a pretty good dish; we have heard, but we hardly can repeat it, that much is consumed in the *guinguettes* round Paris, where the artless customers are far from thinking that anything else but veal can be served to them.

The modern restaurateurs of the Barrières of Paris, have, perhaps, read the biography of Mecænas, and endeavour to render popular the dish so honoured by the celebrated favourite. Who can blame them?

The Dog.

We must beg pardon of the reader for informing him that the dog presented a very relishing dish to many nations advanced in culinary science. To them, one of these animals, young, plump, and delicately prepared, appeared excellent food.

The Greeks, that people so charming by their seductive folly, their love of the arts, their poetic civilization, and the intelligent spirit of research presiding over their dishes—the Greeks (we grieve to say it) ate dogs, and even dared to think them good; the grave Hippocrates himself—the most wise, the least gluttonous, and therefore the most impartial of their physicians—was convinced that this quadruped furnished a wholesome and, at the same time, a light food.

As to the Romans, they also liked it, and no doubt prepared it in the same manner as the hare, which they thought it resembled in taste.

However, it is but right to add, that this dish, which we will not even hear mentioned, was never favourably received by the fashionable portion of Roman society, and that the legislators of ancient gastrophagy even repulsed it with disdain.

There is every reason to believe that the people regaled themselves with a roast or boiled dog, especially once a year, at the period when they celebrated the deliverance of the Capitol from the siege of the Gauls. It is known that, at this solemnity, a goose, laid on a soft cushion, was carried in triumph, followed by an unhappy dog nailed to a cross, whose loud cries greatly amused the populace. In this manner they commemorated the signal service rendered by one animal, and the fatal negligence of the other. The Gauls scaled the Capitol while the dogs slept, and Rome had been lost if the deafening cries of the geese had not given an alarm to the garrison, who, it must be allowed, should have kept better watch.

The quadrupeds last mentioned are the only domestic animals of the kind used as food by the ancients. The case afforded them several others, which we shall mention, after having just glanced at the poultry—one of the most interesting divisions in natural history for the serious and reflective appreciator of gastronomic productions.

CHEF TO ALL NATIONS

Poultry.

The Cock.

An object of divine worship in Syria, the cock was considered by almost every nation as the emblem of vigilance and courage. Thus, heathen antiquity consecrated it to the god of battles. Themistocles, marching with his army against Xerxes, King of Persia, met with some cocks fighting furiously; he made his troops halt, that they might observe them, and he then addressed a spirited discourse to them on the subject. He conquered, and on his return to Athens, desired that every year a cock-fight should commemorate his victory. These cruel games soon spread throughout Greece, and feathered champions were reared with great care, and obtained at a high price from Rhodes, Bœotia, Mela, and Chalcis.

Italy also wished to enjoy this barbarous pastime. At Pergamus, any spectator might throw a cock into the arena, and a prize was awarded to the lucky possessor of the bird who remained master of the field of battle.

This warlike bird has never enjoyed a high culinary reputation; nevertheless, it was eaten when old, that is to say, at that period of its life when its flesh, hard, fibrous, and tough, possesses neither juice nor flavour—then this wretched food was left to those among the common people who joyously feasted in the drinking-shops of Rome. They, however, always avoided making fricassees of white cocks, because they were consecrated to the month, and proclaimed the hours.

The Capon.

The cock being banished from the table of all respectable people, the necessity of dressing hens became evident, for it was necessary to live. Now, you are aware that there are two sorts of hens; one sort consumptive looking and tough, the other tender, plump, and before which an epicure banishes every other thought, and sighs with pleasure. These last were preferred, and, in order to render them more worthy of the voluptuous epicures for whom they were intended, they learned from the inhabitants of the island of Cos the art of fattening them in dark and closed places, with certain wonderful pastes, which increased their delicacy and tempting whiteness.

This ingenous invention belonged to Greece and Asia. Rome possessed herself of it, and even improved it; but soon the constant tyrant of the kitchen, the Consul, C. Fannius, who thought bad what others thought good, and who pretended that in consequence of the immense consumption made of them, the result would be that not a living hen would be left in the empire, ordered that for the future the Romans should dispense with fattening and eating this delicious winged animal.

Fortunately, the law said nothing about young cocks; this silence saved Roman gastronomy, and the capon was invented. It is not necessary to relate with what transports of delight this new creation was greeted; it will be easily understood. Rome was moved; the famous Greek cooks, who consecrated their science to *her*, were on tip-toe. Everywhere, from mouth to mouth, spread the name of the skilful enchanter, who could in such a manner metamorphose the clarion of the farm yard. Fannius, himself, it is said, wished to be assured of the truth of the prodigy: he was served with a roast capon, and the praises he bestowed on it were assuredly the triumph of the bird, of epicures, and of art. From this remarkable epoch, nearly all chickens underwent the ingenious transformation which rendered them so welcome to all

119

Lucullian tables; and it caused such a destruction of birds, that the consul repented, but too late, that he had only named hens in his sumptuary law.

The Hen.

The cackling of hens infalliably announced, among the ancients, some dreadul calamity for the person who had the misfortune to hear it. This fatal omen must have rendered a great number of people unfortunate; for whether she lays eggs, or conducts her young family, a hen generally cackles.

They therefore sought to diminish the number of these birds of ill-omen; they fattened them for eating, and they did right, since, according to learned physicians, the flesh of these birds is good for weakly persons, as well as those who are convalescent. Healthy individuals also find this food suit them perfectly. In Greece there would have been something wanting at a feast, if fat hens had not been served. They embellished the celebrated wedding repast of Caranus; and Athenæus often speaks of them when describing a grand banquet.

At Rome, the art of fattening them became a serious occupation, which was long studied, and had its precepts and rules. Marcus Lœlius Strabo, belonging to the order of knights, invented aviaries in which hens were confined; others sought and discovered the means of giving to their flesh that particular flavour unperceived by uncultivated palates, but which the experienced gastrophilist always appreciates. They patiently gave themselves up to laborious experiments: a warm, narrow, dark spot received these interesting *volatiles*; the feathers of their wings and tails were plucked, and they were gorged twice a day during three weeks with balls of barley flour mixed with soft water. Great cleanliness was combined with this diet: their heads were well cleansed, and care taken that no insect should enter the aviary.

Afterwards barley flour, kneaded with milk, was preferred: then, instead of milk, water, and honey were employed. Excellent wheaten bread, soaked in good wine and hydromel, was also used with success.

Skilful breeders by these means obtained magnificent hens of an incredibly exquisite flavour, and which weighed no less than sixteen pounds.

The Fannian law unfortunately came, and, as we have before observed, brought impediments to these beautiful results by interdicting aviaries and skilfully prepared pastes. It is true that this law allowed a farm-yard hen to be served at every repast— *mais une poule par jour est-ce contentement?* It became necessary, then, to have recourse to a *mezzo-termine*, which was discovered in the capon. but the favourite dish forbidden by the consular authority was not altogether abandoned: some faithful epicureans always possessed in the shade well-furnished aviaries; and it was even then, we are assured, that Rome and the universe were enriched with the *poularde*.

The Chicken.

It is certainly surprising that a people so serious as the Romans generally were, should make the success of the greatest enterprise depend on the appetite of their famous sacred chickens. They were brought from the Island of Negropont, and were kept shut up in cages; their guardian was designated by the name of Pullarius.

Publius Claudius, constrained to consult these strange prophets before engaging in a naval combat, ordered them to be fed; they refused to open their beaks. The incredulous general ordered them at once to be thrown into the sea, and laughingly exclaimed to the dismayed Pullarius: 'Since they will not eat—well! then let us make them drink.'

Diodorus of Sicily, and some ancient writers, tell us that the Egyptians, from a remote period, hatched chickens in ovens. This process is decidedly of the highest antiquity, and was applied to the eggs of all kinds of poultry. In the last century, Réaumur tried various experiments, and recovered this art, which was thought to have been lost; others again have followed the steps of this skilful observer, and, at the present day, obtain the most satisfactory results.

Chickens have ever been considered an estimable food, and hardly yielded to the two glories of their family—the fattened hen and the capon. The Greeks served them at all their feasts of ceremony, and the Romans granted them a distinguished place among the dishes of the second course.

The Goose.

When a flock of geese are obliged to pass Mount Taurus—the dreaded abode of their enemies, the eagles—each of them takes the precaution to hold a stone in its beak, in order that he may keep a profound silence, which, otherwise, his natural loquacity would render impossible. This, if true, would justify Aristotle in attributing foresight to the goose; a quality which Scaliger also claims for this bird.

The ancients highly esteemed its flesh. Homer and Athenæus speak with praise of the fat geese and goslings which the Greeks ate.

The Egyptians served them at their meals every day; it was, with veal, the favourite dish of their monarchs, and they did not forget to offer some to King Agesilaus, when he was travelling through the country.

Some eastern nations were impressed with such deep veneration for this bird that they swore by nothing else. The Britons honoured it, and forbad all persons to do it the least harm. It remained for Queen Elizabeth to prove, at her joyous dinners of the 29th September, that tastes and usages are modified by time. And moreover, many centuries before, her ancestors had been greatly wanting in respect towards a particular kind of goose, which they roasted without any ceremony. A well-deserved sentiment of gratitude rendered them dear to the Romans; their noisy clamour had formerly saved the Capitol. They became for them, as for the Egyptians, a symbol of safety, and were reared, both in town and country, to guard the houses.

Those which were kept, out of gratitude, in the Capitol, were consecrated to Juno, Isis, Mars, and Priapus, and every year one of them was chosen for the brilliant and solemn ceremony we have already mentioned.

But, alas! time obscures and effaces all the glories of the world; and that of the Roman geese, no doubt, had to submit to this sad fate, for they were eaten at least a century before the time of Pliny. Unfortunate bird! Yes, a perfidious art fed them delicately in the shade, in convenient aviaries, where nothing was wanting for their comfort, and at the end of a few days the poor victims made but one step from this dangerous retreat to the place of execution. The Emperor Alexander Severus became so fond of this dish, that on his great festival days they served him with a goose and a pheasant. Nothing, in his estimation, could equal the exquisite flavour of these two birds.

The luxurious Romans, however, neglected the entire animal, and thought only of the liver. They invented the art of fattening this viscera, and of increasing its size to such an extent that it often weighed two pounds. To obtain this result, they simply fed their victims of sensuality, during twenty days, with a paste of dried figs and water. As soon as the goose was killed, the liver was put to soak in milk and honey.

It is not known exactly to whom we are to attribute this gastronomic discovery. Scipio, Metellus, and Marcus Sejus disputed the glory of the invention. At all events, it is certain that the same method was used in Greece as in Italy; that white geese were chosen in preference, and that the fat livers were served roasted, or fried in the frying-pan, and enveloped in the *omentum*, a membrane which we term the caul. Pliny assures us that Apicius found means to increase livers to a monstrous size, which almost equalled in weight the whole body of the animal.

In the sixteenth century they had dark cages, in which they fattened poultry with ground tares, wheaten flour, and barley meal. Capons fattened in hutches, where they could not turn, nor even stir, were esteemed delicious. They fed pigeons on the crumb of bread, steeped in wine; peacocks on the sediment from cider.

On Michaelmas Day, the 29th of September, many persons in England eat roast goose for their dinner. It is said that this custom dates from the time of Queen Elizabeth, who was being served with a piece of goose on Michaelmas Day, at the very moment when news was brought of the defeat of the famous Armada. Some persons affirm that the Queen expressed a desire that this dish might, each year, serve to perpetuate the remembrance of so signal a victory. Would it not be more simple to suppose that Elizabeth herself already conformed to a custom which had existed before her time?

The Turkey Hen.

'There must be two to eat a truffled turkey,' said a gastronomist of the 18th century, to one of his friends—a noted *gourmand*—who had just come to pay him a visit. 'Two!' replied the visitor, with a smile of sensuality. 'Yes, two,' answered the first; 'I never do otherwise: for instance, I have a turkey to-day, and of course we must be two.' The friend, looking earnestly at the other, said: 'You, and who else?' 'Why,' answered the gastronomist, 'I and the turkey.'

In Greece, more than one stomach would have been capable of challenging nobly the voracity of this modern polyphagus: witness the insatiable greediness of the well-known glutton who complained that nature ought to have given him a neck as long as the stork, that he might enjoy for a longer period his eating and drinking.

But for a long time the Greeks were quite ignorant of the culinary value of the turkey; it was looked upon as an uncommon curiosity, and not condemned to the spit. Sophocles, the first who spoke of it, pretended that those marvellous birds came purposely from some distant climate beyond the Indies, to bewail the death of Meleager, who took possession of the throne of Macedonia (279 years B.C.), and who was soon driven from it. This Prince, it is reported, carried them away from barbarous regions, that they might enjoy the charms of Greek civilization; and hence could there be anything more natural than to find those compassionate volatiles shedding tears for their benefactor, in one of Sophocles' tragedies? They have been called since, Meleagrides, and this name perpetuated 'misfortune, favour, and gratitude.'

Aristotle hardly supplies us with any details upon turkey hens: he merely says that their eggs are distinguished by little specks from those of the common hens, which are white; but Clytus of Miletis, his disciple, gives an exact description of them, by which no mistake can be made.

Egypt also possessed some of these birds; but there they are still more rare than in Greece, and formed one of the principal ornaments in the triumphal pomp of Ptolemy Philàdelphus, when he entered Alexandria. Large cages, containing meleagrides, were carried before the monarch, and on that day the people knew not which to admire most—the prince or the turkey.

They were introduced into Rome about the year 115 before our era; but, for a long time, they were objects of uncommon curiosity; and Varro, the first of the Latins who speaks of them, confounds these birds with the guinea hens, or hens of Numidia.

A century later, turkeys greatly multiplied, and vast numbers were reared in the Roman farms. Caligula, who had the good sense to make his own apotheosis during his life-time, through fear lest it might be refused after his death, ordered a sacrifice of peacocks, guinea hens, and turkeys to be made daily before his statue.

The Wild Boar

It was in the year 63 before the Christian era: the consul Marcus Tullius Cicero had just accused and convicted Catilina, and Rome, free from present danger, had forgotten all transitory solicitudes of the past to welcome joyous banquetings.

A worthy citizen, excellent patriot, distinguished gastronomist, and posessor of an immense fortune, of which he made the best use (at least so said several choice epicures, his habitual guests), Survilius Rullus—such was his name—thought of celebrating by an extraordinary banquet the triumph of the illustrious consul, and the deliverance of the country. His cook, a young Sicilian slave of the greatest promise, and whose mode of cooking a dish of sows' paps procured him one day a smile of approbation from Lucullus, succeeded especially in those eminent performances which command the admiration of the guests, and give new strength to their exhausted appetites.

Rullus sent for him, and spoke thus: 'Recollect that in three days Cicero will sup here: let the feast be worthy of him who gives it.'

The Sicilian even surpassed himself. As soon as the guests had tasted the enticing delicacies of the first course, the hall echoed with an unanimous concert of applause, and the proud Amphitryon, intoxicated with joy, was going to ask that a crown might be presented to his beloved slave, when the cook appeared, followed by four Ethiopians, who gracefully carried a silver case of prodigious dimensions, in the shape of a large mortar. This extraordinary dish contained a wild boar; baskets of dates were suspended to his tusks, and charming little wild boars, in exquisite pastry, no doubt—for never was there a more tempting culinary exhalation—artistically surrounded the enormous animal. Every voice was hushed; the guests waited in silence the most profound. The tables of the second service were placed round the guests, who raised themselves on the couches with greedy curiosity. The blacks deposited the pecious burden before another domestic, a skilful carver, who opened the wild boar with incredible dexterity and precision, and presented to the astonished eyes of Rullus and his friends a second entire animal, and in this a third; then came fresh delicacies, all gradually diminishing in size, until, at length, a delicious little fig-pecker terminated this series of strange viands, of which Rome, wondering and astonished, long preserved the gastronomic remembrance.

Man seldom prescribes to himself reasonable limits in the vast field of vanity and ostentation. At first it was thought an enviable boldness to have dared to serve an entire boar of a large size. Every one did the same thing, and at length it became quite common. It was necessary then to do better. One thought of having three at the same time; another had four; and soon the extravagant—and they were not few—caused eight wild boars *à la Troyenne* to appear at a single repast. The Macedonian, Caranus, a man of spirit and of merit, placed himself at once on an eminence which baffled rivalry. He invited twenty guests to his wedding, and he had twenty wild boars served.

It must be confessed that such magnificence rather resembles folly; but, alas! has not every nation its failings? Besides, the flesh of the wild boar enjoyed an astonishing reputation in Rome and Greece, and no one could, with credit to himself, receive his friends at his table without presenting them with the fashionable dish,—the animal appointed by nature to appear at banquets.

At length, however, they began to tire of this enormous dish; they divided it into three portions, and the middle piece obtained the preference. Ultimately they served only the fillet and head; the latter of which was more particularly esteemed by the Romans.

Under the Norman kings the wild boar's head was considered a noble dish, worthy of the sovereign's table. This, we are told, was brought to the king's table with the trumpeters sounding their trumpets before it in procession. 'For,' says Holinshed, 'upon the day of coronation (of young Henry), King Henry II., his father served him at table as sewer, bringing up the bore's head with trumpetes afore it, according to the ancient manner.'—Strutt, *'Manners and Cutoms,'* Vol ii., p. 19.

'A very small consumption is made of the old wild boar; the flesh is hard, dry, and heavy; the head only is good. The young wild boar is a fine and delicate game, also, when a year old. The ancients submitted those they could take away from their mother to castration, and left them afterwards to run about the woods, where these animals became larger than the others, and acquired a savour and flavour which made them preferable to the pigs we rear.'—Sonnini.

The Hare.

Plutarch contends that the Jews abstained from eating the hare, not because they thought it unclean, but because it resembled the ass, which they revered. This is only a pleasantry on the part of the celebrated writer, with no other foundation than the fabulous tale of the grammarian Apion, who asserts in his book against the Jews that they preserved in Jerusalem an ass's head, which they adored. We know that a sanitary motive was the cause of this animal being interdicted to the Israelites; and it has been also remarked that the ancient Britons abstained from it.

This mammifer, everywhere very common, swarmed in the East, if we are to believe Xenophon, who saw a great number of them when marching with his troops to join young Cyrus. Greece was abundantly stocked with them: the inhabitants of islands of the AEgean sea had more than once to deplore the ravages which hunger caused these timid animals to commit, and whose fecundity they cursed.

Hegesander relates that, under the reign of Antigonus, an inhabitant of the island of Anaphe brought two hares into the neighbourhood. Their posterity became so numerous that the people were obliged to implore the gods to preserve the harvest, and to annihilate their formidable enemies. As the immortals turned a deaf ear to these complaints, recourse was had to Apollo alone, and the Pythonissa deigned to return this oracle: 'Train hunting dogs, and they will exterminate the hares.' The advice was good, and deemed worthy of being adopted.

The Greeks esteemed highly the flesh of this quadruped, which was served roasted, but almost bleeding, or made into delicious pies, much in vogue in the time of Aristophanes. Hippocrates had, however, forbidden the use of it. 'The hare,' said he, 'thickens the blood, and causes cruel wakefulness;' but epicurism will always think lightly of Hygeian precepts which do not accord with its own ideas. At all events, Galen was not of the same opinion as his colleague, and Galen must be right.

The Emperor Alexander Severus ate a hare at each of his repasts. Perhaps that prince shared the opinion of the Romans, who thought that a person who fed on hare for seven consecutive days became fresher, fatter, and more beautiful. A lady, named Gellia, had a large share of that unfortunate gift of nature which we call ugliness. She resolved to make a trial of this regimen, and submitted to it with a regularity really exemplary. She showed herself at the end of the week, and we are informed that no one thought her any the prettier for it.

The epicures of Rome contented themselves with eating the shoulder of the hare, and left the remainder to less fastidious guests.

The Rabbit.

'The conies are but feeble folk, yet make they their houses in the rocks.' They taught mankind, it is said, the art of fortification, mining, and covered roads. These skilful engineers come originally from warm climates; from Africa, perhaps, whence they were brought to Spain.

They there became so numerous, and dug so well their holes beneath the houses of Tarragona, that the city was completely overthrown, and the greater part of the inhabitants buried beneath its ruins.

Catullus calls Spain *Cuniculosa Celtiberia* (Celtiberian rabbit warren); and two medals, struck in the reign of Adrian, represent that peninsula under the form of a beautiful woman, clothed in a robe and mantle, with a rabbit at her feet. This animal was called in Hebrew, *Saphan*, of which the Phœnicians have made *Spania*, and the Latins *Hispania*.

Strabo relates that the inhabitants of the Balearic Islands, despairing of being able to oppose the extraordinary propagation of rabbits, which nearly rendered their country uninhabitable, sent ambassadors to Rome to implore assistance against this new kind of enemy. Augustus furnished them with troops, and the Roman arms were once more victorious.

Aristotle says nothing of the rabbit, which, probably, was then little known in Greece. It afterwards became common enough, and that of Macedonia, in particular, found favour at tables renowned for delicacies.

The Romans, those bold innovators in cookery, so desirous of strange and unheard of dishes, would only consent to eat rabbits on condition of their being killed before they had left off sucking, or taken alive from the slaughtered mother, to be immediately transferred to the ardent stoves of their kitchens. It was certainly reserved for that people to frighten the world by all kinds of culinary anomalies.

The Fox.

A young fox, fattened on grapes, and roasted on the spit, is a tid-bit for a king during the autumn. Such was the idea of the Roman peasants; but we must be allowed, however, to differ from their opinion.

Feathered Game.

The Quail.

The dead may be raised by the means of a quail, said the ancients. Now for the proof: Hercules having been killed in Lybia, Iolaüs took one of these birds, which fortunately happened to be at hand, and placed it beneath his friend's nose. The hero no sooner smelt it than his eyes opened to the light, and Acheron was forced to give up his prey.

The learned Bochart denies this prodigy. He affirms that Hercules was subject to epileptic attacks, and that, during a fit, they caused him to smell a quail, whose odour quickly cured him.

The Phœnicians insisted that he was quite dead, and they all cried out, 'A miracle!' The reader must decide between them and Bochart.

In the Desert the Israelites fed on quails; and this food, reserved for them by Divine goodness, caused no discomfort among the fugitive tribes. The Greeks served them on their tables with partridges: they raised them in aviaries, and ate them all the year round. Aristotle speaks most highly of them, and does not attribute to them any dangerous property. However, quails were banished from all Roman tables: they were no longer carefully fattened: they were cursed, and accused of causing epilepsy in those who partook of their fatal and seductive flesh. The authority of Galen confirmed this strange prejudice, and these innocent birds, having lost all reputation in Italy, no doubt easily consoled themselves for the happy ostracism which delivered them from a too expensive glory.

At all events, it is probable that Rome had wickedly calumniated quails; two skilful men, devoted to the cause, undertook to defend them: they were called Hippolochus and Antiphanus. Their eloquent pleadings caused a sensation; the epicureans were moved, and some of these birds were recalled, fattened, and roasted.

Quails, like cocks and partridges, seem born to fight to excess. The Grecians encouraged their warlike ardour, and threw them into the arena, where they contemplated their furious attacks with as much pleasure as they experienced at the sight of gladiators murdering each other in order to amuse them. Solon—the wise Solon—required that young men should be trained to courage at the school of these bold champions, and learn from them to despise danger, pain, and death. We know that sensibility was little thought of in the plan of education formed by the great legislator. Long after him, however, the Areopagus gave a dreadful proof of this, by condemning to death a little boy who had amused himself by pulling out the eyes of all the quails unfortunate enough to fall into his hands. This precocious monster was too promising.

The Thrush.

The immortal author of the Iliad did not disdain, it is said, to compose a poem in praise of thrushes. These verses were so beautiful that the Greeks learned them all by heart in their infancy. The singular love of the ancients for this bird renders these poetical honours tolerably probable. More than once Comus has borrowed the lyre of Apollo.

In Greece, children were not allowed to eat thrushes, because it was feared that their delicious flesh might cause them to contract too early habits of gluttony and effeminacy. Young girls received them as presents from their betrothed on the day of their marriage. They were served at the most sumptuous feasts, and Attica enriched with its gold the bird-catchers of that Daphne, so celebrated for her luxury and scandalous voluptuousness.

Rome inherited this gastronomic rage. One of Varro's aunts reared thrushes in the country, and sold 60,000 of them every year, to the numerous epicures of the metropolis of the world. She derived an immense revenue from this speculation. Magnificent aviaries were soon seen in all rich Roman villas; they were filled with thrushes; and the multitude of these birds became such that they furnished a plentiful manure for the land. They were fed on crushed figs, mixed with wheaten flour; they had also millet, and great care was taken to preserve in the aviary a current of fresh and pure water to slake their thirst. On days of triumph and rejoicing, a dozen of these tempting thrushes cost no less than twenty-seven shillings.

On those solemn occasions more than one generous citizen, consulting his prodigality more than his purse, ruined himself for love of his guests. More than one obsequious dependant spent his last sesterces in composing ingenious crowns of thrushes, which his haughty patrons deigned to receive as a homage. It is true he was sometimes allowed to become a spectator of the repast which his gift was to embellish—certainly a most flattering recompense for his gratitude and servility!

Heliogabalus ate only the brains of these birds. This dish appeared to him most excellent, for it was very costly.

The extreme delicacy of this volatile, which poetical connoisseurs have celebrated in their verses, recommends it to those with weak stomachs and to convalescents. Pompey being ill, his physician ordered him a thrush, but it was impossible to find one in Rome. Some one advised the celebrated general to apply to Lucullus, who fattened them throughout the year. 'What,' cried Pompey, ill-humouredly, 'shall I have to thank Lucullus's pompous luxury for life!' He refused to eat the thrush, and he recovered.

The Starling.

Drusus and Britannicus, sons of the Emperor Claudius, had a starling which spoke admirably the Greek and Latin. Alone he studied his lessons, and afterwards recited them to the astonished princes. Science protected the learned bird from the fate reserved by the Greeks and Romans for the rest of its family, less distinguished by their erudition than by their culinary qualities. Starlings, roasted in the kitchens, honourably associated with partridges, blackbirds, and thrushes, and the disciples of Galen recommended them to their patients, who willingly submitted to so nourishing and light a food.

The Flamingo.

A profound study of the art of good cheer caused the Romans to discover that the thick tongue of the phenicopter, or flamingo, presents towards its root a rather considerable adipose appendage. They tasted this lump of fat, and Rome was enriched with another dish.

It has been asserted that the glory of inventing this refinement in gluttony is due to Apicius. Italy possessed three gastrophiles of this name: the first flourished a short time before the dictatorship of Julius Cæsar; the second, Marcus Gabius, held a school of sensuality at Rome, under the reigns of Augustus and Tiberius; the third, Cælius, was contemporary with Trajan, and poisoned himself for fear of dying of hunger.

We possess, under the name of this last, a Latin work in ten books, from which we have borrowed largely, as the reader may have already remarked. It would be difficult to decide to which of the three Apicii it belongs. The author speaks of the flamingo, but does not mention its tongue: the treatise, then, is not the work of M. Gabius, who would doubtless have indicated the preparation of a dish of which Pliny assures us he was so fond. As to Cælius, if he were the compiler of this curious volume, as it is thought, how comes it he has forgotten a dish so justly celebrated, in this magiric catalogue, in which no detail, however minute, seems to escape him? It would appear that this contested paternity rightfully belongs to the first Apicius, unless some of the learned contest it on the ground that the style of the work nowise agrees with the latinity of his century.

May one of the learned societies of Europe some day take up this arduous question, and restore the ancient masterpiece to its admirable author. In the meantime the writer of the present work will continue to venerate the memory of Cælius Apicius, and offer him crowns of smallage, roses, and parsley, for his name embellishes the frontispiece of those pages which reveal to us the secrets of Roman cookery; and we repeat, with Sosie:—

'Le véritable Amphitryon
Est l'Amphitryon où l'on dine.

Honour is due also to the other Apicius for his ingenious sauce of flamingo tongues. True, we have never tasted it, for this expensive fancy can only be satisfied in the marshes of the Nile. It is still little known in Europe, but the most fastidious of the Romans regaled themselves with it. Three Emperors, Caligula, Vitellius, and Heliogabalus—immortal triumvirate of incomparable polyphagists!—carried to indigestion their gastronomic delirium, their love for this famous *ragoût*. These great authorities are conclusive.

The traveller, Dampier, wished to try the flesh of the flamingo, and he thought it very good, though lean, and very black.

'The flesh of the phenicopterus is a dish more sought after in Egypt than in Europe; however, Catesby compares it for its delicacy to the partridge; Dampier says it has a fine flavour, although lean; Dutertre finds its excellent notwithstanding its marshy taste; the tongue is the most delicious part.'—Vieillot.

Fig-Pecker, or, *Becafico.*

The Duke of C**** had received from nature one of those culinary organizations which the vulgar assimilate with gluttony, and the man of arts calls genius. Greece would have raised statues to him; the Roman emperor Vitellius would have shared the Empire with him. In France he gained the esteem of all parties by inviting them to sumptuous banquets.

This rich patrician brought up with tender care a young *chef de cuisine*, whom his *major-domo* had bequeathed to him on his death-bed, as Mazarin did Colbert to Louis XIV. The disciple profited by the learned lessons of the Duke; already the young *chef's* head, eye, and hand possessed that promptitude and certainty whose union is so rarely combined: there remained for him only the instruction of experience.

One day, in the month of September, some guests of the highest class, all professed judges in the order of epicureans, met together at the residence of the noble Amphitryon, who often claimed the authority of their enlightened judgment. The learned Areopagitæ had to pronounce on certain new dishes: it was necessary, by dint of seduction, to captivate the favour and patronage of these judges by disarming their severity.

Everything was served to the greatest nicety, everything was deemed exquisite, and they only awaited the dessert—that little course which causes the emotion of the great culinary drama to be forgotten—when the young *chef* appeared, and placed in the centre of the table a silver dish, containing twelve eggs. 'Eggs!' exclaimed the Duke. The astonished guests looked at each other in silence. The cook took one of the eggs, placed it in a little china boat, slightly broke the shell, and begged his master to taste the contents. The latter continued to remove the white envelope, and at length discovered a savoury and perfumed ball of fat. It was a fig-pecker of a golden colour—fat, delicate, exquisite—surrounded by a wonderful seasoning.

The good old man cast on his pupil a look full of tenderness and pride; and, holding out his hand to him: 'You are inspired by Petronius,' said he; 'to imitate in such a manner is to create. Courage! I am much pleased with you.'

This classic dish—a revival from the feats of Trimalcio—enjoyed only an ephemeral glory. Europe was on fire; a warlike fever raged everywhere; and Paris soon forgot the eggs of Petronius.

The fig-pecker merits the attention of the most serious gastronomists. The ancients reckoned it among the most refined of dishes. The Greeks made delicate pies of this bird, which exhaled an odour so tempting, that criticism was disarmed beforehand.

The Romans gave it their entire esteem, and prepared it with truffles and mushrooms. Among them, men who knew what good cheer means, thought there was nothing worth eating in birds but the leg and lower part of the body. Fig-peckers were the only exception to this rule: they were served and eaten entire.

'In the southerly parts of France, and in Italy, all different species of linget, and almost all birds with a slender beak, are commonly called becafico, because in the autumn they attack and eat the figs, and thereby the flesh of these birds becomes then fat and exquisite; but that really known as the becafico is remarkable for its delicacy; therefore it has at all times been *recherché* as an excellent eating. It is like a small lump of light fat—savoury, melting, easy of digestion; and, in truth, an extract of the juice from the delicious fruits it has fed upon.'—Vieillot.

The Ostrich.

There were tribes formerly in Arabia who fed on ostriches, and who for this reason were called strutiophagists. Marmot asserts that, in his time, they were eaten in Africa, although their flesh was glutinous, and had a bad smell. When the people of Numidia took any that were young, they reared and fatted them, and led them to feed by flocks in the Desert; and as soon as they were fat they killed and salted them.

The Arabs of the present day abstain from them; but it is said they seek much the fat, which they use plentifully in cooking.

They were served at Rome on a few tables. This was nothing but a depravation of taste.

Heliogabalus, who understood good living better, contented himself with the brains of ostriches. Six hundred of these animals furnished enough for one meal. The devastation was great, but the emperor had made a good supper.

The ostrich's eggs are very hard, very heavy, and very large; their weight often equals three pounds. The colour is of a dirty white, with light yellow veins; they are good to eat. In Africa they are sought after as a *friandise*, and cooked in various ways. The commonest and the best is, after breaking, to mix and cook them with a good deal of butter. They are large enough and sufficient for a man's meal.

When the Arabs have killed an ostrich they open its throat, and make a ligature under the opening; three or four men take the bird, and shake it, the same as rincing a pouch; after which, the ligature being undone, a considerable quantity of a greasy substance comes out, mixed with blood and fat as thick as coagulated oil. One ostrich produces as much as twenty pounds of it, and it is used for the preparation of dishes, for the cure of rheumatism, *humeurs froides*, and paralysis. The Romans used this grease for the same purposes, and believed it possessed the most precious qualities.

Fish.

Perhaps it has not been sufficiently remarked that the science of ichthyophagy is generally developed in a direct ratio with the civilization of a people. Man began at first by satisfying the imperious necessities of his stomach; he then eat to live, and all was good to him. Experience by degrees gave rise to *eclectism*—choice. It was then discovered that a coarse and solid food might be replaced by a delicate and savoury alimentation; joyous appetite, and sensuality, its effeminate companion, took the place of hunger, and this happy couple gave birth to the more amiable of fairies, who, under the name of Gastronomy, was soon to govern the world and prescribe to it imperishable laws.

It is asserted that the art of preparing fish was one of the first boons of this powerful sovereign, and that, instructed by her, Thetis rendered ichthyophagist the god of light and the fine arts.

The Jews, an agricultural people, living far from the borders of the sea, attached but very little importance to fishing and the researches necessarily attendant on it; so much so, that we hardly perceive any trace among them of this kind of food, which Moses did not entirely interdict, since that wise legislator was satisfied with prohibiting fishes without scales or fins. What an immense wealth remained unexplored! Let us pity them for not having known how to profit by it, notwithstanding the good will of the Phœnicians, inhabitants of the coast, who brought them the produce of their maritime excursions.

Let us say it: the Hebrews were tolerably bad cooks. They possessed most admirable laws, a fertile country, courage and many virtues, but their sobriety never would allow them to understand the art of good living. In that, they are to be pitied.

With great pleasure we turn to the Greeks, that charming people who had only to set their foot on the most barren soil to cover it with flowers, and who laid the foundation of ichthyophagy as well as all other sciences.

It appears, however, that, at first, they thought but little of fish as an aliment. None had ever been served to the heroes of Homer, and Ulysses, relating that his hungry companions had partaken of some fish, seems to excuse them, by saying: 'Hunger pressed their digestive organs.' To be sure a celebrated philosopher, and also an amiable epicurean, attributed this grievous abstinence of those warriors to the fear of being enervated by dishes too delicious. And then, the terrible Achilles and the impetuous Ajax could not, perhaps, make up their minds to degustate under their tents a sole *au gratin*, or a fried herring, with the slow precaution more humble mortals willingly submit to.

But shortly after that, fresh and salt fish became one of the principal articles of diet with the Hellenes.

Aristophanes and the gastrophilist Athenæus, allude to it a hundred times in their writings, and various personages are the subjects of biting sarcasms on account of their excessive partiality to the mullet, scar, and turbot. We may name, among others, Philoxenes of Cythera, who learning from his doctor that he was going to die of indigestion, for heaving eaten too much of a most exquisite fish: 'Be it so,' he calmly exclaimed, 'but, before I go, allow me to finish the remainder.'

The Romans inherited the predilection of the Greeks, 'For the dumb companions of the fair Amphitryte;' but, excited by the love of the marvellous, they stocked the sea with imaginary beings; and they saw whales of four acres, fishes of two hundred cubits, and even that eel, or that serpent, which veridical navigators have seen again in our days. It was then thirty feet in length, but now it is much longer!

Pliny, who believed so many things, swore to these by the twelve great gods of Olympus. At all events, we are much indebted to that laborious naturalist for very precious information. He has made us acquainted with the scare, which the Roman epicures preferred to every other species. After the scare, the eel-pout or lotas'-liver enjoyed a great reputation. The red mullet, which is still much esteemed, was considered as one of the most delicate of dishes, and the Romans in fashionable circles employed it in a refinement of pleasure of a singular kind.

It is well known that this fish, when the scales are removed, still remains of a fine pink colour. The fops of Rome having remarked that, at the death, this colour passed through a succession of the most beautiful shades, the poor mullet was served alive, inclosed in a glass vessel; and the guests, attentive and greedy of emotions, enjoyed this cruel spectacle, which presented to them a gradation of colours, which insensibly disappeared.

The greatest sensualists killed it in brine, and Apicius was the first who invented this kind of luxury. The brine most in use, in such cases, was made with the blood of mackerel, and that was one of the varieties of that famous garum so highly praised by the Latin authors, and which was to them, at that period, what the fish sauces of the English are now. We will give, in this work, the various preparations of this so celebrated condiment, and the reader will then be able to judge for himself.

Apicius, the man of culinary progress, proposed a prize to any one who could invent a new brine made with the liver of red mullets. History has not transmitted to us the name of the fortunate conqueror; but Juvenal informs us that Asinius Celer offered sixty pounds for one of these fishes which weighed six pounds.

This was, after all, but a trifling folly, in the midst of so many extravagances which several writers have carefully registered. Lucullus, the most ostentatious of the patricians, had a mountain cut through in the neighbourhood of Naples, so as to open a canal and bring up the sea and its fishes to the centre of the gardens of his sumptuous villa.

The love of fish became a real mania: turbots excited a *furore* of admiration—the *muroena Helena* was worshipped. Hortensius, the orator, actually wept over the death of the one he had fed with his own hands; the daughter of Drusus ornamented hers with golden rings; each had a name, and would come with speed when it heard the voice of the master, whose happiness depended on his fish.

Sometimes, in a moment of over tenderness for his dear *muroena Helena*, Vedius Pollio, a Roman knight of the highest distinction, and one of the intimate friends of the Emperor Augustus, could find nothing better to do than to feed them with the flesh of his slaves, who were thrown to them alive. It is true that these wretched creatures generally deserved this terrible chastisement; for instance, Seneca speaks of one who had the awkwardness to break a crystal vase while waiting at supper on the irascible Pollio. This unfortunate slave having managed to escape from the hands of those who were conducting him to this horrible death, he went and fell on his knees at the feet of Cæsar, whom he implored to inflict some less frightful torture. Augustus, moved to the very soul, granted him his liberty, had all of Vedius's vases broken, and ordered that the pieces should be used to fill up the reservoir in which the barbarous knight fed his *muroena Helena*.

Sturgeon.

This enormous cartilaginous inhabitant of the ocean, the Mediterranean, the Red, Black, and Caspian Seas, received from the Greeks, after its death, honours in which none of the most delicate or renowned fish participated. It was announced to the guests by the sound of trumpets; and slaves, magnificently dressed, placed it on the table in the midst of garlands and flowers.

Joy brightened every face; a more generous wine filled fresh goblets, and some flatterers—for the sturgeon possessed many—with eyes fixed on the noble accipenser, compared its flesh to the ambrosia of the immortals.

The high price of the sturgeon contributed in no small degree to such brilliant praise. This king of banquets would have ruined a modest citizen of Athens, and hardly did the exiguity of its proportions permit its figuring among the expensive rarities of an Attic supper, when it had cost only a thousand drachms, or about £16 sterling.

The Romans, imitators and emulators of the luxury of the Greeks, were almost equally fond of this fish; and, like them, reserved it for princely tables, or aristocratic opulence. It would seem, however, that the enthusiasm excited by the sturgeon somewhat cooled under the reign of Vespasian. Perhaps at this period it became more common, or was sold at a more moderate price. Nothing more was requisite in Rome to deprive a dish of its most brilliant vogue and most powerful patronage.

An alimentary substance, called caviar, furnished almost exclusively by Russia to the rest of Europe, is prepared from the spawn of several kinds of sturgeons.

The spawn of the large sturgeon produces caviar of an inferior quality; that of the common sturgeon, and the sterlet, is prized as being more delicate, when it is carefully separated from the vessels and membranes with which it is intersected, well impregnated with brine, pressed, and slightly dried. White caviar, it is said, is the best of all. It is reserved for the court.

There are two sorts of caviar: granulated caviar, and sack caviar.

The manufacture of the first names is performed by pressing the spawn on a sieve, and rubbing it in every direction to remove the pelheles which adhere to it, after which it is put into strong brine for one hour, then drained in a sieve, and, finally, pressed close into barrels, so as to entirely fill them before the head is fastened down.

The manufacture of the other kind of caviar only differs in two particulars. The spawn is manipulated while in the brine, in order to soften it, and it is put, in small portions of about half-a-pound each, into linen bags, which are powerfully twisted to extract all the brine before it is pressed into the barrels.

The workmen employed in these operations make a third kind of caviar with the refuse. This sort, used only by the poorest classes, deserves no notice.

Red Mullet.

Philoxenes, of Cythera, supped one night with Dionysius, tyrant of Sicily. It happened that the prince was served with a magnificent mullet, whereas a very small one was presented to his guest. The philosopher took his fish in his hand, and, with a very serious air, held it to his ear. Dionysius asked him what he was doing. 'I am busy with my Galathea,' replied Philoxenes, 'and I am questioning him on the subject of Nerea; but I can obtain no answer from him, because he was taken at too early an age. I am certain, however, that the other, evidently much older, which lies before you, is perfectly well acquainted with what I wish to know.' The tyrant, who happened that evening to be in good humour, laughed at the joke, and offered the larger mullet to the witty gastronomist.

The unbridled and cruel luxury of ancient Rome required that this fish should be cooked by a slow fire, on the table and under a glass, that the guests might gloat on its sufferings before they satiated their appetites with its flesh. It is true this barbarous gratification was very expensive, and it was necessary to be very rich to indulge in it—consequently it was decidedly very fashionable, quite natural, and in the very best taste.

Ordinary mullets weighed about 2 lbs.; these hardly deserved that their dying agonies should for an instant amuse the guests; they were worth only about £15 or £20 each. But sometimes fortune threw in their way much larger ones; and the opulent amateur esteemed himself only too fortunate when he could obtain a fish of three or four pounds for a much higher sum than he had paid for the slave, tutor of his children.

Crispinus was fond of mullets. He obtained one weighing four or six pounds, for which the fishmonger asked only £60. This was giving it away; and certainly the man did not understand his trade. Crispinus, on becoming the possessor of this wonderful treasure, was astonished at his good fortune, and the whole of Rome long refused to believe it.

In the reign of Tiberius, three of these fish were sold for 30,000 sesterces, or £209 9s 8d.; and this emperor was one day generous enough to give up to P. Octavins, for the low price of 5,000 sesterces, a very fine mullet which had just been presented to him.

And yet some persons of culinary authority paid but little attention to the flesh of this delicate fish; they sought only the liver and head; and if they paid for it so dearly, it was solely to find some few mouthfuls more in these two parts, to which caprice, enthusiasm, that fever of admiration, and we know not what extraordinary gastronomic rage, gave an inestimable price, which at the present day excites only a smile of incredulity.

Pliny speaks of a mullet caught in the red sea, which weighed eighty pounds. 'At how much,' adds this great naturalist, 'would it have been valued had they caught it in the environs of Rome!' We may suppose, without the least exaggeration, that many a senator would have offered £1,500 to become its possessor.

It is thus that the mistress of the world foolishly dissipated in ephemeral whims the immense treasures poured into her lap by tributary kings—conquered and spoliated nations. Each day her patricians, knights, and nobles, tired of their importunate opulence, solicited new diversions, and invented new excesses. The mullet for a moment satisfied their prodigality, and amused their barbarity; but Heliogabalus appeared, and he imagined prodigies of gluttony which excited at once admiration and envy. The liver of this fish appeared to him too paltry; he took it into his head to be served with large dishes completely filled with the gills. Now, we know that the mullet possesses only two. This dish, whose price would have enriched a hundred families, was worthy of the Sardanapalus of Rome, who, at the age of eighteen, had exhausted the treasures of the empire, and whom a violent death seized most *à propos*, at the moment when he had attained the extreme limits of crime and infamy.

Sea-Eel.

The sumptuous abode of L. Crassus echoes with his sighs and groans. His children and slaves respect his profound sorrow, and leave him with intelligent affection to solitude—that friend of great grief; so grateful to the afflicted soul, because tears can flow unwitnessed. Alas! the favourite sea-eel of Crassus is dead, and it is uncertain whether Crassus can survive it!

This sensitive Roman caused this beloved fish to be buried with great magnificence: he raised a monument to its memory, and never ceased to mourn for it.

This man, who displayed so little tenderness towards his servants, had an extraordinary weakness concerning his fine sea-eels. He passed his life beside the superb fish-pond, where he lovingly fattened them from his own hand. Ornamented with necklaces of the finest pearls, and earrings of precious stones, all, at a signal, swam towards him; several fearlessly took the food he offered them; and some, as familiar as their absent and regretted companion, allowed their master to caress them without seeking to bite or avoid him.

This singular passion, which at the present day we can hardly believe, in spite of the respectable authority of the most serious writers, was very common at Rome, amongst those who were rich enough to rear such fish. C. Hirtius was the first to construct fish ponds on the sea shore, to which many visitors were attracted by their magnificence. The family of Licinius took their surname of *Muroena* from these fish, in order thus to perpetuate the most silly affection, and the remembrance of their insanity.

Sea-eels necessarily pleased men cloyed with pleasures, and who substituted a kind of cold and cruel curiosity for the terrible emotions which beings peculiarly organized hope to find in evil-doing: gladiators murdering each other; lions or tigers lacerating the *bestiarii*; all these agonies of the amphitheatre had long since lost the attraction of novelty. It was a much more exciting spectacle to witness a swarm of sea-eels tearing to pieces an awkward or rebellious slave; besides, it greatly improved the fish. The atrocious Vedius Pollio, who understood these matters, never failed to have sea-eels served him after their odious repast, that he might have the pleasure of eating some part of the body of his victim.

Thank Heaven! however, some amateurs of this dreaded fish were not so barbarous; they fattened them very well without having recourse to such criminal food. Veal was cut into thin slices, and steeped in the blood of the animal for ten days, after which the fish greedily regaled themselves with it.

It was, doubtless, in this manner that the skilful speculator, Hirtius,—the same already mentioned—nourished his sea-eels, which produced him an immense revenue. His fish ponds contained so great a number that he was able to offer six thousand to Julius Cæsar on the occasion of the public feast that general gave the day of his triumphal return from the conquest of Gaul.

The greater part of the Roman emperors were exceedingly fond of sea-eels. The greedy Vitellius, growing tired of this dish, would at least only eat the soft roes: and numerous vessels ploughed the seas in order to obtain them for him. This exquisite rarity again appeared too common to the maniac child, who dismayed and astonished Rome for the space of three years. Heliogabalus brought the soft roe of the sea eel into disrepute by ordering that the peasants of the Mediterranean should be gorged with it. This folly amused him, and only cost several millions. That was a trifle when compared with the blood which almost always flowed to satisfy his whims.

Shell Fish.

The Emperor Caligula had made immense preparations to invade Great Britain. He set off, and when he arrived in sight of that Albion he was going to attack, he commanded his troops to form in close array along the shore, the trumpets to sound the charge, and sat himself on the quarter-deck of his galley, from whence he might have directed the action. For a short time he contemplated his warlike cohorts, and having thus gratified his pride, he ordered his troops to pick up the shells which abounded on the strand, and returned to Rome, where he showed the *'spolia opima'* the ocean had delivered up to him. Caligula expected to receive the honours of a triumph; but the senate, having some sense of modesty left, would not award them, and the implacable Cæsar, from that moment, swore the ruin of the senators.

Oyster.

The pontiffs of pagan Rome, men of exquisite delicacy and matured taste, caused oysters to be served at every repast. This little piece of epicurism was very expensive, and it was necessary for these grave personages to carry the whole of the devotion which characterized them in their love of good cheer to the highest degree, to dare eat of a dish still uncommon a century before the Christian era. At this epoch a *borriche* (a sort of basket) of oysters was worth one hundred sesterces (£9). It is unnecessary to remark that the poor never tasted them.

The Greeks and Romans, like ourselves, were remarkably fond of this delicious shell fish, and eat them (French fashion) at the beginning of a banquet. For this reason Athenian epicures called oysters 'the gastronomic prelude to the supper.' They were often served raw, and were then dexterously opened by a slave on the table, in presence of the guests, whose experienced eyes greedily sought the light purple net which, according to them, surrounds the fattest and best.

The inhabitants of Italy preferred large oysters, and exacted that this dainty manna of the sea should be always fresh and abundant at their feasts. This displayed wisdom on their part: this delightful fish excites the appetite and facilitates digestion. To add to its delicate flavour, the 'Roman club of epicureans,' a useful association, which modern Europe envies antiquity, caused to be sent from Spain, at a vast expense, that precious garum, the recipe of which seems to have been lost, and the condiment itself forgotten by the whole of the Peninsula.

The magiric genius of Rome did not hesitate to demonstrate that oysters do not form an exception to the law of perfectibility which governs all beings, and that it is possible to render their flesh more succulent and delicate by transporting them from their damp cradle into reservoirs exposed to the mild influence of the sun. Sergius Orata or, perhaps, Fulvius Hirpinus, was the first who received this happy inspiration. He caused to be constructed, near Pouzzole, a short time before the civil war of Pompey, a fishpond, where he stowed oysters, which he fattened with paste and cooked wine worked into the consistence of honey—*sapa et farre*. This worthy Roman enriched himself by the sale of them, and bequeathed a name to posterity—a two-fold happiness for the gastronomist Fulvius, whose good fortune the poet Homer did not partake.

Apicius esteemed highly oysters from the lake of Lucrinus, from Brindes, and Abydos, and studied deeply the succulent qualities of this shell fish. He knew how to preserve them fat, fresh, and alive, during long and fatiguing journeys; and, thanks to a delicate attention on the part of this immortal *bon vivant*, the great Trajan was enabled to regale himself with oysters sent from Rome while carrying on a distant war against the Parthians. This present of the king of epicureans to the master of the world was worthy of both the giver and receiver, but it completed the ruin of the generous Apicius.

The Roman ladies shared their husbands' taste, and eagerly partook of oysters from the lake of Lucrinus, brought into fashion by Sergius Orata, and when their fatigued stomachs struggled painfully with gluttony, this delicacy soon obtained an easy triumph by disposing the appetite to fresh exertions. The means of defence, however, were not very formidable; sometimes a little warm and limpid water— oftener a dazzling plume from the bird of Juno—hastened the struggle, and, without effort, decided the victory. This ingenious method was very much relished by polyphagists, and the Emperor Vitellius particularly honoured it.

Cape Pelorus furnished the Greeks with highly prized oysters, which were eaten alone, fried, stewed, or nicely dressed with marsh-mallows, dock-leaves, and with some kind of fish.

The Romans at length became disgusted with those found on the coasts of Italy, or in the Dardanelles; an instinct of greediness caused them to prefer oysters from the Atlantic ocean, and especially from the shores of Armorica, now called Britany. Bordeaux supplied imperial tables, and this high distinction is sufficient for its praise.

It may not be useless to remark here, that no sooner had Ausonius praised this fish in his lines than it was forgotten, and did not re-appear till the 17th century on the tables of distinguished personages. May our descendants be more just than our forefathers.

The Cook.

The author of a rare and very curious work, which no one at present has time to read, formed the charitable project of reconciling medicine and gastronomy. This was a noble enterprize, worthy of a true philanthropist, and which assuredly presented less difficulties than people may think. In effect, what was the moot question? To agree, *de forma*, without interfering with the substance; to examine whether culinary preparations poison, as has been said, the food which nature gives us, and unceasingly paralyze the salutary action of the dietetic, which the faculty prescribe.

For many centuries cooking has been exposed to these odious reproaches, the gravity of which we do not pretend to attenuate; and yet, ever pursuing its brilliant career amidst revolutions and ruins, the magiric art, endowed with eternal youth, embellishes each new era of civilization, receives its most constant homage, and survives it when it fades away. Let us speak plainly: mankind has thrown on cooks all the faults of which they ought to accuse their own intemperance. It was no doubt easier, than to avoid the fatal abuse of pleasure, and the evils it brings with it; but there was the crying injustice, which we do not hesitate to denounce; *there* lay the obstacle it was necessary to overcome, in order to bring about a peaceful understanding between the disciples of Galen and the followers of Apicius.

Gourmandise would never have rebelled against the kitchen if all polyphagists had obtained from the good Ceres the gift she granted to Pandarea—a celebrated eater, who could pass days and nights at table, without experiencing the slightest indigestion.

'But,' say you, 'Seneca, the philosopher, perpetually combats, with the authority of his virtuous language, those dangerous men who are busied with a single stomach, and who lay the foundation for a train of maladies.'

The reply to this is, that Seneca, the pedant, should have thundered against the stomach, which alone is guilty (he has sometimes done so); that this atrabilarious preceptor of Nero, attacked with an incurable consumption, could only eat very little, which much enraged him; and that his imprecations on the subject of the excessive riches and prodigious luxury of the Romans of his age, neither hindered him from possessing, and unceasingly increasing, a more than royal fortune; nor from feeding—well or ill—several thousand slaves; nor from pompously displaying in his palace five hundred tables—only five hundred—of the most elaborate workmanship, of the rarest wood, all alike, and ornamented with precious incrustations.

How often have people extolled the Lacedæmonians and their legislator, Lycurgus. Well, Lycurgus mercilessly commanded poor little children to fast when they looked fresh and fat. Strange law-giver of a strange people, who never learned to eat, and yet who invented the celebrated 'black sauce,' the *jus nigrum*, for which the entrails of the hare served as the foundation. So true it is that cookery always preserves certain imprescriptible rights over the most fervent disciples of frugality.

Moralists do not cease to repeat that Rome would have have had sumptuary laws had it not been corrupted by cooks from Athens and Syracuse. This is an error. All the ordinances of the consuls proscribed profusion, excess—in a word, all the ruinous expenses of a passionate and ridiculous gastrophagy, at the same time, respecting the magiric art itself; that is to say, that industrious chemistry which composes, decomposes, combines, and mixes—in a word, prepares different substances which gluttony, delicacy, the fashion, or luxury may confide to it for the space of a few minutes.

Why render the cook responsible for the extravagant tastes and follies of his age? Is it for him to reform mankind? Has he either the means or the right?

What is asked of him? and what can be asked? To understand exactly the properties of everything he employs, to perfect, and correct, if necessary, the savours on which he operates; to judge with a true taste, to degustate with a delicate palate, to join the skilful address of the hand, and the prompt and comprehensive glance, to the bold but profound conceptions of the brain; and above all it cannot be too often repeated—to identify himself so well with the habits, the wants, even the caprices and gastronomic eccentricities, of those whose existence he embellishes, that he may be able, not to obey them, but to guess them, and even have a presentiment of them.

Mankind had long obeyed that imperious and periodical necessity which has been called hunger, when it announces its presence with its brutal exigencies, before any one thought to form a code of doctrine calculated to guide a sensation which, by its energy and duration, procures us the most thrilling and lasting pleasures.

The primitive nations no doubt gave themselves up to their native gluttony. They eat much, but they fed badly. They did not yet possess gastronomy; and, consequently, they had no cooks, in the serious and complete acceptance of the word.

The heroes of Homer prepared their repasts with their own hands,—and what repasts, gods of taste!—and prided themselves on their culinary talents. *Où la vanité va-t-elle se nicher?* Ulysses surpassed all others in the art of lighting the fire, and laying the cloth. Patroclus drew the wine, and Achilles very carefully turned the spit.

The conquerors of Troy shone more in the combat than under the tent which served them as kitchen.

At length the aurora of the magiric ages began to dawn: it is not a revolution, it is a creation which is preparing to appear. Man has only known hunger; he shall now become acquainted with the charms of an appetite. The King of Sidon learns how to eat, and it is Cadmus, the grandfather of Bacchus, the future founder of Thebes, who takes upon himself to instruct this august mouth.

And since that time how many illustrious followers have descended into the arena, how many glorious names will not culinary annals have to register!

Somebody will, perhaps, one day publish a chronological history of celebrated cooks. In the meantime, it may not be amiss to recall to memory a few illustrious men, whose services and genius an ungrateful posterity has too soon forgotten.

Thimbron, among the Greeks, took the culinary art from its cradle: he watched devoutedly over its development, and only descended into the tomb after having won the heart of the whole of Greece, for his favourite science. Timachidas of Rhodes, cook and poet of the highest renown, composed an epopee on the art which he professed, in the midst of emanations from the stoves and the spit. His verses, glowing with the sacred fire which inspired him, lighted up the magiric vein of several of his disciples, among whom Numenius, Hegemon, and Metreas, are still cited.

Artemidorus collected and commented on all the words in use in the kitchens of his time. Greece owed to this patient terminologist the possession of a culinary language, subject to certain unchangeable rules.

Mithœcus gave the 'Sicilian Cook'—a remarkable type of a multitude of tiresome and insipid imitations.

At length Archestratus appeared. He was of Syracuse, and passed all his life in profoundly meditating on the functions, strength, anomalies, and resources of the stomach. He discovered the laws which govern that organ, and presented to the world his magnificent treatise on gastronomy—an inestimable master-piece of laborious investigation of which time has deprived us, together with the works of his useful predecessors.

We must not omit the names of some celebrated theoricians, to whom the art owes its rapid progress:— Philoxenus of Leucadus, devoted himself to the difficult study of degustation, and practised several experiments, which were, however, ill-appreciated by his contemporaries. Thus, in the public baths, he accustomed his mouth and hands to the contact of boiling-water, in order to be able to seize and devour burning viands, the instant they were placed on the table. He recommended cooks to serve everything very hot, so that he alone exercised mastication and deglutition, while other guests less inured, were obliged to content themselves with looking at him.

Pithyllus invented a sheath that covered the tongue, and protected it, without paralyzing its action, against a caloric dangerous to its delicate tissue. This ingenious cuirass was not appreciated, and history, in its thoughtlessness, has not even transmitted to us a description of it.

It was then the good time of Athens: gluttons had made way for epicureans: hunger, to a less fierce and gross sensation, already subjected to examination and discussion. The magiric art possessed its rules, its various partisans, its professors, and disciples. Great masters studied deeply the appetite—indispensable basis, on which will always rest the culinary exegesis; and they finished by classing it definitively, according to the three degrees of intensity which observation discovers in it.

The bold appetite, said they, is that which is felt when fasting. It reflects but very little; is not squeamish about viands, and loses all reserve at the sight of a very indifferent *ragoût*.

The indolent appetite requires to be encouraged. It must be enticed, pressed, irritated. At first, nothing moves it—but after having tasted a succulent dish, it rouses, is astonished, its ardour becomes animated, and is capable of performing prodigies. It is this appetite which has consecrated the trivial but true proverb: '*L'appétit vient en mangeant.*'

The *eclectic appetite* owes nothing to nature; it is the child of art. Happy, thrice happy, the skilful cook to whom it says: 'Thou art my father!' But how difficult is this creation—how rare! It is the work of genius—but listen. Some guests, chosen amidst veteran epicureans, seat themselves round a table covered with culinary offerings worthy only of the God of Feasts, and a small number of the faithful. Their *indolent appetite* examines, compares, judges, and, at length, abandons itself to the incomparable dainties from which it unceasingly seems to draw new ardour. But alas! pleasure, like pain, has its limits here below. Strength grows less, and becomes extinguished; the eye loses its greedy covetousness; the palate languishes; the tongue becomes paralysed; the stomach sinks, and that which before pleased, now creates only fatigue and disgust. It is then that a *cusinier hors ligne*, tries a bold diversion, which must never be risked if the artist does not feel in himself that force of generous efforts which is no other than genius. By his orders, three or four dishes, prodigies of science and of luxury, appear on the altar, which the sacrificers no longer heed. At this sight, their looks brighten; desire revives; the smile reappears; the magiric *facies* shines forth with all its splendour; the chest dilates, and you no longer distinguish your former guests. A man has transformed them. Each one chooses, tries, tastes— is silent, and lost in wonder. The appetite is perhaps tired, but not satiated; and the skilful cook at length enjoys a deserved triumph.

In this solemn moment he received, among the ancients, a crown of flowers— sweet and noble recompense of his arduous toil. Nay, a more substantial proof of gratitude often greeted his new dishes. In Greece, the inventor alone had a right to prepare them during a whole year, and drew from it all the honour and profit. It was necessary, in order that these culinary preparations should fall into the public domain, that some one of his colleagues should succeed in surpassing him.

At this epoch, the best cooks came from Sicily. Trimalcio was one of the most celebrated. Athenæus tells us that, when he could not procure rare and highly esteemed fish, he understood so well how to imitate their form and flavour with common fish, that the most cunning epicures were always entrapped. This reminds us of a certain cook of Louis XIV., who, on Good Friday, served the king with a dinner, apparently composed of poultry and butcher's meat, which, in reality, offered nothing but vegetables, and prepared, too, *au maigre*.

The Romans, inheritors of the luxury of Asia and Greece, did not erect a temple to the greedy Addephagia, goddess of good cheer, who possessed altars in Sicily; but they thought it impossible to repay too highly those who knew how to extend the limits of the pleasures of the table, and a generous senator offered his *chef* at least four talents, or more than £800 a year.

This is yet but little compared with the magnificence of Antony. He gave a supper to Cleopatra; that princess praised the delicacy of the feast, and immediately her lover called for the cook, and presented him with a city, in recompense.

How times are changed! We, at the present day, treat all this as pompous and ridiculous prodigality. It is because our somewhat mean epoch judges the olden times by the narrow ideas of order, foresight, and economy. The ancients enriched their *Archimagiri*, wasted their revenue in feasts, and then killed themselves. We have adopted a very different style of living. But, at the same time, how far are our most sumptuous banquets behind the most modest collations of Greece and Rome! Lucullus caused to be served to Cicero and Pompey a little *ambigu*, which cost £1,000. There were only three of them to partake of it!

The Emperor Claudius had generally six hundred guests at his table.

Vitellius did not spend less than £3,200 for each of his repasts; and the composition of his favourite dishes required that vessels should unceasingly ply between the Gulf of Venice and the Straights of Cadiz.

It must be confessed that cooks of that gastronomic era had to fulfil an incessant and most laborious task. What was then more natural than to abandon to them some thousands of those sesterces, which the profusion of the master devoured by millions, in the form of phenicopters' tongues, scarus or parrot-fishes' livers, and peacocks' brains?

We see that the Cæsars encouraged this frightful gastronomic monomania. Tiberius gave more than £3,000 to the author of a dialogue, in which the interlocutors were mushrooms, fig-peckers, oysters, and thrushes.

Galba breakfasted before day-break, and the breakfast would have enriched a hundred families. AElius Verus invented the *pentapharmacum*, a kind of *Macèdoine*, composed of sows' flanks, pheasants, peacocks, ham, and wild boars' flesh. Geta insisted upon having as many courses as there were letters in the alphabet, and each of these courses must contain all the viands whose name began by the same letter.

These follies, which cooks were forced to obey, continued to astonish the world until the moment when Rome—with her gods, the monuments of her ancient glory, and of her recent turpitudes—crumbled beneath the invincible weight of that horde of barbarians, that mysterious and impacable scourge, which Divine vengeance reserved for the punishment of unheard-of crimes.

Seasonings

Garum.

When we have read all that has been written by the ancients on this famous preparation, we become convinced, in spite of the obscurities and continual contradictions of commentators, that if Garum is no longer manufactured in the present day, it is not on account of the impossibility we find in discovering the recipe of the Greeks and Latins, but solely because this rather strange brine has not the same charm for us that it had for them. Let us, however, scan the authorities.

The Greeks called the shrimp *garos*, the Romans *garus*: it may hence be supposed that garum had originally for basis the flesh of shrimps, if Pliny had not taken the trouble to inform us of the fact. It was afterwards composed of other fish, but it always retained the name which recalled its origin. In like manner the signification of certain words is now applied to things quite different from the original type; chicory, or succory, is received under the mask of coffee; a certain pottage boldly usurps the honours due exclusively to turtle soup. Nothing more easy than to multiply these examples of catachreses: there are few figures which have become so common.

Well, then, they macerated the intestines of fish in water, saturated with salt, until putrefaction began to show itself; they then added parsley and vinegar.

A thick garum was also frequently obtained, by allowing the entrails and other parts, generally thrown away, to liquefy in salt.

In the time of Pliny, mackerel was preferred, of which they employed either the gills and intestines, or only the blood, directly the fish left the water, and while yet living. They thus obtained a precious liquid, and which the care necessary for its production rendered so dear, that eight pints of it cost no less than from fifteen to twenty pounds.

This expensive garum was especially esteemed when it came from Spain: it was then called 'garum of the allies'—*garum sociorum*—because it was received from a nation allied with the Romans; or, again, perhaps in allusion to the 'band of gluttons,' of Rome, a sort of fraternity of free-livers, who made great use of it.

The blood and entrails of the tunny fish, mixed with salt in a vase, produced also a most elaborate garum. A hole was made in the vessel at the expiration of two months, and the rich seasoning flowed from it.

This brine became exquisite, and obtained an exorbitant price when made from the liver of anchovies macerated in vinegar, pepper, salt, parsley, garlic, white wine, and sweet herbs. But Apicius attained at the first step the apogee of refinement of the most sensual gluttony, by inventing garum made from the liver of red mullet. What we have already said elsewhere with regard to this fish will enable the reader to appreciate the value of this new preparation.

Amateurs who were more economical contented themselves with very little saxatile fishes, of which only the intestines were taken, or which were thrown whole into a vase with a great quantity of salt. These were exposed to the sun, and the mixture long and often stirred. When heat had caused fermentation, and the vessel contained only a kind of pulp, or paste, almost liquid, a kind of willow basket was introduced, into which the garum alone could penetrate. The thick part—the dregs which remained at the bottom of the vase—was termed *alec.*

The following method was also frequently adopted:—

Mackerel, or small fish, were placed in a small vase with a large quantity of salt;

this was well stirred, and the mixture was then left quiet all night. The next day it was transferred into an earthen pot, which remained uncovered in the sun. At the end of two or three months, it was hermetically closed, after having added a quantity of old wine equal to one-third of the mixture.

When it was wished to obtain garum without waiting any length of time, they took brine, carefully filtered, and so saturated with salt that an egg would float on it; this was placed with the fish in a new saucepan; wild marjoram was added, and the whole boiled over a gentle fire, until the fish was entirely dissolved. Then wine, reduced to two-thirds by boiling, was added. It was left to get cold; the liquid was several times filtered, till it became quite clear, and was then finally laced in an uncovered vase.

Although fish was generally used, the flesh of several animals was sometimes employed in the formation of garum. It was, hwoever, submitted to the same preparations as those already mentioned.

Such was this wonderful seasoning, forming the chief delight of the ancients, whose praises poets have sung, and the composition of which formerly exercised the singularly mad intelligence of Maitre Françoise Rabelais. The reader will doubtless remark, that the principal elements of garum are almost invariably the same: fish, salt, and a greater or less fermentation. But perhaps some one may exclaim: 'this must be detestable!' No doubt, but then no one ever thought of regaling himself with this liquid; it was never taken alone; it was but reserved as a seasoning for a host of dishes, in order to heighten their flavour.

It must also be observed, that a skilful cook always took care to modify the garum before he sent it to table, by the help of various ingredients, such as pepper, vinegar, Falernian wine, water, and oil, according to the use to which it was destined, or the degree of strength it was expedient it should possess. Hence that variety of seasonings with garum,—sweet, sharp, mixed with water, wine, vinegar, and many other substances which changed or corrected the acid flavour of the primitive condiment, though without in the least depriving it of the qualities which fermentation had communicated to it.

It results from the different citations of which this chapter is composed, that recipes for the making of garum are to be obtained more easily than people seem to think at the present time. Everyone may not be of the same opinion with regard to the kind of fish generally used by the ancients to obtain this liquid, although all difficulties would be removed by admitting—which certainly is nothing but right—that they chose at one time mackerel or tunny fish; at others, gudgeons and small sardines; sometimes even the red mullet, in spite of its rarity and price. But it is evident that garum was prepared by either dissolving and liquefying these fish in their brine, either whole, their intestines, or their liver, and that, to effect this, it was only necessary to expose to the sun the vessel containing them; or that they simply put small fish into a dish, with vinegar and parsley, placed it on a charcoal fire, and stirred it for some time, when it was wanted for immediate use.

Truffle.

A truffled turkey was to be eaten at a dinner where Buffon was invited. A few minutes before setting down to table, an elderly lady inquired of the celebrated naturalist where the truffle grew. 'At your feet, madame.' The lady did not understand; but it was thus explained to her: *'C'est au pied des charmes'* (yoke elm tree). The compliment appeared to her most flattering. Towards the end of the dinner, some one asked the same question of the illustrious writer, who, forgetting that the lady was beside him, innocently replied: 'They grow *aux pieds des vieux charmes'* (old yoke elm trees). The lady overheard him, and no longer thought anything of his amiability.

Nevertheless Buffon was right. It was around the yoke elm trees of Lampsachus, Acarnidea, Alopecomesia, and Elis, that those famous truffles were discovered, whose reputation was spread in all parts and which Italy envied Greece.

The truffle! beloved treasure that the earth conceals within her bosom—as she does the precious metals, which she seems to have yielded grudgingly to the patient researches of the gastronomist; the magiric records do not tell us at what memorable epoch this exquisite tubercle astonished, for the first time, the palate of man; but a doubtful tradition maintains that a vile animal (a pig), guided by his marvellous gluttony, found out the existence of this pearl of banquets.

Pliny was very much inclined to range the truffles amidst astonishing prodigies. He fancied that he saw it at its birth increase without roots, without the slightest fibre, without the least capillary vessel likely to transmit to it nutritious juices; therefore he believed that, sown by thunder-bolts in the autumnal storms, this daughter of thunder grew like minerals by juxta-position, and relates on this subject the history of Lartius Licinius, governer of Spain, who, while biting a truffle with avidity, broke one of his teeth against a Roman denarius which chance alone had inclosed within it.

The Greeks thought a great deal of a delicious species of truffles, smooth outside, red within, which were found just under the surface of the ground, and did not show the slighest appearance of vegetation. Another kind was also much sought after by amateurs, probably on account of their scarcity. They were originally from Africa, and called cyrenaic, white outside, of an excellent perfume, and exquisite flavour.

The Athenians, enlightened appreciators of all sorts of merits, accepted with gratitude a *ragoût* with truffles, invented by Cherips. That culinary genius did not long enjoy his glory; a premature death carried him off from his stoves, his honours, and his fortune; but the Greeks did not bury their gratitude in his tomb; his sons became citizens of Athens, and the name of their father, more fortunate than that of Christopher Columbus, clung for ever to his brilliant discovery.

Mushrooms.

Agrippina, desirous of securing the crown to her worthy son, Nero, went to a celebrated female poisoner, and procured a venomous preparation which defies the most powerful antidotes. The Princess slipped this terrible poison in a very fine *morel* (a species of mushroom), which Claudius ate at his supper. The unfortunate Emperor died according to the desire of his amiable consort, who was, of course, inconsolable for a long time, and placed among the gods the husband she had murdered. Nero ascended the throne, and every time that mushrooms were served at his table, true to the memory of his father-in-law, he facetiously called this preparation the 'dish of the gods.'

To the poisonous effects of this vegetable have been attributed, also, the death of the Emperor Tiberius, that of Pope Clement VII., King Charles VI. of France, and many other important personages, who either knew very little of good cooks, or of *morels*. Notwithstanding these tragical events, mushrooms always retained a proud position, among the ancients, above the most inoffensive culinary plants; and their rather doubtful reputation has not prevented them from maintaining their ground down to our time, for we find that they now claim the same rank which they formerly occupied in the gastronomic *réunions* of Athens and Rome: a sad image of those fortunate criminals, whom society dreads, and yet often loads with its favours.

This 'voluptuous poison,' as Seneca, the philosopher, calls it, which compels us to eat of it again, even when not hungry, was much relished by the wealthy inhabitants of Rome and Italy. These free-livers, careless of the morrow, preferred the field mushroom, which they devoured with delight, having previously covered it over with a pungent sauce, which they afterwards neutralized with various iced beverages. It is true that this dish, worthy of the gods, often inflicted a severe penalty on those who yielded to its irresistible seduction; but what mortal could think of the anguish of an uncertain poisoning, when he had the good luck to meet with some *boleti*, or mushrooms, of the rarest description, which the price of a beautiful toga would hardly have purchased, and which promised some mouthfuls of ineffable, although ephemeral enjoyment? Besides, does not pleasure possess more piquant charms when danger is attached to it? The greater part of mushrooms are very dangerous, say the ancients; but blind destiny, perhaps, reserves for uncertain kinds which are not so. Re-assured by this judicious reflection, they gave orders to their cooks to stew some, and season them with vinegar, oxymel, and honey.

However, reasonable people—and there were still some to be found—abstained entirely from this vegetable, or procured it by the method which Nicander recommends; that is to say, they frequently watered the trunk of a fig tree after manure had been laced around it. That philosopher assures us that by these means we may grow mushrooms perfectly wholesome.

Those of our readers who are in possession of fig trees will be able to give their opinion on the merit of Nicander's method.

King Soyer resigning the Great Stewpan (from *Punch*)

Beverages.

Of which water is the foundation.

Water is certainly the most ancient beverage, the most simple, natural, and the most common, which nature has given to mankind. But it is necessary to be really thirsty in order to drink water, and as soon as this craving is satisfied it becomes insipid and nauseous. What is then to be done? Cyrus would have said: 'Drink no more;' so would a teetotaler of the present day. In the first ages of the world, the human race, bound by no oath of temperance, succeeded, by sheer application of their ingenuity, in finding something better, or perhaps worse, according to the ideas of certain moralists, whose wise teaching, however, commands respect. Certain it is that water, continuing to be regarded with peculiar flavour, was called to play a principal part in various combinations by which it lost its insipidity and inoffensive properties, and required the wonderful power of provoking a sort of madness, known by the name of drunkenness.

Those beverages which man imbibes when he is no longer thirsty, which cloud his weak mind, and render him ill when in good health, are called fermented liquors.

Beer is one of the most ancient. If we are to believe Diodorus of Sicily, Bacchus himself invented it. However, it is certain that the absolute injunction not to drink wine, caused the inhabitants of Egypt to have recourse to a factitious beverage obtained from barley, often mentioned in history under the name of *zythum* and *curmi*, and whose invention has been often attributed to Osiris—which means, that its precise origin is entirely unknown.

It was a kind of beer composed of barley, and capable of being preserved for a long time without decomposing; for instead of hops, utterly unknown in that country, a bitter infusion of lupins was added.

The Egyptians also used Assyrian corn in its composition, and probably other aromatic plants, in which each one followed his peculiar taste. The method of brewing varied much among them; but the one here mentioned was that most generally in use to procure zythum in Lower Egypt, where it was converted, like our beer, into vinegar, which the Greek merchants of Alexandria exported to the European ports.

The Egyptians long drank nothing but this fermented liquor, because the followers of Osiris believed that when Jupiter crushed the Titans with thunderbolts, their blood, mixing with the earth, produced the vine. They invented the zythum as a substitute for wine.

It is not probable that the Greeks, whose wines were so renowned in antiquity, thought much of beer. Nevertheless, Aristotle mentions drunkenness being caused by drinking a beverage drawn from barley. AEschylus and Sophocles mention a liquor procured from the same cereal.

The Danes and Saxons gave themselves up to an enormous consumption of zythum and curmi, kinds of ale and beer, varying in no other respect than in the manner of preparing them. The warlike piety of their ingenuous and coarse-minded heroes, desired no greater recompense, after a life of fatigue and rough combats, than to sing the praises of Odin amidst eternal banquets, where these exhilirating beverages might unceasingly maintain the joy and bravery of the warriors.

The ancient Britons had many vines, but they esteemed them only as ornaments to their gardens; and they preferred, says Cæsar, the wine of grain to that of grapes. It

146

is historically demonstrated that the English, at a very early epoch, applied themselves to the making of beer.

It is mentioned in the laws of Ina, Chief, or King, of Wessex; and this liquor held a distinguished rank among those that appeared at a royal feast in the reign of Edward the Confessor.

Under the Normans, ale acquired a reputation it has ever since maintained. Two gallons cost only one penny in the cities; in the country, four gallons might be obtained at the same price. Happy age! happy ale drinkers! At that period—the golden age for the apostles of the Britannic Bacchus—the brewers rendered no account of the preparation of this beloved beverage. The English nation did not yet purchase the right of intoxicating themselves: it was not till the year 1643 that this authorization was to be bought.

The use of hops would appear to be of German invention. They were employed in the Low Countries at the beginning of the 14th century; but it was not till the 16th that they were appreciated in England.

Can it be true that beer or ale possessed, in certain cases, strange curative properties? We find the following fact in a statistical account of Scotland.

A poor coal miner of the county of Clackmannan, named William Hunter, had been long suffering with acute rheumatism, or obstinate gout, which deprived him of the use of his limbs. The eve of the first Monday of the year 1758, some of his neighbours came to pass the evening with him. Ale was drunk, and they got merry. The jolly fellow never failed to empty his glass at each round. Scotch ale is a seductive drink, and as perfidious as pleasure: it bewilders the senses, and finally masters the reason. William Hunter lost his, completely; but his legs were restored, and he was able to make marvellous use of them for more than twenty years. After that happy evening, never did his old enemy, the gout, dare approach him; and the worthy coal miner took care to keep it at a distance, by reiterating the remedy which had proved so beneficial. Nobody could blame him. Ale had become so dear to him! Gratitude and prudence combined to make it a duty to remain unalterably attached, and he was faithful to it till he breathed his last.

It was also the custom to serve very cold water, in which certain plants had been infused, and which was freshened by being surrounded with snow after it had been boiled for some time. The invention of this iced water is attributed to the Emperor Nero, who made great use of it; and who appears to have bitterly regretted it when, dethroned and flying from his assassins, he was constrained through excessive thirst to drink muddy water from a ditch. The unfortunate Cæsar then, for the first time, thought of the strange vicissitudes of fortunes, and casting a sorrowful glance at the disgusting fluid he held in his hand, 'Alas!' he exclaimed, with a sigh, 'is this the iced water that Nero drank?'

Wine.

Modern science, agreeing with holy writ, looks upon the east as the common cradle of the vine and the human race.

Palestine was renowned for its vines. Pliny speaks in praise of them. The vineyards constituted a part of the riches of the country, and they were preserved with the greatest care; so much so that Moses, with an especial view to vines, forbade the sowing of different seeds in the same field, on pain of confiscation: and it was done to encourage their cultivation, that that wise legislator exempted every person who had planted one from military service, and from all public duties, until the first vintage.

The growths of Lebanon, of Helbon, and of Soree, enjoyed an extraordinary reputation, and the delicious wine they produced was capable of inspiring the lyric David with that celebrated praise by which intemperance has often dared to authorize reprehensible excesses.

However, the Hebrews, a sober people, like all eastern nations, rarely made use of pure wine; they generally mixed it with a quantity of water, and only drank a little at some ceremonial feasts, and at the end of their repasts. They sometimes mixed with it perfumes and odoriferous drugs.

Some nations seem to have had a great horror of wine. The Persians drank nothing but water; and the inhabitants of Pontus, the Seythians, and the Cappadocians, partook of this strange taste. The Arcadians, who lived on chesnuts and acorns, were not worthy of the favours of Bacchus; neither were the troglodytes, the ichthyophagists, and other swarms of hydropotes who were as yet too little civilized to ask of drunkenness its illusions and its enchantments.

The Egyptians would have thought it a profanation of their temples to carry in a flagon of the rosy liquid; but Psammetichus came (670 B.C.), and that wise prince made them understand that a pot of beer is not worth a cup of good wine.

The Romans asserted that their old king, Janus, planted the first vine in Italy, and that, later, Numa taught them how to trim it. That noble people knew how to appreciate such blessings, and in order to demonstrate that wisdom is always to be found in wine, they never failed to place on their altars the statue of Minerva beside that of Bacchus.

The inflexible muse of history has preserved to us the name of the individual who doomed himself to a sorry sort of immortality by inventing the custom of mixing water with wine; it ws Cranaüs, King of Athens, 1532 B.C. The gods, doubtless to punish him, caused a great part of Greece to be inundated, and it was not long before he was dethroned. Pliny accuses the obscure Staphil, son of Sithen, of this depravation of taste, which gained upon imitators to such an extent that, in the time of Diodorus of Sicily (45 B.C.), the guests still mixed water with their wine at the end of the repast. It is true that they were then all intoxicated.

Lyerugus was, no doubt, ignorant of this practice, when he had the barbarity to destroy the vines of the Lacedæmonians, under pretext of putting an end to the disorders caused by intemperance. It would have been preferable, says Plutarch, to have united the nymphs with Bacchus. The ingenious philosopher insists on the mixture being made by a fourth, a fifth, or an octave, in the same manner as the chords in music, which charm our ears. The fifth was obtained by pouring three measures of water on two of wine; one part water and two parts wine made the octave; a quarter of wine and three quarters of water produced the fourth, a most inharmonious chord, struck only by inexperienced and unskilful hands.

Hippocrates, great physician as he was, had already somewhere advised this deplorable dereliction from all wise doctrines, so true is it, that science sometimes goes astray; but, happily for his glory, that learned man, further on, recommends us to drink pure wine, and to drink enough for joy to dissipate our griefs, and rock us in the sweet errors of hope.

The god of grapes had everywhere fervent admirers, except, perhaps, among the Scythians. These schismatics refused to worship a divinity who caused the faithful to become intoxicated. In other places they sacrificed to him a tiger, in order to show the power of his empire; and zealous disciples, with their heads crowned with branches of the vine, holding in one hand a crater and in the other a torch, ran with dishevelled hair about the streets, shouting to the son of Jupiter, the terrible Evius, in the silence of the night.

The Romans addressed to him special prayers twice a year, on the occasion of the wine festivals, which took place in the months of May and September. In the first, they tasted the wine; and, during the second, they implored the god to grant Italy fine weather and abundant vintages.

The method of making wine was precisely the same both in Greece and Italy.

The vine gatherers carefully rejected the green grapes, and piled the others in deep baskets, the contents of which were instantly emptied into large vats. There men, hardly clothed in the lighest garments, trampled them under their feet, whilst joyous songs and sounds of flutes hastened their movements, and animated them to work faster.

Wine obtained in this manner was much esteemed, and kept very well. The wort which escaped from the vat as soon as they had thrown in the grapes, and which came from the pressure occasioned by their laying one on the other, enjoyed the preference. This first liquor was transformed into an exquisite wine.

The grapes, crushed by the feet, were placed under the press, and an opening made in the lower part of the vat allowed the wort to flow into earthen jars, whence it was subsequently poured into the barrels.

The press was always raised at a little distance from the cellar and kitchen. Its mechanism was very simple. The antiquities of Herculaneum will furnish us with an example. Two trees were firmly fixed in the ground, at a few feet distance one from the other, and a strong horizontal beam rested on their summit. Other pieces of wood, similar to the top piece, were placed underneath. The grapes occupied the space between the vat and the lower plank. Between each of the cross planks wedges were introduced, and two persons kept striking them with hammers, one on each side; it is thus the pressure was effected. Wine from the press, inferior to those just mentioned, served for the ordinary consumption of the family, and for the servants. It was not racked, but simply taken from the barrel as it was wanted.

The lees were taken from the press when it yielded no more liquor; a certain quantity of water was poured over them, and the whole subjected to a second pressure. The weak kind of wine obtained by this new operation must have somewhat resembled that acrid stuff called *piquette*, in France; it was the beverage of the people, and especially of the country people during the winter.

A part of the wort—that which was required for immediate use—was put aside, and clarified with vinegar. A portion of that obtained from the crushed grapes was put to boil on furnaces, supported on three legs, at a little distance from the press, in coppers, the contents of which were continually stirred. This liquor, reduced by a third, was called *carenum*; when the half only remained, it was called *defrutum*; and, lastly, when the ebullition left only a third part remaining, this substance, very similar to honey, took the name of *sapa*. It was mixed with flour, to fatten the snails reared by skilful speculators, who reserved them for the Roman sybarites.

This wort, thus prepared by night, when the moon did not shine, and carefully skimmed, served to preserve wines, to give more body to those which were thought too weak, and became the base of several beverages sought in preference by Roman ladies, at that period of life when maturity of years made alliance with sensuality.

Those who wished to preserve sweet wine during a whole year, filled with the second wort—that is to say, that which was produced by the pression of the feet—

some amphoræ covered with pitch inside and out. They were then hermetically sealed, and buried in the sand, or plunged in cold water, where they remained at least two months.

There still was left a large quantity of wort as it came from the grapes. This was taken into the cellar, which was always situated a little below the level of the ground; or to the ground floor, where no kind of smell was allowed to penetrate, or any emanation capable of spoiling the bouquet of the wine it contained.

Fine wines were kept in the wood for two, three, or four years, according to their different properties; after which they were transformed to amphoræ, and that operation required the greatest care.

The amphoræ were earthen pitchers with two handles, reserved for choice wines. To prevent evaporation through their pores, they covered them with pitch, and stopped the neck with wood or cork, covered with a mastic composed of pitch, chalk, and oil, or any other fat substance. The name of the wine was inscribed on the amphora; its age was indicated by the designation of the consuls who were in office when it was made. When the amphora was of glass, it was ticketed with these details. For this kind of vessels they had store-rooms which were commonly at the top of the house. By exposing them to the sun and to smoke the maturity of the wine was hastened. The discovery of this means of ripening, which the Roman œnophiles never failed to practice, was attributed to the Consul Opimius.

The following are the made wines most in vogue in olden times.

The *Passum* was one of those most esteemed in Rome, particularly when it came from Crete. It was made with grapes, spread in the sun until they were reduced in weight to one-half. The pips, thus dried, were then put into a butt containing some excellent wort. When they were well soaked, they were crushed with the feet, and then subjected to a slight pressure in the wine-press. Sometimes they simply plunged the fresh grapes into boiling oil, instead of exposing them to the sun, and the result was the same.

The *Dulce* wine was obtained by drying the grapes in the sun for three days, and crushing them with the feet on the fourth, at the time of the greatest heat. The Emperor Commodus thought this a most delectable drink.

The *Mulsum*, or honeyed wine, was an exquisite mixture of old Falernian wine and new honey, from the Mount Hymettus. The physician, Cœlius Aurelianus, recommends the holding of warm mulsum in the mouth as a palliative in cases of violent head-ache.

The name of *Anisites* wine was given to that in which some grains of aniseed had been infused.

The *Granatum* was prepared by throwing thirty broken pomegranates into a pipe of wine, and pouring over them ten pints and a half of a different wine, hard and sour. This drink was fit for use at the end of thirty days.

Apicius gives us the recipe for the *Rosatum*:— 'Put,' says he, 'some rose leaves into a clean linen cloth; sew it up, and leave it seven days in the wine; take out the roses, and put in fresh ones; repeat the operation three times, and then strain the wine. Add some honey at the time of drinking. The roses must be fresh, and free from dew.'

The *violatum* is made in the same manner, only violets are used instead of roses.

Rosatum may also be obtained without roses, by putting a small basket filled with green lemon leaves into a barrel of new wine before the fermentation has taken place, and leaving them there for forty days. This wine is to be mixed with honey before it is drunk.

Myrrh wine—*Myrrhinum*, among the ancients—was wine mixed with a little myrrh, to render it better and make it keep longer. They thought much of it.

All these wines, like those previously mentioned, were strained through the *colum vinarium* before they were served to the guests. This strainer was composed of two round, deep dishes, of four inches in diameter. The upper part was pierced, and received the wine, which ran into the lower recipient, whence the cups were filled.

Repasts.

Mortals were formerly remarkably sober, and the gods themselves set them the example, by feeding exclusively on ambrosia and nectar. The most illustrious warriors in the Homeric ages were generally contented with a piece of roast beef; for a festival, or a wedding dinner, the frugal fare was a piece of roast beef; and the king of kings, the pompous Agamemnon, offered no greater rarity to the august chiefs of Greece, assembled round his hospitable table. It is true that the guest to be most honoured received for his own share an entire fillet of beef.

The vigorous but uncultivated appetites of these heroes were hardly satisfied when everything disappeared, and none of them thought to prolong the pleasures of good cheer. Happy times of ingenuous and ignorant frugality! what has become of you?

It must not, however, be imagined that they were entirely destitute of more refined aliments. Homer gives to the Hellespont the epithet of *fishy*; Ithaca, and several other islands of Greece, abounded in excellent game; but the magiric genius was asleep—it awoke at a later period.

Beware, however, of a mistake: those men—with so little choice respecting their viands—all possessed stomachs of astounding capacity. Theagenes, an athlete of Thasos, eat a whole bull; Milo of Crotona did the same thing—at least once. Titormus had an ox served for supper, and when he rose from table, they say not a morsel remained. Astydamas of Miletus, invited to supper by the Persian, Ariobarzanes, devoured a feast prepared for nine persons. Cambis, King of Lydia, had such an unfortunate appetite, that one night the glutton devoured his wife! Thys, King of the Paphlagonians, was afflicted with voracity nearly similar. The Persian Cantibaris, eat so much and so long that his jaws were at last tired, and then attentive servants used to press the food into his mouth.

These are facts of which we do not exactly guarantee the truth, for history—it is no secret—has some little resemblance to the microscope: it frequently magnifies objects by presenting them to us through its deceitful prism.

We close this singularly incomplete list of the ancient polyphagists by adding that the Pharsalians and the Thessalians were redoubtable eaters, and that the Egyptians consumed a prodigious quantity of bread.

In more modern times, some men have acquired, by the energy of their hunger, an illustration they would have vainly demanded from their genius or their virtues. The Emperor Claudius sat down to table at all hours and in any place. One day, when he was dispensing justice according to his own fashion in the market-place of Augustus, his olfactory nerves scented the delicious odour of a feast which exhaled from one of the neighbouring temples. It was the priests of Mars, who were merry-making at the expense of the good souls in the surrounding locality. The glutton emperor immediately left his judgment-seat, and, without any further ceremony, went and asked them for a knife and fork. Never, no, never, adds the biographer of this prince, did he leave a repast until he was distended with food and soaked with drink, and then only to sleep. Yes, the ignoble Cæsar slept; but still, the 'peacock's feather,' an unseemly invention of Roman turpitude, was called into requisition to prepare the monarch for new excesses.

Galba could taste nothing if he was not served with inconceivable profusion. His stomach imposed limits upon him, but his eyes knew none; and when he had gloated to his heart's content upon the magnificent spectacle of innumerable viands for which the universe had been ransacked, he would have the imperial dessert taken slowly round the table, and then heaped up to a prodigious height before the astonished guests.

Vitellius, the boldest liver, perhaps, of the whole imperial crew, and the most active polyphagist of past times, caused himself to be invited the same day to several senatorial families. This deplorable honour often caused their ruin, for each repast cost not less than 400,000 sesterees (£3,200). The intrepid Vitellius was equal to the whole, thanks to the peacock's feather, which, doubtless, was cursed more than once by the unfortunate victims of his dreadful gluttony.

True, this poor prince was continually tormented with a hunger that no aliment seemed capable of satisfying. In the sacrifices, like the Harpies of whom Virgil speaks, he took the half-roasted viands from the altars, and disputed the sacred cakes with the gods. As he passed through the streets he seized the smoking-hot food spread out before the shops and public-houses; he did not even disdain the disgusting scraps that a miserable plebeian had gnawed the evening before, and which a hunger-stricken slave would have hardly contested with him.

Such were the masters of the world, the proud Cæsars! before whom haughty Rome bowed the head and trembled, and from whom it basely implored a smile, up to that day when some soldiers, tired of their shameful obedience, kicked the imperial corpse into the Tiber, after having mutilated it in presence of the populace, who crowded joyously around the Gemoniæ.

These terrific examples of insatiable voracity have become rare and obscure. A few isolated facts may perhaps be met with at very distant periods, which remind us of the polyphagic celebrities of Greece and Italy. There are, however, two which would have merited the attention of Vitellius himself.

The ingenuous Fuller speaks of a man, named Nicholas Wood, to whom the county of Kent proudly claims the honour of having given birth, who once ate a whole sheep at one meal. One day three dozen pigeons were placed before him, of which he left only the bones. Another day, being at Lord Wootton's, and having a good appetite, he devoured eighty-four rabbits and eighteen yards of black-pudding for his breakfast. We leave to Fuller the responsibility of the figures. Any how, the brave Nicholas Wood must have been a vigorous trencher-man!

The second anecdote is from Berchoux:—

Marshal Villars had a house-porter who was an enormous eater. 'Franz,' said he, one day, 'tell me, now, how many loins you could eat?' 'Ah! my lord, as for loins, not many: five or six at most.' 'And how many legs of mutton?' 'Ah! as for legs of mutton, not many: seven or eight perhaps.' 'And fatted pullets?' 'Ah! as for pullets, my lord, not many: not more than a dozen.' 'And pigeons?' 'Ah! as for pigeons, not many: perhaps forty—fifty at most, according to the appetite.' 'And larks?' 'Ah! as for that, my lord—little larks—for ever, my lord, for ever!'

M. Soyer's Symposium (from *The Illustrated London News*)

A truce to gluttons. Let us speak of epicureans.

It is to them that gastronomic civilization owes the laws by which it is regulated; they were the legislators of the table: they introduced regularity and order at repasts. The breakfast, dinner, collation, and supper were created by those sages. Fashion has often modified the nomenclature, but assuredly it will never be able to supersede it.

The Greeks submitted to it for many years; and then, that fickle people, whom everything wearied, declined the drudgery of masticating so frequently. The lower orders and the army ate twice a day; the fashionable people contented themselves with one repast, which some had served at mid-day, but the greater part just before sunset. The party of resistance had, as yet, yielded only on one point—the collation; and they continued bravely to breakfast, dine, and sup. But the monophagists were not sparing in their jokes, and the new fashion triumphed at last over the prescription of ancient usages. Pagan sobriety was doubtless far from suspecting that the Book of Eccliastes, in accordance with it on this subject, pronounced an anathema against the kingdom whose princes ate in the morning.

The Greek manners were introduced in Rome, and persons of a certain rank, who did not make a profession of gluttony, gave themselves up to the pleasures of the table only once a day.

The tyranny of fashion was not, however, such that all persons thought themselves bound to obey it under pain of being shamed and ridiculed. Many unscrupulously transgressed its laws, and more than one respectable Greek of good family, following the example of Ulysses, who prepared his breakfast at sun-rise, had the *acratism* brought so soon as the crowing of the cock announced the return of day. This frugal breakfast was composed of bread steeped in pure wine. The adults restricted themselves to this slight repast, but the children received more substantial nourishment.

The Romans, when they were not asleep, breakfasted at three or four o'clock in the morning. A little bread and cheese, or dry fruits, enabled them to wait for the solemn hour of the banquets.

It would appear that the Jews dined at mid-day; it was the hour at which St. Peter was hungry. This repast took place also among the Greeks about the middle of the day, if we are to believe Athenæus. However, Cicero relates that the philosopher Plato appeared to be very much astonished, when travelling in Italy, to see the inhabitants eat twice every day. It will only be necessary to repeat that the supper alone formed the rule, and that the breakfast and dinner were exceptions; they depended entirely upon the casualties of will.

About mid-day the sober Romans had a slight collation. Seneca, who never loses sight of himself in his fastidious treatises on wisdom, informs us that a little bread and a few figs were all that his virtue required.

The senators, the knights, and the luxurious freed-men, spared no expense either for dinner or supper. The priests of Mars, of whom we have already spoken, set them an example too seductive for them not to follow it. It is to be remarked, by the way, that those worthy ministers of the god of war took this repast in the most secret part of their temple, where they hardly allowed any one to come and interrupt them. This gastronomic quietude was also very much the taste of a celebrated modern sailor, the Bailiff de Suffrein. He was at dinner in Achem, India, when a deputation from the town was announced. Being a witty glutton, he conceived the happy thought of sending word to the importunate troop that an article of the Christian religion expressly prohibited every Christian from occupying himself with anything besides eating, that function being of the most serious importance. This reply singularly edified the deputation, who retired with respect, admiring the extreme devotion of the French general.

The collation—*merenda*—was little in use. It took place about the end of the day, before supper, particularly in summer, among the workmen and farm labourers.

We now come to the principal repast, to that which threw such brilliancy over the latter centuries of Rome, when a culinary monomania, a sort of gastronomic furor, seemed to have seized the sovereign people, who, no longer great by their conquests, betrayed a desire to become so by the number and audacity of their follies.

The Hebrews supped at the ninth hour, that is to say, about three o'clock in the afternoon. Their custom of two repasts would be sufficiently proved by the fact that, on fast days, they took food only in the evening. Hence, when they did not fast, they also ate at another hour. Their ordinary aliment was very simple; we shall have to speak of it hereafter.

In the primitive times, kings prepared their own suppers. Beef, mutton, goat's flesh—such were the viands which then satisfied the daintiest palates. Baskets, filled with pure wheaten bread, were carried round to the guests, and heaps of salt, placed on the table, gave proof of the hospitality of those simple and unsophisticated ages.

The fierce warriors of that warlike period never forgot to invoke the gods before they satisfied their appetites: libations of wine rendered them favourable. This pious duty once fulfilled, they gave themselves up without restraint, to the joys of good cheer; and the sounds of the lyre and the buffooneries of mountebanks enlivened the banquet, which again received fresh animation from the copious healths, which persons the least versed in the forms of society never forgot.

It often happened that each one paid his share, or brought provisions with him to these joyous suppers, of which the last rays of the setting sun always gave the periodical signal. The uncertainty of these amicable meetings constituted their charm. Pic-nics, as we see, may be traced rather far back.

It was then that pleasure presided at those repasts; dulness had its turn when luxury proscribed the supper in open air, and in common, after the manner of the Jews, who assembled in gardens, or under trees, and mingled the sweet harmony of music with the less delicate seductions of their banquets.

The breakfast has always taken place after rising; dinner in the middle of the day; the collation in the course of the afternoon; and the supper in the evening. In the 14th century, people dined at ten o'clock in the morning. One or two centuries later, they dined at eleven o'clock. In the 16th century, and at the commencement of the 17th, they dined at mid-day in the best houses. Louis XIV, himself, always sat down to table at that hour. This order was not modified until the 18th century.

The Sicilian cooks taught unheard-of refinements, and were sought after with strange eagerness. The chine of beef and haunch of mutton of the Homeric epoch, gave way to sumptuous banquets, and a learned prodigality divided them into two or three acts, or courses, the order and luxurious majesty of which have been adopted in modern times.

The following is the style of living at the court of the Dauphin of France in the 14th century:

As in all well-regulated houses, there were five repasts, viz.: the morning (except on fast days), the breakfast; the repast of ten o'clock,—(*dix heures*, or the *décimheure*; by abbreviation *décimer*, and by a second abbreviation, *diner*)—the dinner; the second dinner, the supper *(souper)*, at which they ate no more than soup than we do; and lastly, the sight repast, which they called a collation.

As an every-day fare, the Dauphin took for his dinner a rice pottage, with leeks or cabbage, a piece of beef, another of salt pork, a dish of six hens or twelve pullets, divided in two, a piece of roast pork, cheese, and fruit; at supper, a piece of roast beef, a dish of brains, neat's feet, with vinegar, cheese and fruit. Other days, other dishes, which were also pre-arranged with respect to kind and quantity. The barons of the court had always the half of the quantity of the Dauphin; the knights, the quarter; the equerries and chaplains, the eighth. The distributions of wine and bread were made in the same proportions; such a rank, such weight, such measure; so that the young and delicate baroness had four pots of wine, while the chorister and the chaplain had but one.

We are indebted to the learned Monteil for the following details relative to the public repasts of Louis XIV.:—

The usher of the court, at the hour named, goes and knocks with his wand at the door of the hall of the body-guard, and says: 'Gentlemen, to the king's table!' a guard is dispatched, who follow him to the goblet, where one of the officers for the service of the table takes the nave. The guard accompany him, marching by his side, sword in hand.

Having arrived in the dining-room, the officers spread the cloth, try the napkins, the fork, the spoon, the knife, and the tooth-picks; that is to say, they touch them with a morsel of bread, which they afterwards eat.

The usher returns again to the hall of the body-guard, knocks at the door with his wand, and cries: 'Gentlemen, the king's meat!' Four guards then follow him to the ambry, where the equerry of the household and the chief steward, or major-domo, test the dishes, by dipping a piece of bread, which they eat. After this, the king's meat is carried, the guards marching with their drawn swords on either side; the chief steward, preceded by the usher, walking in front. When he arrives near the table, he approaches the nave, and makes his obeisance to it; and if the announcer, or any other person desire also to do it, he may. The gentlemen-in-waiting place the dishes successively, and the table being covered with them, the king then enters.

It is to be remarked, that it is always a prince or a great personage who presents the wet napkin to him with which to wash his hands, whereas it is a simple valet who presents him with the dry napkin to wipe them.

The king takes his seat.

The equerry-carver carves the viands.

The king serves himself on a plate of gold.

When he asks for drink, the cup-bearer calls aloud: 'Drink for the king!' At the same time he makes his obeisance to him, goes to the buffet, takes two crystal decanters, one of which is filled with wine, and the other with water, returns to the king, makes another obeisance, removes the cover of the glass, and presents it to the king, who pours out wine and water according to his own pleasure.

During the dinner or supper of the king, a group of lordly courtiers stand behind his chair, and endeavour—though frequently in vain—to divert him, and make him laugh; and another group, composed of ladies of the court, stand behind the queen's chair, who, on their part, try to amuse her, and excite a smile.

CHEF TO ALL NATIONS

A Roman Supper.

Two lustres had passed since the world obeyed Domitius Nero, son of Agrippina. The Romans, a herd of vile slaves, docile adulators of the infamous Cæsar, had already celebrated nine anniversaries of his happy accession to the empire, and the Flamen of Jupiter solemnly thanked the gods at each of these epochs for all the benefits that the well-beloved monarch had unceasingly lavished on the earth.

Few princes, it is true, ever equalled Nero. He and his mother had poisoned Junius Silanus, the pro-consul of Asia; subsequently the younger emperor made away with Agrippina, and the senate applauded that horrible crime, which was only the prelude to outrageous enterprises which astonish the historian who narrates them.

The Flamen was, indeed, bound to offer up solemn thanksgivings to Jupiter for having hitherto restrained the crowned monster from the commission of evil which afterwards marked his flagitious career.

It was the 64th year of the Christian era. The emperor had passed some time at Naples, whence it was thought he would go into Greece; but suddenly changing his project, he returned to the capital of the world, to prepare, it was said, a spectacle of unheard-of splendour, and such as Nero alone could conceive.

One of his ancient freed-men, Caius Domitius Seba, resolved to celebrate the return to Rome, and the tenth anniversary of the reign of his master, who was now become his patron and friend. That man possessed immense riches, a formidable credit at court, and an insolence which had struck so much terror into the souls of the proudest families of the empire, that they had long since humbled themselves before him. So that it was no sooner whispered among the Roman aristocracy that the magnificent Seba intended to give a banquet, than one and all became anxious to be numbered with the guests of Cæsar's favourite.

However, days past, the time for the nocturnal festival approached, and the Invitor had not made his appearance.

Among the Hebrews, nothing was more simple and unsophisticated than an invitation to dinner; but, with the Romans, etiquette required that the amphitryon should send one of his servants to each person who was to participate in his pompous hospitality. This servant, who was generally a freed-man, went from house to house, and indicated, with exquisite politeness, the day and precise hour of the banquet.

Seba's Invitor was at last announced to the two consuls of the year, Lecanius Bassus and Licinius Crassus, who accepted with tender gratitude the distinguished honour which the enfranchised slave deigned to confer upon them.

After them the same favour was received with the same gratitude by the Agrippas, the Ancuses, the Cossuses, the Drususes, and all those who were the most noble, powerful, and proud in Rome.

The next day, about two o'clock in the afternoon (the repast was to begin at six o'clock), an unusual movement reigned in the Palatine baths, and those of Daphnis, near the Sacred Way. The *mediastini* kept up a steady fire under the coppers; the *capsarii* folded with care the clothes of the bathers; the *unguentarii* sold their oils and unguents; and the *fricatores*, armed with the *strigil*—a sort of wooden, iron, or horn spoon—rubbed and scraped the skin before the *tractatores* came gently to manipulate the joints, and skilfully shampoo the body, which gained by this operation more elasticity and suppleness.

The upper classes of the Romans never sat down to table until they had undergone all these preliminaries of minute cleanliness.

The future guests return home, after the bath, to employ the skill of the barbers (*tonsores*), who are in waiting to give more grace to the hair, and remove, with the aid of tweezers and pumice, the first silvery indications of the lapse of years, which, though incessantly effaced, still re-appeared.

A more serious occupation succeeded. Epicureans should never neglect their teeth—particularly at the approach of a banquet. Nor did the ingenious gastronomy of the first century of our era neglect to invent tooth-powder, which cleaned the enamel without injuring it, and fortified the gums—those fortresses of mastication. Some persons made use of substances which no one would adopt in the present day, because our delicacy revolts against them. But preparations less offensive were employed, and men of good taste, as well as fashionable ladies, extolled ox-gall, goats' milk, the ash of stags' horns, of pigs' hoofs, and of egg-shells.

Thus were the teeth equipped, as the comic Plautus has it; or, rather, thus were they prepared to undergo the labour required of them.

Those who had had the misfortune to lose some of those powerful gastrophagic auxiliaries substituted false ones of ivory, which art found means to render absolutely similar to their neighbours. The eye was deceived: what more could be required?

But the clepsydræ and the celebrated clock of the field of Mars announce that it is time to put on the white, light robe, a little longer than the pallium of the Greeks, and to which the Latins have given the names of *vestis cœnatoria*, *vestis triclinaria*, *vestis convivalis*. This last part of their toilet finished, the guests set out for the magnificent abode of their host, preceded by a few slaves, and followed by their shadows—those hungry hangers-on of whom mention has already been made, and who strive to obtain, on the road, a smile or a word by dint of cringing obsequiousness.

Arrived at the *atrium*, the crowd of Roman nobles are conducted into the interior of the house by the parasites of Seba. The proud freed-man disturbed himself for nobody; but, like the opulent Greeks, whom he aped, he left to these ignoble familiars the care of replacing him in the honours of his palace.

They enter an immense hall, decorated with unheard-of luxury, lighted by lustres, and round which are several ranks of seats, not unlike the folding-stools and arm-chairs we meet with in the present day in the most elegant *boudoirs*. The guests seat themselves, and anon Egyptian slaves approach with perfumed snow-water, which flows from golden vases of the most graceful forms, and cools the hands of senators and Roman knights, whilst other servants disincumber them of their patrician shoes, the end of which represents a crescent. The feet then received a similar ablution, and fresh slaves, skilful orthopœdists, accomplish in a twinkling the delicate toilet of these extremities, and imprison them again in elegant and commodious sandals, fastened by ribands which cross on the top.

Here and there a few persons are remarked who still wear their togas, having doubtless forgotten to substitute the banqueting dress. So soon as the major-domo perceives them he makes a sign to some youths clothed in white tunics, who hasten to present to each of these guests a *synthesis*, or short woollen vestment of different colours, which envelops the whole body, but leaves the shoulders and breast uncovered if the wearer desire it.

These indispensable preliminaries being terminated, the seats disappeared, and the guests stood waiting for the freed-man, Seba, who speedily entered accompanied by the two consuls, for whom places of honour had been reserved on couches beside their pompous amphitryon. The latter deigned to address a few words of welcome to his noble company, and each one stretched himself on his couch of gold and purple. The fourth couch was given up to the parasites and shadows.

Meanwhile, slaves were burning precious perfumes in golden vases *(acerrœ)*, and young children were pouring on the hair of the guests odoriferous essences, which filled the banqueting hall with balmy fragrance. Rome had borrowed this custom from the east.

The golden panelling of the hall shone with dazzling brightness as it reflected a torrent of light from the crystal candelabra, and the melodious sounds of the hydraulic organ announced the commencement of the banquet.

At this signal, servants, richly dressed, place within the circle formed by the couches lemon-wood tables of inestimable price, which they immediately cover with a rich tissue of gold and silk. That done, sylph-like hands spread them over with a profusion of the rarest flowers and rose leaves.

Musicians *(symphoniaci)* then occupy a kind of orchestra or platform, raised at one of the extremities of the hall, among whom the flute and harp players are to be particularly remarked. The former constitute, among the Romans, a special body dubbed with the name of *College*, and they have the exclusive right to attend banquets and enliven the pomp of ceremonies.

These musicians execute a slow, dulcet melody while the slaves are placing on the table the statues of some of the principal gods, together with that of the divine Nero, whom a pusillanimous flattery ranks already with the immortals. At this moment they also arrange here and there the salt-cellars, while the more meditative of the guests invoke Jupiter, before they give themselves up to the pleasures of the feast. Hardly is this short prayer finished when joyous cup-bearers distribute charming little crystal cups, which Æthiopian slaves fill to the brim with a generous, honeyed wine, drawn, in the first instance, from those large pitchers which the Greeks have named *amphoræ*.

Some drops of the exhilarating liquid are offered to the *Lares* (household gods), by sprinkling it in their honour on the floor and the table. This pious libation precedes the entrance of the first course *(antecœna)*, composed of the lightest and least succulent kinds of viands, by means of which a generous host stimulates the appetites of his guests, as a preparative for brilliant exploits.

Lettuces, olives, pomegranates, Damascus plums, tastefully arranged on silver dishes, serve to encircle dormice, prepared with honey and poppy juice, forcemeat balls of crab, lobster, or cray-fish, prepared with pepper, cummin, and benzoin root. A little further, champignon and egg sausages, prepared with garum, are placed by the side of pheasant sausages, a delicious mixture of the fat of that bird, chopped very small, and mixed with pepper, gravy, and sweet sun-made wine, to which a small quantity of hydrogarum is added. Tempting as these delicate viands may be, the practised epicureans seem to have a decided preference for peacocks' eggs, which they open with spoons. These eggs, a master-piece of the culinary artist, who presides over Seba's stoves, are composed of a fine perfumed paste, and contain, each one, a fat, roasted, ortolan surrounded with yolk of egg, and seasoned with pepper.

The first course was removed to the sound of music. Now came chased silver cups, much larger than those of crystal—no doubt because thirst is excited by drinking. Amphoræ of a secular wine were ranged by the major-domo on the mosaic flooring of the hall, at some distance from the triclinium, and they proceeded, by the invitation of the consuls, to the choice of the *symposiarch* (or master of the banquet), upon whom devolved the duty of regulating how often any person was to drink, and of preventing the guests, in the best manner he could, from yielding too easily to bacchic provocations, which commonly led to unseemly gaiety and the loss of reason.

This sort of magiric magistracy was obtained by lot, or the unanimous call for a personage worthy of such a distinction. That memorable evening every voice named the senator Drusillus, one of the most determined drinkers of the Roman aristocracy. Drusillus smiled, snapped his fingers, and, by the order of his master, thus intimated, a slave, who was standing behind him, filled a golden crater with wine, and presented it to the symposiarch.

Thereupon, the latter, slightly raising his head from the downy cushions on which it rested, and supporting it from the left elbow, makes a graceful bow to the amphitryon, the consuls, and the rest of the assembly. Then, with a stentorian voice: 'Slaves,' he cried, 'bring wreaths of flowers. Fugitive images of the spring and of pleasure, they shall bind our brows. At the same time let garlands adorn our craters, in which the cherished liquor of the son of Semele sparkles; and let us bestow no thought, during the fleet joys of the banquet, on the uncertain and fatal hour when Atropos shall pronounce our doom.

This speech, slightly impregnated with the epicurean philosophy so much in fashion during the reign of Nero, had at least the merit of a praiseworthy conciseness. Nor did it fail to attract applause from the auditors, whose brows and cups were speedily adorned with wreaths of roses, which young boys, clothed in white tunics, arranged with marvellous art.

The slight rustling of the flowers were soon drowned by the shrill noise of the trumpets which announced the second course. A flattering buzz welcomed this profusion of viands, which encumbered the tables, and well-nigh crushed them with their weight. There were the peacock, the duck, whose breast and head are so much coveted; capons' livers, peppered becaficoes, grouse, the turtle-dove, the phenicopter, and an infinite number of rare birds, the costly tribute that Europe, Asia, and Africa, exchanged against the gold of the prodigal Seba. Other gold and silver dishes contained those inestimable fishes which Roman luxury brought so much into fashion; the scarus, or parrot fish, sturgeons, turbots, mullets, and those numerous inhabitants of every sea with which the tanks were stocked, to supply the kitchen of the freed-slave.

Moreover, there were wild boars *à la Troyenne*, ranged in the centre of the table, in silver basins of a prodigious value: stuffed pigs, quarters of stag and roebuck, loins of beef, kidneys surrounded with African figs, sows' paps prepared with milk, sows' flank, and some pieces of Gallic bacon, which certain gluttons loved to associate with a piece of succulent venison.

While the carvers were cutting up the meats with incredible address, to the sound of light but animated music, Numidian slaves filled the cups from small leathern bottles with old Greek wine, a servant carried bread round the tables in a silver basket, and others ventilated the apartment, or offered the guests warm and iced water.

In every direction trays circulated, covered with divers kinds of meats, which they took care to humect with peppered garum, that strange condiment, which the freed-slave procured from Spain at a price equal to its weight in gold.

Suddenly the symposiarch commands silence: the musicians obey—the slaves are motionless.

'Let us drain our cups,' said he, 'in honour of Caesar. Let us celebrate the tenth anniversary of his glorious reign, and his happy return to the metropolis of the world. Let us drink, senators and knights, as many craters as there are letters in the cherished name of the emperor.'

Sense and reason must have succumbed, had the patrician assembly toasted Caius Lucius Domitius Nero: it would have been constructive treason not to empty twenty-three cups; but they limited themselves to four, which represented the last of these names.

Joy unrestrained floated with the funny wine, furnished from large glass amphoræ, on which were these words: 'Falernian wine of a hundred leaves, made under the consulship of Opimius.' The consuls and the Roman nobles almost forgot, in the voluptuousness of the splendid repast, that the executioner of Britannicus and Burrhus, the crowned tiger, was doubtless thinking at that very moment of taking some of the heads then present. A funereal spectacle soon aroused their dormant fears.

An officer of the palace presented himself at the door of the banqueting hall. He advanced slowly, followed by two slaves, who laid on the table an object covered with a winding-sheet. 'Pressing occupations,' said the imperial messenger, 'prevent Cæsar from sharing with you the hospitality of Seba; but he thinks of you, and sends you a testimony of his remembrance.'

'Long live Cæsar!' cry the consuls, the freed-slave, and some few trembling voices. The officer retires. The veil which shrouds Nero's present from every eye is removed, and all perceive a silver skeleton, of terrifying truthfulness, and which, by its admirable mechanism, proclaims the artist to be one of those Greeks who have come to Rome to seek fortune and celebrity.

This episode engrossed the thoughts of the greater part of the guests, and the old senator, Lucius Vafra, could not help saying, with a sigh, to his neighbour, Virginius Rufus, one of the consuls of the preceding years: 'Fear the Greeks; fear this disastrous present!'

But the hot wine which was being served, and the healths which succeeded without interruption, drove the sinistrous presage from their minds; and, moreover, the present of the emperor was nowise contrary to the manners of the epoch, and the thought of death would only have enlivened the repast, if it had been presented by any other than Nero.

At first healths were drunk in the Greek fashion,—that is, beginning by the most distinguished personages, he who drank bowed and said: 'I wish you every kind of prosperity;' or simply: 'I salute you.' In pronouncing these words, he who drank the health took only a part of the wine contained in the cup, and sent the remainder to the guest he had just designated.

Many craters were then emptied in honour of the mistress of the house *(dominœ)*; neither were the illustrious dead nor absent friends forgotten. The formula was nearly the same for all: 'to your healths,' said the symposiarch, 'to our own, to that also of the friend whom we cherish.'

Sometimes Drusillus, still fascinated with that dulcet poetry of theGreeks which

Sometimes Drusillus, still fascinated with that dulcet poetry of the Greeks with which, when young, he had stored his mind, would take up the harmonious cadences of Horace, and thus personate, as it were, those divine chanters of Attica who have immortalised themselves by celebrating love, wine, and pleasure.

One of his extempore strains, while sipping the sparkling liquor from his cup, was:—

> This dream of bliss maintain, prolong these happy hours,
> O, all-enchanting wines! perfumed with flowers
>> Which Cos and Cyprus rear;
> Let nothing ever change this soul-felt, rich delight;
> For I would say, when parting for the realms of night,
>> I never knew a tear.

This sensual philosophy found numberless echoes in that vain-glorious Rome, who exhausted her disdain, outrage, and punishments on the (so called) new fantastic folly that the Nazarenes were endeavouring to introduce. A few years more, and their doctrine will subjugate the universe!

Time passed rapidly, and the meats, divided into equal portions, were served to the guests, who frequently did not touch them, but gave their share to their servants, or sent it home.

So soon as the major-domo perceived that appetite began to flag, he ordered the whole to be cleared, and the dessert, spread on ivory tables, to be substituted for the more substantial comestibles, with which the guests were satiated.

Exquisite drinks, artificial wines, delicate and light aliments, still came to titillate the palate and the burthened stomach—pears, apples, walnuts, dried-figs, grapes; a thousand different kinds of raw, cooked, and preserved fruits; tarts, cakes, and those incredible delicacies which the Latins designated by the collective generic term *bellaria*, wooed the epicurean—if we may be allowed the expression—with their mild, material, dangerous, and irresistible eloquence.

Some one proposed to replace the half-faded flowers by Egyptian wreaths, and every brow was soon bound with garlands of roses and myrtle, interspersed with little birds, which, by their fluttering and chirping, soon restored the drowsy company to that animation which seemed to wane.

Then began the amusements of the evening.

A troop of strolling players were admired for their agility and suppleness. Some rolled round a cord like a wheel which turns on its axle; they hung by the neck, by one foot, and varied these perilous exercises in a thousand different ways. Others slid down a cord, lying on the stomach, with their arms and legs extended. Some revolved as they ran along a descending cord. Some, in a word, performed feats of strength and address on the horizontal rope which were truly incomprehensible, and at an elevation from the flooring which would have rendered a fall fatal.

To these acrobats succeeded prestigiators, who appeared to receive a peculiar degree of attention. One placed under cups a certain number of shells, dry peas, or little balls, and he caused them to disappear and reappear at will. The spectators strained their eyes without being able to comprehend anything. Another of these mountebanks wrote or read very distinctly while whirling rapidly round. Some vomited flames from the mouth, or walked, head downwards, on their hands, and beat with their feet the movements of the most agile dancers. Then a woman appeared, holding in her hand twelve bronze hoops, with several little rings of the same metal, which rolled round them. She danced gracefully, throwing and successively catching the twelve hoops, without ever allowing any of the rings to fall. After that, another juggler rushed, with his breast uncovered, into the midst of a forest of naked swords. Every one thought him to be covered with wounds, but he re-appeared, with a smile on his countenance, whole and sound.

These feats were followed by an interlude, in which the parts were amusingly sustained by marionettes. The Greeks knew this childish pastime, and Rome did not disdain it. These little bronze and ivory figures played some comic scenes tolerably well, and obtained the applauses of grave senators, who more than once forgot their senility as they contemplated the grotesque pantomime.

The only thing now wanting to render Seba's supper a worthy specimen of nocturnal Roman feats was, to produce before the guests one of those spectacles which outrage morals and humanity. Nero's freed-man had been too well tutored to refuse them this diversion. Young Syrians, or bewitching Spanish girls, went through lascivious dances, which raised no blush on the brow of rigid magistrates, who forgot, in the abode of the vile slave, the respect due to their age and dignity.

After the voluptuous scenes of the lewd Celtiberians, blood was required: for they seem to have been formed by nature to take a strange delight in sudden contrasts. Ten couples of gladiators, armed with swords and bucklers, occupied a space assigned to them, and ten horrible duels recreated the attentive assembly. For a long time nothing was heard but the clash of arms; but the thirst for conquest animated those ferocious combatants, and they rushed with loud cries on one another. Blood flowed on all sides; the couches were dyed with it, and the white robes of the guests were soon spotted. Some of the combatants fell, and the rattles announced approaching death; others preserved, in their last struggle, a funereal silence, or endeavoured to fix their teeth in the flesh of their enemies standing erect beside them. The spectators, stupified with wine and good cheer, contemplated this carnage with cold impassibility; they only roused from their torpor when one of those men, happening to trip against a table, struck his head on the ivory, and his antagonist, prompt as lightning, plunged his sword into the throat of his foe, whence torrents of black, reeking blood inundated the polished ivory, and flowed in long streams among the fruits, cups, and flowers.

The deed was applauded; servants washed the tables and the floor with perfumed water, and these stirring scenes were soon forgotten. A last cup was drunk to the good genius, whose protection they invoked before returning home.

Meantime a stifling atmosphere pervades every part of the hall, and a hollow noise, rumbling in the distance, excites at intervals in the minds of the guests a sort of undefinable apprehension—the ordinary presage of an unknown but imminent catastrophe. The consuls raise themselves on their couches and listen; their host endeavours to calm their fears; but at this moment a slave, panting for breath, rushes towards Seba, and pronounces a few inarticulate words. 'Fire!' cries the anguished freed man. 'Where is the fire?' inquire all the terrified guests, who have heard but this one sinistrous word. 'Everywhere!' replies the slave; 'it has burst forth simultaneously in every part of the city!' No one waits to hear more. Consuls, senators, knights, musicians, and servants, jostle one another; and, abandoning those who fall, arrive pell-mell at the atrium. The porter still chained, trembles at his post; the flames already envelop the sumptuous edifice—the entire street is one vast brazier! Rome burns, and will soon be a heap of ruins and ashes! Flight is impossible—the flames intercept every issue! Nero has taken his measures well.

We will not attempt to depict the mute but terrible despair of those proud patricians, at bay in the midst of an ocean of fire, in which they are fated ere long to perish. The wreaths of flowers which bind their brows are already parched by the scorching breath of those roaring flames, which engulf and consume everything as they sweep along. A thick smoke begrimes the lustrous robes, whose graceful folds erewhile displayed the exquisite urbanity of Seba's guests, and which now exhibit only a sad emblem of festive joys. The dread of death, and I know not what strange anguish at this all-important moment, blanch those human faces, to which the choicest wines of Greece and Italy had just given a hue of purple. These men feel—instinct tells them—that life is theirs no longer, and they have not the courage to die!

The opulent freed-man calls to his slaves, and promises them their liberty if they consent to risk their lives in an attempt to save his. But the vile herd is already dispersed; the porter alone remains—for no one has thought to liberate him—and he, in his impotent fury, replies by insulting clamours to the cowardly supplications of his quondam master.

This horrible scene soon changed by the very action of that torrent of fire which was pursuing its devastating course; and the next day, when Aurora appeared, a heap of ruins was all that remained of the odious Seba's magnificent palace.

The two consuls and some of the senators were fortunate enough to escape the common danger. Less besotted, perhaps, by the wine and good cheer, and finding in despair that incredible energy which sometimes operates the same prodigies as courage, they rushed through the flames, and gained the country, or those obscure portions of the city which the son of Agrippina had apparently forgotten.

Thus it was that Lucius Domitius Nero celebrated the tenth anniversary of his glorious reign. While the fire was rolling on with its resistless flood of flame from temples to palaces, and from the Circus to the Pantheon, the young, poetic Cæsar, his brow bound with laurel, and holding in his hands a golden lyre, viewed from the top of a tower—where he was surrounded by a troop of histrions and buffons—the conflagration he had just kindled.

And while the imperial Apollo sang some melancholy verses on the fatal destiny of the antique city of Troy, his ignoble courtiers cried with enthusiasm: 'May the Gods preserve Nero, their august son, and the delight of the human race!'

Such was the last gorgeous feast at which the magiric genius presided in that Rome which Romulus had founded, and which engulfed the treasures and wonders of the world. Destroyed by the imperial incendiary, it arose from its ashes with increased beatuy and voluptuousness; and the wild joy of its new banquets caused the thoughtless queen of nations quickly to forget the disasters of the past, and the sinistrous presages of the future.

Chef to the Troops
Soyer's Culinary Campaign

The Gore House fiasco seems, temporarily at least, to have knocked the wind out of Soyer. His grandest enterprise of all, into which he had poured his heart and soul, had not succeeded and (more important) had been seen not to succeed. The whole affair had dented his reputation, and he decided to lie low for a while. Thus, his biographers record, 'during the years 1853 and 1854, Soyer did nothing which calls for comment, but led a retired quiet life'. Hard though it is to imagine, the Gastronomic Regenerator contented himself with his soup kitchens, his writing and the occasional modest banquet.

One reason for this prolonged spell of relaxation was his discovery of what he called 'the Paradis Champêtre of England'. Soyer's previous experiences of English country living had left him a convinced urbanite (on one occasion, at a foxhunt in Shropshire, he had distinguished himself by chasing a dog and being thrown into a hedge—an incident which left him undeniably à la zoug-zoug). So he was overjoyed to visit Virginia Water, with its gentle parklands, two-mile-long lake, pleasant glades and gothic ruins. Here was the countryside, but a section blessedly free from mud and thorns and hills. Above all, it was within a short train and coach ride of central London ('too close for the wealthy, and too far for the people,' crowed Soyer). He spent many happy days in this genteel spot, putting up at the Wheatsheaf Inn and, together with the landlord, entertaining friends and locals with his hospitality and practical jokes. One of the latter is described with relish in the *Memoirs*:

About this period, a laughable event occurred at a dinner party given by the immortal *chef*, at the Wheatsheaf, Virginia Water. The chair was taken by the *chef* himself, faced by his valued friend, E. T. Smith, Esq., lessee of the Theatre Royal, Drury Lane. On a sudden, and after the dispersion of what, in culinary language, are termed the 'removes,' a waiter appeared with what seemed to be either a large sirloin of beef, or a saddle of mutton, at least, surmounted by a large cover; whereupon Mr. Vice rated the man for not bringing it earlier, himself clearing a space on the table before him for its reception. The waiter appeared to be inclined to drop the hot dish as it was placed on the table, Mr. Smith the while sharpening his carver, and calling for customers for his joint, and, on the man removing the cover, out jumped a little squirrel, and leaping right on the shoulder of the astonished vice-chairman, scampered along the heads and plates of his fellow-guests. After passing the entire length of the table, in the manner described, the little thing bounded to the floor, when suddenly a new epoch in the way of dining took place, for no sooner did the astonished animal take to the earth than away vanished the guests' hunger, and there was a general chase to catch the animated joint. After a long hunt the squirrel was captured, and once more let loose amongst his companions in the adjacent wood. During part of the time Soyer sat as grave as a judge, but the merry twinkle of his dark piercing eye ultimately lapsed into one of his uncontrollable fits of laughter, and there he sat, unable to stay his mirth, until the game was captured, when once more hunger returned, and the magnificent banquet placed on the table was speedily demolished.

A CULINARY CAMPAIGN

BY A. SOYER

ILLUSTRATED BY H. G. HINE

Two years of 'retired quiet life', however, were more than enough for Alexis Soyer. He began to chafe at the inactivity. No matter how much he enjoyed his grand picnics by the lake and his carousals at the Wheatsheaf, he knew that he should be making better use of his massive talents. What he needed was a new cause. When, early in 1855 he read a letter to the *Times* from a soldier serving in the Crimea, he knew that he had found one. The letter asked for the great chef's advice on how the British troops might best use their food rations. Soyer was quick to reply, and eagerly began to discuss with his friends how he might be of practical use to the Army. The situation at the Front, vividly and unflinchingly described by W. H. Russell of the *Times*, was appalling. The soldiers huddled on the mud of the Crimean plain without sufficient tents, uniforms or footwear. They had no proper stoves, and little to cook in the first place. Supplies were pitifully short, and supply wagons bogged down in endless mud. The only gleam of light in the whole wretched tragedy came from the Lady with the Lamp, Florence Nightingale, whose selfless labours at Scutari military hospitals at least brought comfort to the wounded and dying.

The tale of Soyer's great Crimean adventure is best told by the man himself, using extracts from his *Culinary Campaign*, which appeared in 1857. Here, more clearly than in any of his other books, we encounter sheer unadulterated Soyer, his radiant personality bouncing off each page in a blur of enthusiasm, sentimentality, wisecracks and swaggerings. All this tends to get in the way of a clear and detailed description of the battle zone: Soyer repeats lengthy conversations with generals and aristocrats, and finds plenty of room for anecdotes illustrating his own ingenuity and wit, but of the conduct of the war itself we hear very little. Yet somehow there is great charm in this egocentricity.

Selection from
Soyer's Culinary Campaign (1857)

'Hurrah! hurrah! bravo! bravo!' For a few minutes rounds of applause and shouts of laughter from the juveniles were heard and loudly re-echoed throughout the vast cupola of Old Drury, sending home the delighted spectators, in fits of sneezing and coughing, through a variegated atmosphere.

In a few minutes the theatre was nearly emptied of spectators, but still full of smoke. Considering myself that evening as free as a butterfly on a spring morning, though unable, like the light-hearted insect, to flit from flower to flower, I was trying to escape, with the swiftness of an eel, down the gigantic and crowded staircase, hoping to get off unobserved, as I had to start early in the morning for the country, when suddenly a friendly hand pressed me forcibly by the arm. The owner of the same cried, 'Stop! stop! my friend; I have been hunting all over the theatre for you.' I at once recognised an old Devonshire acquaintance, whom I was indeed much pleased to see, having received a most kind reception from him at my last visit to that delightful county—so justly named the garden of England.

'Well, my dear sir,' said he, 'myself and several acquaintances of yours are here for a few days, and have ordered a supper this evening at the 'Albion.' We heard you were at Drury Lane, and I have come to ask you to join us.'

'I must say it is very kind of you, Mr. Turner; but you must excuse me, as I am going as far as St. James's-street, by appointment; besides, I leave for the country early to-morrow morning. But I shall be happy to spend to-morrow evening with you and your friends; therefore, I beg you will apologise for me.'

'To-morrow very likely we shall be off again; we only came for a couple of days, to breathe the London air, and then return.'

'I beg your pardon—you mean London fog, not air.'

'Why, yes, fog should be the word; but for all that, I love London in any season; so no excuse—I shall not leave you; you must join us, or your friend the squire will be greatly disappointed. He came from the Great Western Hotel this evening on purpose to see you.'

Finding it almost impossible to get out of it, and my friend having promised we should break up early, I accepted, saying, 'You must allow me to go as far as the "Wellington," as I have an appointment there; I will be back in about half-an-hour.'

My incredulous country friend would not grant permission till I had assured him that I would faithfully keep my promise, and return.

This dialogue took place in the entrance of the vestibule, where a number of ladies and children were waiting—some for their carriages and broughams, others for those public inconveniences called cabs. This bevy of beauty and group of children, the pride of young England, seemed to interest my provincial friend so much, that I had some trouble to get him out. It was then nearly twelve o'clock. The front steps were also crowded; the weather was chilly and damp; a thick yellowish fog, properly mixed with a good portion of soot, formed a shower of black pearls, which, gracefully descending through the murky air, alighted, without asking permission, upon the rosy cheeks of unveiled fair dames, spotting their visages, if not à la Pompadour or à la Watteau, at least à la Hogarth. A few steps lower we entered a dense crowd—a most unpicturesque miscellany of individuals, unclassically called the London mob. 'Mind your pockets,' said I to my country friend.

'By Jove, it's too late,' said he, feeling in his pocket—'my handkerchief is gone!'

'Is that all?' I inquired.

'Well, let me see,' he observed, feeling again: 'yes, thank god! my watch and purse are quite safe.'

'Ah,' I continued, laughing, 'the old adage which prompts us to thank God for all things is quite correct; for you are actually thanking Him for the loss of your handkerchief.'

'Not at all,' he replied; 'I was thanking Him for the safety of my watch and purse.' After a hearty laugh we parted, he going to the 'Albion,' and I to the 'Wellington.'

On my arrival there, I found that my friend had been and was gone. My intelligent cabby soon brought me back through the dense atmosphere to that far-famed temple of Comus, at which crowds of celebrities meet nightly—some to restore themselves internally, others to sharpen their wits at that tantalising abode of good cheer. Upon entering, I inquired of a waiter, a stranger to me, if he could inform me where my six friends intended to stop.

'Yes, sir, directly.' Speaking down the trumpet: 'Below! a Welsh rabbit and fresh toast—two kidneys underdone—scalloped oyster—a chop—two taters! Look sharp below!' to the barmaid: 'Two stouts, miss—one pale—four brandies hot, two without—one whisky—three gin—pint sherry—bottle of port!'

'What an intelligent waiter!' thought I, 'to have so good a memory.' Having waited till he had given his orders, I again said, 'Pray, my fine fellow, in which room are my friends going to sup? They have a private room, no doubt?'

'Yes, sir, a private room for two.'

'No, not for two—for six.'

'Oh! I don't mean that, sir: I want a rump-steak for two,' said he; 'stewed tripe for one—three grogs—bottle pale Bass.' And off he went to the coffee-room.

'Plague upon the fellow!' said I to myself.

As the barmaid could not give me any information upon the subject, and I perceived through a half-opened door on the right-hand side of the bar a table laid for six, I went in, making sure it was for my friends, and that they had not yet arrived. Indeed, I had myself returned from my appointment much sooner than I had expected. I sat down, and was reading the evening paper, when a waiter came in. 'After you with the paper, sir.'

'I have done; you may take it.'

'There's the *Times*, sir, if you have not seen it.'

'No, I have not; let me have a look at it.' After reading one of the leaders, my attention was drawn to a long article written by the Crimean correspondent of that journal. When I had read it carefully a second time, a few minutes' reflection on my part enabled me to collect my ideas, and established in my mind a certain assurance that I could, if allowed by government, render service in the cooking of the food, the administration of the same, as well as the distribution of the provisions.

These were matters in which I could detect, through the description of that eye-witness, the writer of the above-mentioned article, some change was much needed. I therefore wrote the following letter to the *Times*, it being then nearly one o'clock in the morning:—

THE HOSPITAL KITCHENS AT SCUTARI.
To the Editor of the Times.

Sir,—After carefully perusing the letter of your correspondent, dated Scutari, in your impression of Wednesday last, I perceive that, although the kitchen under the superintendence of Miss Nightingale affords so much relief, the system of management at the large one in the Barrack-hospital is far from being perfect. I propose offering my services gratuitously, and proceeding direct to Scutari, at my own personal expense, to regulate that important department, if the Government will honour me with their confidence, and grant me the full power of acting according to my knowledge and experience in such matters.

I have the honour to remain, Sir,

Your obedient servant,

Feb. 2, 1855.   A. Soyer.

After despatching this letter, I again inquired about my friends and my anticipated supper, which for some time had escaped my memory. 'Did you ring, sir?'

'No, I did not, sir, but the bell has;' recognising my stupid waiter.

'Oh, sir! are you here?'

'Of course I am; don't you see me?'

'Well, sir, your friends have had supper; they inquired everywhere for you; I told them you could not wait, as you had two ladies to see home as far as Brompton.'

'You foolish fellow! I never spoke to you about ladies, Brompton, or any such thing; I merely asked you where my friends were to sup; to which you replied,

"Rump-steak for two, tripe for one, two taters, pat of butter, one pale Bass, and three kidneys for a gentleman, underdone." '

'No more you did, sir. It was number three who told me to say so; not you, sir; you're quite right, sir!'

Pausing only to write out a few receipts for the landlord, Soyer staggered out into the fog, hailed a hansom cab, and arrived home in Bloomsbury Street very late. The fire was out, the supper given to the cats, the servants in bed and the gas out.

A most curious dream haunted my mind throughout the night, one of those indescribable phantasmagorian illusions which set all the vibrations of the heart at work without moving the frame, or in imagination only, quite depriving our senses for the time of the true sense of existence. Scarcely had the first gleam of Aurora peeped through my curtains, than a double knock was heard at the street door, apprising me that the time for rising had come, and forthwith brought back my wandering senses to the realities of human life: a minute after, a friend popped into my dressing-room, exclaiming, 'Hallo! so you are going to the seat of the war, I hear.'

'The seat of the war! who told you so?'

'Why, the *Times*, to be sure; I have just read your letter, which, at all events, is very likely to carry you as far as Constantinople.'

'You don't say so! What! is my letter in the *Times* today?'

'Of course it is,' he replied.

'I sent it so late last night, I did not suppose it could appear till to-morrow, if at all.'

'They would not have inserted it, arriving so late, I assure you, had they not thought it of great importance, and that you were likely to improve the hospital diets. No doubt you will soon set them to rights. I read the article, and must say I was much pleased when I saw your letter, and that is what brought me here so early: but mind, it is a long journey, and rather a dangerous one.'

'Well, my dear friend, if Government honour me with their confidence, I shall be happy to start immediately, and rough it for a short time—say a couple of months, which will be about the time required.'

'My opinion is, that you will soon hear from the authorities.'

'I say again, they are perfectly welcome to my humble services.'

I was sitting down to my breakfast, when, to my annoyance, as I had much business to transact, some one knocked at the door, and, without waiting for the reply, came in. It was the landlord, with a face full of anxiety and astonishment, his glasses raised to his forehead, a newspaper in his hand, and looking as serious as if he had just been married, or had lost one of his favourite pups. 'I say, master,' said he, 'do you mean it?'

'Mean what, man?'

'But now, really! do you mean it?'

'I'm puzzled to know to what you allude. Is it about my trip to Paris?'

'Paris! no, that has nothing to do with the letter of yours I have just read in the *Times* of this day.'

'Oh! now I understand you, and can easily account for your long face and evident astonishment.'

'Now you understand me, don't you?'

'Of course I do.'

'Well, allow me to tell you frankly that you are very foolish; you are not a military man, and have made the offer, it is true, very likely in a moment of enthusiasm; but plead any excuse you can to get out of it if you are sent for; remain where you are—"good folks are scarce," says the proverb.'

'Thanks to the proverb first, and you afterwards,' said I.

'And if you do go, it is a hundred to one against your returning.'

'Many thanks for your frank advice; but I am determined to go, and if Government send for me, I wish to be ready at a day's notice; so sure I am that I can render some services to my fellow-creatures by so doing.'

'I have no doubt you can—but you may catch the fever, or God knows what besides! Why, they are dying by fifties and sixties a-day in the hospital at Scutari; look, here is the latest account, the names of the poor fellows defunct, and number of their regiments. There is no mistake in that.'

'I am aware of all that; but mind you, my firm belief is, that no fruit falls from the tree to the ground till it is perfectly ripe; and I also believe that we are never gathered from this frivolous world till we are really wanted in the other.'

With these noble sentiments, Soyer settled down to design a portable field store. He took the plans immediately to a firm of engineers.

The next morning, at half-past nine, Messrs. Smith and Phillips, according to promise, brought me a most beautiful small model of the field-stove, which they warranted first-rate, and to be capable of working in or out of doors, and in all weathers. I immediately proceeded to the War-Office, to show the model, and explain the principle to Lord Panmure. In the waiting-room I had the honour of meeting the Duke of Cambridge, which gave me an excellent opportunity of explaining its merits. The Duke appeared to approve of it, and particularly noticed the great economy of fuel consequent upon the construction and smallness of the furnace. The Duke made some important remarks, and gave me a few hints upon the cooking regulations both in the hospital and in the camps. These I took note of, and after explaining my plan of transport, I was quite delighted at having had such an opportunity of conversing with the Duke on a subject in which I was aware he felt particular interest. Mr. Ramsay, the secretary, having sent for me, I quitted the Duke; and, before leaving, I informed him that I had seen my friend Comte, and that he had given me all the assistance in his power, and had also told me that his highness had presented the hospital with a very nice *petite batterie de cuisine*, which, no doubt, I should find very useful upon my arrival.

'Adieu, Monsieur Soyer, I wish you well, and hope you will succeed.'

On reaching Mr. Ramsay's office, that gentleman kindly informed me that if I wished to see Lord Panmure I had better wait till he went to take his luncheon. I then stated that my object was to show his lordship the model of a stove I had invented for the use both of the hospitals and the army.

'Walk into the next room; Lord Panmure will be there in a few minutes, and you will have plenty of time to show it without interfering with his business.'

I had not waited ten minutes before Lord Panmure came in alone.

'Ah, Mr. Soyer, what have you there?'

'The model of a stove I wish to submit to your lordship. It is one which will, I believe, suit admirably for cooking both in and out of doors.'

After closely examining it, and listening to the details I had previously given to the Duke of Cambridge, Lord Panmure approved of it, and requested me to have another made, which he might keep by him for inspection.

He then inquired how many cooks I should take with me.

'Only a few from Paris,' I replied, 'as I wish to make a trial before engaging many people; besides, I hope to be able, in a very short time, to instruct the soldiers, who, being under discipline, might prove as useful as any cooks.'

Lord Panmure seemed pleased at my anxiety to instruct the soldiers; and, as he very justly remarked—'We want them to learn how to cook their rations to the best advantage, and that your instructions should remain for ever among them. Well, I have settled all you wished me to do; and my secretary, Mr. Ramsay, will remit you all the letters you require. When do you think of starting?'

'By the next mail.'

'Well!' said his lordship, shaking me heartily by the hand, 'Good-bye, if I do not see you again before your departure.'

'It would only be troubling you; I therefore beg to take this opportunity of thanking your lordship for the kind reception and encouragement I have received, and, still more, for the confidence with which you have honoured me. I assure you that it will cause me to be most careful and economical, and it will be my pride to improve the diet without increasing the expense to Government. This may not be effected at first; but when the system is once introduced, and fairly established, I will answer for both a great amelioration as well as a saving.'

'I am confident, Soyer, that you will do your best.'

The outward journey, via France and Greece was marked by rough weather. However Soyer characteristically seized any opportunity to enjoy himself. In Marseilles he gleaned a receipt for bouillabaisse from a local restaurateur: in Ajaccio he visited the kitchen of Napoleon's birthplace—writing off a letter to the *Times* which unfortunately got lost in the post. At Athens he lugged his Magic Stove to the Parthenon and cooked a meal for his fellow travellers. At last the vessel *Simois* passed through the Dardanelles and docked at Constantinople. Here, Soyer had his first sight of Scutari:

My mind was quite overpowered when I learnt that the monster building before us was the Scutari Hospital—a town in itself—and I reflected that it was full of sick and wounded; that each patient would require from three to four articles of diet daily, making a total of several thousand per diem to be provided in some shape or other; and that I had undertaken to reform and introduce a better organization in the cooking department, where all was confusion, in so strange a country. I must confess that, for an hour or so, I was quite at a loss to think how I should commence operations. I did not know one official there. I had not the least idea how I should be received; and after all, I might probably catch the fever, or some other complaint at the time raging within its walls. Suddenly I recollected the plan I had explained to the Duchess of Sutherland and her noble circle, which was to be tried upon a hundred patients. This had entirely escaped my memory; and, in a few minutes my puzzled brain was as clear as a bell, and I felt confident of success. 'If I succeed with a hundred,' said I, 'in a very short time I can manage a thousand, providing I meet with proper support.'

I afterwards learnt from the doctor on board, that the large red brick building on the right, about half a mile from the Barrack Hospital, was called the General Hospital, in which there were at least five or six hundred patients. My resolution as to how I should act was then fixed; nothing appeared difficult to me; and, instead of fearing the undertaking, I was most anxious to begin.

Our two caidjees rapidly flew away with us from the side of the *Simois*, and soon landed us at the Tophané tumble-down stairs. We are now on shore; but what a contrast!—the fairy scene has disappeared, and we appear to be in the midst of a penny show. The Tophané landing place is nothing but a heap of rotten planks, parts of which have given way, and the holes are rather dangerous, as one might easily slip and break a leg. The very clean and picturesque caidjees are waiting amidst heaps of manure and the carcass of a dead horse, which had been thrown into the Bosphorus and had drifted on shore. A number of ill-looking, half-famished dogs were feeding upon that heap of corruption. On inquiring of the son of the proprietor of the hotel, who accompanied me, he coolly told me that it had only been there a day or two, and would probably remain for months—particularly the skeleton—when the dogs had devoured all the flesh. The odour arising from the carcass, and the filth daily cast into the water, was very unwholesome, and quite unbearable; and very glad was I to quit the great landing-place of Tophané—so called, no doubt, from the extraordinary amount of daily traffic between the shipping above and the Asiatic shore. About seventy or eighty caiques are always waiting there, as it is the principal landing point at Constantinople.

Following my guide, we passed through a number of dirty narrow streets, full of a black liquid mud, very ill paved—if they could be called paved at all, amidst which numerous leperous and villainous-looking dogs were snarling and fighting. Donkeys loaded with tiles, stones, and long logs of wood filled up the filthy road; besides gangs of powerful and noisy Turkish hamals or porters, carrying enormous loads upon long poles. The enchanting mirage of the panoramic Constantinople vanished rapidly from before my disenchanted eyes; this ephemeral Paradise of Mahomet changing at once into an almost insupportable purgatory. I could not imagine how such a mass of ruins and of miserable wooden houses could, from so short a distance, take such a brilliant aspect or create such ravishing sensations, as the first view of Constantinople had raised in my mind from the deck of the *Simois*. I now envied the fate of our fair fellow-traveller who so much regretted that she could not disembark—were it only for a few hours. Those few hours, nay, the first, would have sufficed to break the spell. Reader, though this is an exact description of our entrance into Constantinople, I reasoned thus—It is an immense metropolis, and no doubt something great exists within its walls. I must wait patiently and try to find it out.

Reproaching my dragoman for bringing me through such a vile part of the city, he quietly replied, in English, 'There is no other road, sir; it has rained very much lately, which is the cause of so much mud.' I now perceived, that as far as the names of pavements go, the difference between Constantinople and London was not so great,— the former being *much-muddy-mised*, and the latter *macadamised*.

At this moment we were turning the corner of the Grand Mosque of Sultan Soliman; and a pacha, in all his obesity, mounted upon an Arabian horse, and followed by his suite, six in number, rode full gallop through a pond of liquid slush, splashing every one from head to foot on either side the narrow street. An English soldier at once sent him his military blessing; and the Turk, spurring his horse, exclaimed, 'Not Bono Johnny; Not Bono Johnny;' that being the name given to the

English by the Turks. After passing through several similar streets, consisting of ruinous wooden shanties and shops of the lowest order, 'viz., chibouque tube and pipe-bowl makers,' the interior of which were dirty and mean, with scarcely any kind of stock, we arrived at a fountain, in front of which was a semi-perpendicular and narrow street. My guide informed me that my hotel was at the end of this street. 'It is,' he continued, 'the Hôtel d'Angleterre, called by the English—Messerie's Hotel.'

'Thank God for that,' said I.

The next day, Soyer got down to work.

The hospital being on an elevated spot, and not more than a thousand yards distant, appeared three times as large as it did from the deck of the *Simois*; and here again, at sight of such a gigantic establishment, my courage failed me, and for the second time I regretted having undertaken such a difficult task. I immediately went to the grand hospital entrance, the residence of Lord W. Paulet, thanking my stars that I had the honour of being known to him. I was shown the general's quarters, and sent in my card. I was desired to follow, and had no sooner entered, than his lordship came to meet me, and shook hands cordially.

'Monsieur Soyer,' said he, 'we have not had the pleasure of meeting since 1847, when I saw you in Dublin,—the year of the famine in Ireland.'

These words recalled the scene to my mind.

'I was at the Royal Barracks, with the Duke of Cambridge, when you opened your kitchen in the Barrack Square—in fact, before our window. The Duke and myself paid you a visit the day the Lord-Lieutenant opened it. You had nearly a thousand visitors that morning, and fed between four and five thousand poor people in the course of the day. The samples of food prepared by you were excellent, though made at such a moderate price, I assure you,' his lordship continued, speaking to some gentlemen present, one of whom knew me while at the Reform Club.

'Indeed, my lord, you give me much pleasure by recalling reminiscences of my success at that period; and I accept the same as a good omen for my present undertaking, especially when taken in connexion with your valuable support.'

'Monsieur Soyer, you may depend upon my support; but I tell you beforehand, you will have no end of difficulties.'

'Well, my lord, with your support, a good will, and perseverance, I have no doubt of doing some good.' I then presented Lord Panmure's letter respecting my mission. While his lordship was reading it, I was asked by several officers present, 'What are you sent out for?' Lord William Paulet, overhearing them, replied, 'To set us to rights in our kitchen department, to be sure. This letter from the Minister-at-War shall be closely attended to, Monsieur Soyer, and I will this day give orders to that effect.'

From this I understood that Lord Panmure had given instructions for everything I might require.

'Well,' said his lordship, 'how many cooks have you brought with you?'

'Four, my lord.'

'Only four! I thought you would want many more than that. However, let me know what you require. You are staying at Pera?'

'Yes; but I intend coming over to-morrow, to make a beginning.'

'I must get you a house in town; we are so full here, we have no room to spare.'

'I'm not sorry for that—it will be a change of air—though I shall require a small room in the hospital.'

'We'll see about that—but tell me, of how many does your staff consist?'

'About seven or eight.'

'I'll try and get you a house to yourself.'

'Many thanks, my lord. I assure you that the kind reception accorded to me will never be forgotten by your humble servant. In order that no time may be lost—and I am aware that your lordship's is highly valuable—will you kindly instruct some one to show me Dr. Cumming's apartment, as I have a letter of introduction to that gentleman from Dr. Andrew Smith; and I am anxious to confer with the Doctor upon the subject of the new diets, and submit them for his special approval.'

His lordship then directed Dr. Rutherford to show me to Dr. Cumming's office, which we reached through a long corridor lined with beds on either side, and occupied by sick and wounded. The apartment was full of persons waiting to see the doctor. On sending in my card I was immediately admitted, and very politely received. Dr. Cumming was, of course, full of business. He read the letter from Dr. A. Smith, and then said, 'Monsieur Soyer, you may depend upon it that I will do all in my power to assist you.'

I then stated my plan of commencing with a hundred patients, of which he highly approved. 'The next thing,' I observed, 'will be to find a suitable place for a kitchen.'

'I think,' said he, 'the General Hospital will be the best to begin at, as it has always been used as an hospital. You will find everything more appropriate there.' I expressed a great desire to commence with the Barrack Hospital, to which Dr. Cumming immediately consented.

'Dr. Rutherford, you will perhaps be kind enough to show Mr. Soyer over the hospital, and assist him in selecting a suitable spot to commence operations.' Doctor Cumming again repeated his promise of giving me every support, and said, 'You know my office, and I shall at all times be glad to see you upon matters of business.'

'You may depend on it, Doctor, that I shall only trouble you with indispensable matters, and such with which it is most important you should be acquainted.'

We then parted. The Doctor and myself walked round the whole of the corridors, both sides of which were filled with patients. The numerous wards round the barracks, each of which held about thirty patients, were also full. These melancholy sights have been so often depicted in letters in the public press, that it would only be re-opening an old wound were I to dilate upon them. There is a wide difference between seeing the thing upon the spot, in all its painful and wretched truth, and in merely reading a well-written description. This fact all who have witnessed such spectacles have felt, without being able or willing to describe. I must say that, in spite of the *sang froid* and energy I possess, the sight of such calamities made a most extraordinary impression upon me, and produced an effect which lasted for several days afterwards. At length I found a place on one of the large staircases, in which I could make an excellent model kitchen, and of this discovery I at once informed Dr. Cumming. The afternoon was drawing to a close, and being obliged to return to Pera, I was compelled to leave without seeing Miss Nightingale, for whom I had brought several letters—one in particular, from the Duchess of Sutherland.

The next morning we started as agreed upon. On arriving at Scutari, I met a soldier who informed me that a house in Cambridge-street was being prepared for my reception. 'It is not two minutes' walk from here,' said he; 'will you go and see it?'

'Thank you, not this morning; my friend is in a great hurry. When will it be ready?'

'To-morrow, or next day, at the latest.'

'That will do very well. Where can I find you if I want to see you?'

'At the Engineers' office; my name is Corporal Hardy.'

'I thank you.'

As the Doctor was on his way to head-quarters, and Mr. Bracebridge was going in another direction, we continued our journey, which, though short, was very fatiguing, the roads being very bad in consequence of a continuance of heavy rain. At last we arrived at the hospital, which, although the smallest, is certainly the most elegant. It was one of the Sultan's Kiosques, and was divided into three departments—one for the officers, and two for the men. About three hundred and forty men and twenty officers were there at the time, as I was told; the latter complained very much about their cooking, the inferiority of which was unavoidable, as there was only a very small kitchen, badly built, which smoked all day, and was without ventilation. It was there that the Duke of Cambridge and staff remained during his indisposition; but I must observe that the Duke had a first-rate culinary artist, who went through the campaign with him. The Duke was only attended by a few gentlemen, and consequently it had not at the time of my visit twenty occupants. Nothing could be done properly for them, till I had built a rough wooden kitchen, and placed a civilian cook under the orders of the doctor and purveyor who had the regulation of the diets. This hospital, though very pretty, was never considered healthy, it being surrounded by gardens and marshy meadows.

After inspecting the mess-kitchen, we retired, and thence went to the General Hospital. The doctor-in-chief not being there, we were shown round by a staff-doctor. I found the kitchen very dark, and badly built, for such a number of patients; but the distribution of food and the regulation of the same were on a much better footing than at the Barrack Hospital. On noticing this to the head cook, he gave the credit to Dr. O'Flaherty. Upon being introduced to that gentleman, I recognised him as one of my visitors in Dublin, at the same time as Brigadier-General Lord W. Paulet. I promised to have the kitchen altered as soon as it could possibly be done, and started for the Barrack Hospital to visit Miss Nightingale. I entered the great Barrack Hospital alone. The entrance was crowded with officers of rank and medical gentlemen. The High-street, facing the General's quarters, was literally crammed with soldiers, more or less conscious of the state of warlike affairs. Most of them kept vandyking from the gin palace to their quarters, their red jackets forming a strange contrast to the quiet dress and solemn air of the Moslem soldiers upon duty.

After shaking hands with some officers and doctors whom I had the pleasure of knowing in England, I inquired of a sentry for Miss Nightingale's apartment, which he at once pointed out to me. On my entering the ante-room, a Sœur de Charité, whom I addressed, informed me that somebody was with that lady. She added, 'I am aware that Miss Nightingale wishes to see you, so I will let her know that you are here.' I hoped to have a few minutes to myself in order to take an observation of this sanctuary of benevolence; but my project was defeated by my being immediately admitted; and this compels me to trace this picture from memory.

Upon entering the room, I was saluted by a lady, and not doubting that this was our heroine, 'Madam,' said I, 'allow me to present my humble respects. I presume I have the honour of addressing Miss Nightingale.'

'Yes, sir. Monsieur Soyer, I believe?'

'The same, Madam.'

'Pray take a seat. I hear you had a rough voyage out.'

'Very much so, especially from Marseilles to Ajaccio.'

'So I heard, Monsieur Soyer.'

'I have brought several parcels and letters for you; among the latter, one from the Duchess of Sutherland.'

After having perused this epistle, Miss Nightingale remarked: 'I believe her Grace is right; you will no doubt be able to render great service in the kitchen department.'

'For which I shall need the good-will and assistance of all the heads of this monster establishment; and I must beg, above all things, that you who have already done so much for the sick and the wounded, will be kind enough to give me the benefit of your valuable experience.'

'I will, Monsieur Soyer; but first of all, I should advise you to see Lord William Paulet, Dr. Cumming, and the Purveyor-in-Chief, Mr. Milton.'

'Many thanks for your kind advice. I had the pleasure of seeing Lord William yesterday, as well as Dr. Cumming. To Mr. Milton I shall pay my respects upon leaving you.'

'You had better do so; for the principal part of your business you will have to transact with those gentlemen.'

'A very excellent remark, which I shall not fail to attend to.'

'Another gentleman you must see in the purveyor's department, is Mr. Tucker. You will then be able to commence operations.'

'Very true: I shall not think of commencing before I am well acquainted with every one in each department that has reference to the cooking. I shall submit every sample of diets, with a statement of the quantity and kind of ingredients of which they are composed, for the approval and opinion of the medical authorities; as I shall have to deal with patients, and not with epicures.

'Perfectly right,' said Miss Nightingale.

'That no time may be lost, I should very much like this afternoon to visit the kitchens now in use, inspect the stores, and procure a statement of the daily rations allowed to each patient, if I can have one of the inspectors to go round with me.'

'Certainly you can; I will send for somebody who will be happy to accompany you.'

'Perhaps you would favour us with your company, as I should be most happy to attend to any suggestion you might like to make.'

'I will go with you with greatest pleasure; but here comes Doctor Macgregor, the under-superintendent, who will be our guide. He told me that he had met you before.'

'Yes; we met yesterday at Lord William Paulet's.'

'Doctor,' said Miss Nightingale, 'Monsieur Soyer wishes you to accompany him round the various kitchens and store-rooms.'

'I will do that with the greatest pleasure; but he had better be introduced to Mr. Milton and to Mr. Tucker. Mr. Milton is out, but Mr. Tucker will do instead.'

Our visitorial pilgrimage then commenced. We first visited Miss Nightingale's dietary kitchen, in which I immediately recognised the whole of the little *camp batterie de cuisine* which my friend Comte told me that the Duke of Cambridge had presented to the hospital. Justice was indeed done to it, for every separate article of which it was composed was in use. Miss Nightingale had a civilian cook as well as an assistant. Everything appeared in as good order as could be expected, considering what there was to be done. I noticed the very bad quality of the charcoal, which smoked terribly, and was nothing but dust. Of course, this interfered materially with the expedition of the cooking, which is a subject of vital importance in an hospital, where punctuality is as essential as quality. Addressing the Doctor, I said, 'Suppose you have fifty or a hundred patients under your direction—according to the disease you vary the diet, and according to the state of the patient you vary the hour of his meal.'

'Of course we do.'

'Then, this defect, simple as it may appear, should be reported and immediately remedied.'

'The only excuse I can find for the rations and diets not being ready at the time required is entirely owing to the bad quality of the charcoal, which, as regards time, would deceive the best of cooks, and is quite sufficient to upset the best of culinary arrangements. However, I will take note of the various things which strike me as being out of order or bad, and this will give me a good chance of effecting an immediate improvement.'

'You are perfectly right,' said Miss Nightingale. 'I assure you that Dumont, my cook, is always complaining of the charcoal, which, as you see, is so full of dust that it will not burn; and some days he cannot manage to cook at all with it.'

'Well, I will endeavour to remedy this great evil.'

'Doctor,' said Miss Nightingale, 'you had better tell Monsieur Soyer to whom he is to apply in this matter.'

'Oh, Mr. Milton or Mr. Tucker will be able to give him the necessary information. We will now visit another.'

About half-way down the long corridor, we found another extra diet kitchen, managed by soldiers; but it was far from being in good order—on the contrary, all was in the greatest confusion. The kitchen was full of smoke, and everything was boiling too fast. In consequence of the bad quality of the charcoal, a wall of bricks had been raised round each stove, and thus wood and charcoal were used *ad libitum*, burning the rice-pudding, and over-doing everything. In fact, everything had the disagreeable flavour of being burnt. As I did not wish to alarm them, I merely remarked that the fire was too fierce; and, on the following morning, I took one of my men with me to teach them how to manage better.

We then visited several other kitchens, all of which were, more or less, in the same state. To this there was, however, a single exception, to which I must do justice by observing, that, though not quite perfect as a model—being short of cooking utensils—still it was clean, and everything we tasted was far superior in flavour. Nothing was burnt, except a slight catch in the rice-pudding; but this was a mere trifle, compared with the way the viands were spoilt in the other places. The beef-tea, chicken-broth, &c., were nicely done, although they all wanted seasoning. At my first visit to the various diet kitchens, I tasted the soups made for the patients, which I found quite free from the slightest suspicions of seasoning, and consequently tasteless. I then asked to have a couple of basins filled with this. To one I added the requisite seasoning, and requested Doctor Cumming to taste of both. The Doctor complied with my request, and could scarcely believe it possible that such an improvement could be effected by so trifling an addition. He then expressed his approval and decided that in future the cook should season the soup, instead of leaving the same to the irregular tastes of the patients.

'Well,' said Doctor Macgregor, 'this is by the doctor's order, you may be sure.'

'I have not the pleasure of knowing that gentlemen, yet, though I admire his kitchen very much, and must admit that he keeps it in good order, I shall certainly tell him when I see him that I do not agree with his method of not seasoning the broths,

&c., while in course of preparation. It is very true they ought not to be too highly seasoned; but it is the province of the cook, as I before said, to season for the patient, and not the patient for the cook. Instead of giving so much salt in the ward, I would allow each patient but little or none at all; because in all cookery it is the combination of good and wholesome ingredients properly blended which constitutes the best of broths or diets; and this rule holds good for the bill of fare of all nations.'

'This seems logical enough,' said the Doctor; 'nor do I approve of the quantity of salt and pepper given in the wards.'

'But, Doctor, there is another evil; some people are more partial to salt than others, and, only a few minutes ago, I saw a patient begging his neighbour to give him a portion of his share.'

'I am aware they do that, Monsieur Soyer.'

'Be kind enough to favour me with the name of the doctor.'

'His name is Dr. Taylor; he will be glad to see you, Monsieur Soyer,' said Miss Nightingale, smiling. 'I can assure you he is a great cook, and manages his own kitchen. He comes down here two or three times every day. He is attending a board this morning, or he would certainly have been here.'

'If that is the case, we shall have no difficulty in understanding each other. I will do myself the pleasure of calling upon him.'

'You will be sure to find him in his office at nine o'clock to-morrow,' said Dr. Macgregor. We then crossed the yard to the general kitchen, as Miss Nightingale called it. Upon entering it, I found, to my surprise, a superb kitchen, built, I believe, by the Turks, and fitted up with twenty copper boilers, set in white marble, holding about fifty gallons each. About sixteen soldier cooks were employed cleaning the boilers, to make the tea, as the men's dinner had just been served.

'This is a magnificent kitchen,' I observed to Miss Nightingale. 'I was not aware there was anything of the kind here.'

'So it is, Monsieur Soyer; but see how badly everything is managed.'

'Well, this can be remedied.'

On going to the top of the marble steps, about eight in number, I perceived that every boiler was made of yellow copper, and screwed to its marble bed. I immediately inquired about the tinning, as I perceived the boilers were much in want of this. Copper is, as I have before remarked, the worst metal which could possibly be employed for hospital uses. I took notes of all, and having inquired of the men how they cooked the patients' dinners, I told them to go on as usual, and that I would be with them at seven the next morning, to put them in the right way. As it was getting late, I was about taking my departure, when Miss Nightingale informed me that there was a similar kitchen on the other side of the yard, and advised me to go and see it.

'Like this one, do you say, Mademoiselle?'

'Yes, exactly like it.'

'You astonish me. Of course I will go directly. I shall, however, be sorry to trouble you to come so far.'

'Oh, no trouble at all, Monsieur Soyer. I am much interested in any improvement or amelioration which may be introduced in so important a department.'

We did, indeed, find just such another kitchen as the last, partitioned off in the centre. 'This one,' said I, 'will be large enough for all that we require.'

'You don't say so,' observed Dr. Macgregor.

'Quite large enough, I can assure you; the only inconvenience is its great distance from the building. However, I shall try and manage somehow. This kitchen is cleaner than the other, and the head man appears more intelligent; still there is a great deal to be done, in order to set the whole to rights.'

'I was certain you would say so,' Miss Nightingale observed.

'Oh, but I am far from despairing. Indeed, I feel confident that I shall succeed. All I require is, that they will go on just as if I had not arrived. I shall come to-morrow at seven o'clock, and watch their proceedings, without removing any one from his post, and have no doubt I shall be able to introduce a much better system.'

After we had examined this kitchen, Miss Nightingale prepared to leave us. I promised to call upon her the following day, to go round the wards, and see the dinners served.

At half-past six the next morning I was in the kitchen. The soldiers were at that hour making the coffee and tea for breakfast. I went with the serjeant on duty to inspect the quality of the meat, the quantity allowed, and the place of distribution. I found the meat of a very inferior quality, the method of distribution too complicated. When the weight of the quantity allowed was explained to me I found it correct. I was at first much puzzled at finding that some patients upon full diet received three quarters of a pound, some half a pound, and some a quarter of a pound of meat, accordingly as they were placed upon full, half, or quarter diet allowance—a system unavoidable in a hospital, but which would deceive the best cook. On some days, in providing for a hundred patients, this could make a difference of from ten to twenty pounds of meat, according to the number of half or quarter diets. Yet the same quantity of soup would nevertheless be required.

I made a note of this, and next perceived that every mess took their meat separately. Some messes numbered fifteen, twenty, or even thirty. The meat was spitted upon a rough piece of wood about two feet long, and then tied as tight as possible with a strong cord. Although this was a very bad method, I did not choose to interfere, as it was important for me to show them the evil effects of their system, and ensure a reform by pointing out a better. We then went to the store-rooms, and looked over what the contractor called the mixed vegetables, though they were principally of one kind, and half of these unfit for use. After having seen the rations weighed, I sent orders to the cooks not to commence operations until I arrived. We examined all kinds of preserved meats, soups, sweetmeats, &c. I next went to see the poultry, which I found of very inferior quality, consisting principally of old fowls, badly plucked and drawn. The gizzards, heads, and feet, which make such good broth, were thrown away. Mr. Bailey, whom I had not yet seen, then entered. When I had explained what we had already done, and the plan it would be most advisable to adopt for the future, he promised to bring the contractor, that we might talk the matter over. I examined the bread, which was very good indeed.

Mr. Bailey accompanied me to the various kitchens, where I had ordered the men to proceed as usual, and the same in the extra diet kitchen. During our progress I had the pleasure of meeting and being introduced to most of the medical gentlemen as they were visiting the patients in the corridors and wards. Having been informed that Mr. Milton, the purveyor in chief, had arrived, I called at his office, but unfortunately he had just gone to some storeroom—no one could tell which. I left my compliments, and a message to say that I should call again. I went to see Dr. Cumming, and report progress, and engaged to let him taste some of my cooking the following day. My next visit was to Lord W. Paulet, whom I found surrounded by military gentlemen of all ranks. He called me in, and, in a most good-natured manner, introduced me to his visitors, saying, 'Now M. Soyer is come, I fear he will feed the sick soldiers so well, that they will be sorry to recover and leave the hospital.'

It was then noon, and about dinner-time. So I returned to the kitchen, where all was in the greatest confusion. Such a noise I never heard before. They were waiting for their soup and meat, and using coarse language, without making the least progress in the distribution. The market at old Billingsgate, during the first morning sale, was nothing compared to this military row. Each man had two tin cans for the soup. They kept running about and knocking against each other, in most admirable disorder. Such confusion, thought I, is enough to kill a dozen patients daily. As a natural consequence, several must go without anything; as, owing to the confusion, some of the orderly waiters get more and others less than their allowance. Any attempt to alter this at the time, would have been as wise as endeavouring to stop the current of the Bosphorus. As I did not wish to lose the chance of seeing the rations served out in the wards, I went for Dr. Macgregor, and we called for Mr. Milton—but the latter had not returned. I then fetched Miss Nightingale, and we went through the wards. The process of serving out the rations, though not quite such a noisy scene as that I had before witnessed, was far from being perfect. In the first place, the patients were allowed to eat the meat before the soup. As I was confident that this could not be by the doctor's order, I asked the reason. The reply was, 'we have only one plate.' (What they called a plate, was a round and deep tin dish, which held a pound of meat and a pint of soup.) I therefore recommended them to cut the meat as usual into small pieces, and pour the pint of boiling soup over it. This method had the advantage of keeping the meat hot.

'It will enable the patients,' I said, 'to eat both the soup and meat warm, instead of cold—the daily practice, in consequence of the slow process of carving.'

'Very true,' said Dr. Macgregor. 'Nay, more, the soup will comfort and dispose the stomach for the better digestion of the meat and potatoes. When the men are very hungry, they will often swallow their food without properly masticating it, and the meat is also probably tough.'

We then tasted both the soup and meat. The former was thin and without seasoning; the latter, mutton, tough and tasteless. The potatoes were watery. All these defects I promised to rectify the next day. We proceeded to a ward where they complained bitterly that the meat was never done; in fact, it was quite raw, and then of course the cook was blamed.

'Now,' said I to Miss Nightingale, 'I will wager anything that we shall find some parts very well done, and some, no doubt, too much done, though it is all cooked in the same caldron.'

'How do you account for that, Monsieur Soyer? is it owing to the bad quality of the meat?'

'Not at all; that may come from the same sheep, and yet vary.'

At another mess, the meat was well done; a small piece at the end only being over-cooked.

'I will explain this to you, madam,' said I. 'I remarked this morning that the man tied all the joints together very tight, after having put them upon a 'skewer,' as he calls it, almost as large as a wooden leg. The consequence is, that when the meat is thrown into boiling water, it is not properly done; the meat swells, and it is impossible for the heat or the water even to get at it.'

'Ah, I noticed that several of the men did exactly as you say this morning,' said Miss Nightingale. 'The parts which are well done were placed loose upon the stick; and this explains the mystery—but I shall alter that to-morrow.'

Having afterwards inspected several extra-diet kitchens, and tasted various things, I perceived what I could accomplish, both as regarded convalescents and extra diets. Miss Nightingale having again offered to render any assistance in her power, left us; as she had a great deal to attend to. I retraced my steps to Dr. Cumming's, and stated my opinion of the present system of cooking; and explained what I proposed doing, of all of which he approved highly. I then returned to the kitchen, and sent a requisition for six rations of everything allowed for making the soup. I proceeded thus:—

To eight pints of water I put four pounds of meat, a quarter of a pound of barley, a little salt and pepper, and the allowance of vegetables, and in about an hour I produced a very good soup—some of which I sent to several doctors. They tasted and praised it highly, as being very nourishing and palatable. I then carried some to Dr. Cumming, who approved of its composition; but expressed his opinion that it would probably be too expensive. I then informed him I had made it with the ration allowance, taking the meat at half-diet scale. He was much pleased with the meat, which he pronounced highly palatable, and thought that the seasoning should be put in with the other ingredients. I explained that I could still improve it by the simple addition of a small quantity of sugar and flour.

'The purveyor will not, I am certain, refuse that,' said he.

'Oh, I am aware of that; but I wish to manage it without increasing the expense. I must accomplish that, if possible.' Miss Nightingale and Dr. Macgregor, to both of whom I sent some, praised it even more than the others had done, particularly the meat, which they stated to be of a very excellent flavour, and they had the opportunity of tasting the former.

I was up at six, and in the kitchen by seven. None of my orders had been attended to. My own people were not there as they ought to have been; and the men told me they could not get the rations till ten o'clock, that being the usual time for issuing them.

'Really,' said I; 'and pray who told you so?'

'The serjeant and some of the orderlies,' was the reply.

'We shall see all about that; come with me.'

The truth is, I did find it very difficult to get anything; but, in less than half-an-hour after I had been to the purveyor's head-quarters my new regiment began to manoeuvre admirably under my command. By eight o'clock everything was ready for the cooking, except my cooks, who had been sleeping in a store-room upon some straw, and had a regular fray with the allied rats. These animals, it appears, had come to welcome them to Scutari.

Upon inspecting the boilers, my first fear was realized—there was nothing but copper—all the tinning had worn away. And very difficult was it to ascertain this fact, these immense and deep caldrons being securely screwed to the marble basement, and extremely difficult, not only to remove, but also to tin when removed. I consider it most advisable that all large establishments should have their cooking apparatus made of malleable iron, which is extremely clean, is much cheaper, and does not require tinning: the lid may be made of copper for appearance's sake, but not so the boiler. The kitchen battery of the wealthy alone should be copper, as they can afford to employ professional persons for the preparation of their diet, who never would attempt using them when coppery. (For my important visit to the Consumptive Hospital at Brompton, see Addenda.)

That day I was obliged to use them. Having put the proper quantity of water into each copper, with the meat, barley, vegetables, and salt and pepper, we lighted the fire; and after allowing the ingredients to simmer for two hours and a half, an excellent soup was made; I only adding a little sugar and flour to finish it.

The receipt for this excellent soup, so highly approved of and immediately adopted by the medical men, will be found in my Hospital Diets, with a scale of proportions from ten to a hundred.

The meat was so poor that there was no fat to skim off the soup. It was therefore served out at once, as described in the receipt. Several doctors went round with me, and asked the men how they liked it. They were all highly delighted with it, and praised it very much. I also took care that the rations of meat should not be tied together on the skewer.

The orderlies were now ordered not to tie their rations of meat so tight. Upon inspection I found that they had a most curious method of marking their different lots. Some used a piece of red cloth cut from an old jacket; others half a dozen old buttons tied together; old knives, forks, scissors, &c., but one in particular had hit upon an idea which could not fail to meet with our entire approval. The discovery of this brilliant idea was greeted with shouts of laughter from Miss Nightingale, the doctors, and myself. It consisted in tying a pair of old snuffers to the lot.

All this rubbish was daily boiled with the meat, but probably required more cooking. On telling the man with the snuffers that it was a very dirty trick to put such things in the soup, the reply was—'How can it be dirty, sir? sure they have been boiling this last month.'

When all the dinners had been served out, I perceived a large copper half full of rich broth with about three inches of fat upon it. I inquired what they did with this?

'Throw it away, sir.'

'Throw it away?' we all exclaimed.

'Yes, sir; it's the water in which the fresh beef has been cooked.'

'Do you call that water? I call it strong broth. Why don't you make soup of it?'

'We orderlies don't like soup, sir.'

'Then you really do throw it away?'

'Yes, sir; it is good for nothing.'

I took a ladle and removed a large basinful of beautiful fat, which, when cold, was better for cooking purposes than the rank butter procured from Constantinople at from ten to fifteen piastres per pound. The next day I showed the men how to make a most delicious soup with what they had before so foolishly thrown away. This method they were henceforward very glad to adopt. Not less than seventy pounds of beef had been daily boiled in this manner, and without salt. It would hardly be credited, but for its truth I can appeal to Miss Nightingale and others who were present.

Nothing was needed but a sharp look-out after the cooks in order to ensure complete success. The day after I had the coppers tinned. The next thing was to have a charcoal stove built, an oven, a store-room, and a larder partitioned off; and a kitchen dresser and chopping-block made. Through the kindness of the Chief Engineer, Captain Gordon, these things were accomplished in a few days, and at a trifling expense. If not a very magnificent, it was, as will be seen, a very spacious and handy kitchen.

In a short time, and without much trouble, I initiated the soldier cooks into my method, and taught the serjeant to see it properly executed. I shall here describe the process fully, as it will be generally useful for hospitals or public institutions. In the first place I drew up two receipts—the one by weight and the other by measure, the former for beef and the latter for mutton soups. Mutton was the principal meat used for patients in a state of convalescence. These receipts I had carefully copied and hung up in the kitchen, at the same time supplying the cooks with weights and scales. I also taught them how to stew the meat well, and to manage the fires so as to prevent over-boiling or burning, as well as to economize the fuel. It was no longer a matter of much difficulty. Every soldier had become a cook; and if in case of any of them being removed to their regiments, one of the initiated, under the direction of the above-mentioned serjeant, who was not changed, soon made a new recruit capable of cooking for any number. So simple was this plan, that it was as easy to cook for thousands as it had before been for hundreds, and to do it to perfection.

Although this was as perfect as possible, a great difficulty still remained, as the number varied daily, some days increasing, others decreasing; and as the whole was cooked by messes, the same caldron was required to cook for two hundred and fifty persons one day, and perhaps for one hundred and seventy the next. This caused great confusion and delay, as well as continual quarrelling, among the cooks and orderlies, the latter complaining of not getting their full share; and if this happened, it was a matter of vital importance to the patient, who was thus deprived of the proper quantity of sustenance ordered by the medical man. In fact, it led to many very serious results. I therefore settled that all the caldrons should be filled every day; and as each boiler would cook for one hundred and fifty, in one only was it necessary that the quantity should vary. As it was most probable that this one would vary daily, I made a supplementary scale for it, from five diets to one hundred, leaving only a few pounds to be guessed. If any mistake occurred, it could be of no material consequence. I also had tinned iron skewers made, with numbers to each, to prevent the meat being mixed in the boilers, as expedition, cleanliness, and proportion should be the motto of all such establishments. This plan was followed to the last.

Just as I had set everybody to work in the various hospitals, and my Scutari kitchen was nearly finished, an entirely new plan suggested itself to my mind. It was as follows:— Instead of commencing with a hundred patients at a time, as I had at first intended, I changed my mind, and preferred making a grand opening, resolving to invite all the heads of the medical department in the various hospitals, as well as some of the most eminent among the French and Turkish medical staff. This, I was aware, was a cold experiment; for had I failed—and many unforeseen events might have caused such a result—my reputation would have suffered. I was, therefore, well aware that I was risking the labour of twenty years against an uncertainty; as all those I was about to invite would come to watch my proceedings with the eyes of Argus, and would judge of my plans accordingly. At all events, my sample trials had already given great satisfaction to two eminent doctors. In pursuance of this plan, I went to Lord William Paulet, explained it, and begged him to send, or cause to be sent, invitations to all the principal officers to honour me with their presence upon the occasion, which his lordship kindly promised to do. I also apprised the doctor-in-chief, who promised to attend himself, and invite the principal medical gentlemen to do the same.

The opening day was fixed for the following Monday—it was then Tuesday—leaving me till Thursday to finish my preparations. On the Friday morning, after having inspected several kitchens, and gone through a number of wards, I was suddenly taken ill. I seemed to have forgotten everything, and experienced at the same time a sensation of brain fever. There were, however, none of its symptoms. Although I was quite conscious of what I had to do, I was entirely incapable of doing it, or of ordering anything or directing any one. In fact, I began to fear that all my former endeavours would prove useless, and the opening of my kitchen be a marked failure. The day appointed by Lord Paulet could not easily be changed, and such a course would have caused the success of my project to be doubted. Though I had a couple of assistants, neither of them could carry it out for me, as they did not know my plans. This sudden indisposition I only mentioned to my people and to Doctor Macgregor, who told me to keep quiet, and gave me some soothing medicine. It was Sunday afternoon before my head was clear, and, after a good night's rest, I felt myself again, and quite able to open my kitchen on the day appointed.

The doctor attributed this mental disorder to the effect produced by the immense number of sick and wounded I was in the habit of seeing daily, and the numerous dead bodies passing before the windows to be buried. I had also witnessed several cases of autopsy and some operations. 'This,' he said, 'with the constant worry of business, has unnerved you to that extent, that had you unfortunately taken the fever, you would perhaps never have recovered your senses.' However, thanks to a kind Providence, I was able to open my kitchen at the appointed time. It met with perfect success, and the entire approbation of all the medical gentlemen and visitors present. They all expressed themselves highly gratified, and declared that the various samples of diets I then submitted for their opinion were much preferable to those produced under the old system, besides having the merit of being concocted with the same ration allowance.

The plan I adopted was this:— my samples of diets and extra diets being prepared, I arranged the basins containing the different diets on the table, and in juxtaposition I placed those prepared by the soldiers, affixing a number to each, to enable the people present to make a comparison. All was ready by eleven o'clock, and one being the time appointed for the arrival of the visitors, I fetched Doctor Cumming, and requested him to taste the several samples, and give me his candid opinion; observing that everything was made from the usual allowance, and cost about the same, or even less, when made in large quantities.

No. 1, was beef-tea. Tasting my sample first, Doctor Cumming pronounced it good; the other, without taste or flavour. No. 1 was adopted.

Then followed chicken-broth, mutton-broth, beef-soup, rice-water, barley-water, arrowroot-water, ditto with wine, sago with port, calves'-foot jelly, &c. Everything was found superior, and so highly commended by the doctor-in-chief, I no longer had any doubt of success, nor of the general approval of all the faculty. I promised to lay the recipes for my new diets before the doctor the next day, and he retired.

About half-past twelve, the kitchen was crowded to excess with military and medical men. Lord William Paulet entered, followed by his staff, and accompanied by Mr. Milton, Mr. and Mrs. Bracebridge, &c. They were much pleased with the cleanly appearance of the kitchen, and equally surprised at the alteration which it had undergone in so short a time. I then showed his lordship round, carefully pointing out to him the simple but useful alterations I had effected; and requested him to taste the various samples, compare the one with the other, and give his candid opinion thereupon. Having done this, Lord W. Paulet expressed his high satisfaction, and to confirm it, while in the kitchen, wrote the following letter:—

THE SELECTED SOYER

Lord William Paulet to Monsieur Soyer.
It is with great pleasure that I state I have carefully viewed and tasted the new diets introduced by Monsieur Soyer in the hospitals this day; and had I not seen and tasted them, I could not have believed that such an amelioration could have been produced from the same materials as allowed by Government.   W. Paulet.

Above a hundred officials from the various hospitals were present, and many of the Sisters of Mercy. Not one person had anything to say in disapproval; but, on the contrary, praised everything. This was sufficient to stamp it with success. The only thing I regretted was, that—owing to the rough state of the Bosphorus that day— Lady Stratford de Redcliffe, as well as a number of military men and medical officers from the French and Turkish hospitals, were not present. However, they visited my kitchen some days after, and having inspected everything, added their testimonials of approbation to those I had already received. They were particularly struck with the cleanliness and order in a place where so much was done daily.

The day after the opening, I proposed to Doctors Cumming and Macgregor, the superintendent, to take one wing of the hospital, and supply these with all which they might require. This I did with the greatest ease, and without the least confusion, much to the satisfaction of the patients. I continued to do this for three days, and then took half of the hospital in hand. As I wished fully to impress the patients with the superiority of my newly-adopted diets, I then took the other half in hand, and put the first back to the old *régime*, for a day or two, as I was not quite prepared to undertake the whole at once. The patients immediately became dissatisfied, so I was obliged to go with Dr. Macgregor to them and explain the reason of the sudden change, which was only momentary, three cheers from my numerous guests closing my laconic, though effective, speech.

On May 2nd, Soyer, Miss Nightingale and others sailed for the Crimea itself. On board, he met a travelling gentleman called Peter Morrison (known as P.M. hereafter), whose professed bravery and actual cowardice caused great amusement on the trip. At Balaklava, Soyer proceeded to visit the hospital.

We went to the kitchens, which we found were built of mud, exposed to the open air, unroofed, and burning much fuel. I immediately fixed upon a spot to build a kitchen, and sketched a plan, which I submitted to the doctor and Miss Nightingale, who had then joined us. We also visited those mud mounts called cook-houses, looked over the provision stores, and departed. Miss Nightingale, Dr. Henderson, and yself, returned together by the same road, Miss Nightingale intending to visit an officer patient who was at the doctor's house. Mr. Bracebridge being on horseback, was compelled to take another road. On reaching the doctor's house, Miss Nightingale was introduced to the patient, who was suffering from a very severe attack of typhus fever. I stayed in the front room, making my sketch for the new hospital kitchens. At length Miss Nightingale retired, after giving words of consolation to the patient, and promising the doctor to send a nurse who would set him to rights.

As we were returning to the vessel, I could not help remarking that Miss Nightingale seemed much fatigued; upon which she replied, 'I do feel rather tired, those roads are so bad.' I inquired about the patient she had visited.

'The poor young man,' said she, 'is very ill. I very much fear for his life.' She then stated what a bad attack of fever it was. Upon this, I remarked, that it was very imprudent of her to remain so long near him.

'Oh, Monsieur Soyer, I am used to that.'

'Very true, Mademoiselle, but then it is in large airy wards, and not in small rooms, like the one you have just left.'

'I must say that I have been very fortunate through my Scutari campaign, and I hope to be as fortunate in the Crimea.'

'I hope so too, but would recommend you to be careful of your health, as I am sure the army cannot spare you.'

By this time we were near the *Robert Lowe*—a boat was ready to take us on board, and Mr. Bracebridge was anxiously waiting our arrival, to inform Miss Nightingale that Lord Raglan had been on board, and also to the General Hospital, in order to see her, and was very much disappointed at not having had that pleasure. It was arranged that we should visit the camp next day, and that I should go and deliver my official letter, and present my humble duty to Lord Raglan. Miss Nightingale decided upon taking that opportunity of returning his lordship's visit. Doctor Sutherland and Mr. Anderson, of the Sanitary Commission, who happened to be on board, arranged about the horses, and the time of our departure the next morning.

At nine, we were all on shore and mounted. There were about eight of us ready to escort our heroine to the seat of war. Miss Nightingale was attired simply in a genteel amazone, or riding-habit, and had quite a martial air. She was mounted upon a very pretty mare, of a golden colour, which, by its gambols and caracoling, seemed proud to carry its noble charge. The weather was very fine. Our cavalcade of all nations assembled at Balaklava, who were astonished at seeing a lady so well escorted. It was not so, however, with those who knew who the lady was.

On the road to head-quarters, we met several officers whom I had the pleasure of knowing in England. All made inquiries respecting the lady in our party. As I knew that Miss Nightingale wished to preserve her incognito as much as possible, and especially in the camp, I referred them to Mr. Bracebridge. At that time the number of the fair sex in the Crimea numbered four, always excepting the Sisters of Mercy, who were never seen out.

It took us about half-an-hour to go from the Col of Balaklava to Kadikoi (about a mile distant), having to fight our way through a dense crowd of Greeks, Armenians, Jews, Maltese, &c.—hundreds of mules, horses, donkeys, artillery waggons, cannon, shot and shell, oxen and horses kicking each other, waggons upset in deep mud-holes, infantry and cavalry passing and repassing. The road was execrable, and not nearly wide enough for the immense amount of traffic. Amidst this Babel of tongues and deafening noise, we were obliged to speak at the top of our voices in order to make ourselves heard. Our horses, by way of enjoying the fun, kept prancing and kicking in all directions, particularly our fair lady's palfrey, which could not be kept quiet. Many females would have felt very nervous in such a position; but Miss Nightingale appeared to rise above such weakness, and even, on the contrary, to take considerable interest in this her first introduction to the turmoils of war. We at length emerged from the crowd, without having sustained much damage. One of our cavaliers had part of his mackintosh carried away by a log of wood that projected from the back of a mule, and P.M. lost a strap, which nearly unseated him. His mule kept kicking and prancing about, which, one is constrained to confess, is not over pleasant, especially in a crowd—and such a crowd. As we were at last out of danger, we could not help laughing at the misfortunes of our friends. Such was our début on the soil of the seat of war.

Our first visit was to the hospital at Kadikoi, in a small Greek church at the end of the village. Upon our arrival, we were informed that the doctor was not in, so we promised to call again. We then galloped to the top of a high hill on the left, on which we could not help making a halt, as we were quite struck by the grandeur and novelty of the scene. We could plainly distinguish everything for five miles around us. The camps, with their myriads of white tents, appeared like large beds of mushrooms growing at random. The sound of trumpets, the beating of drums, the roar of cannon from Sebastopol, made a fearful noise, whilst military manœuvres, and sentries placed in every direction, gave a most martial aspect to the landscape, backed by the bold and rugged range of mountains by which Balaklava is surrounded.

Having gazed for some time, highly delighted with the scene, so novel to us, we proceeded on our journey. As Miss Nightingale wished to see one of the small regimental hospitals, Doctor Sutherland recommended us to visit that of the 11th Hussars. We were received by the doctor, who very kindly showed us over. Miss Nightingale and myself inspected the kitchen, which, though far from being comfortable or convenient, was, at all events, very ingeniously contrived. Having made my notes, we called at two other regiments, and afterwards proceeded direct to head-quarters. Mr. Bracebridge and myself at once rode to Lord Raglan's house, the front of which was crowded with staff officers and gentlemen on horseback. On asking whether his lordship was within, we were answered in the negative, and were informed that he would probably not return before dinner-time. I then inquired for Colonel Steele, his lordship's secretary, for whom I also had a letter. That gentleman received us cordially, and having read Lord Panmure's letter, promised to give me his utmost support. Mr. Bracebridge stated he had come to thank Lord Raglan in Miss Nightingale's name, for his kind visit of the day before. I next inquired when I could see Lord Raglan. Colonel Steel replied, 'When you like, Monsieur Soyer, but for a day or two he will be very much engaged, as he is preparing for the reception of the Sardinian army, which is shortly expected. Lord Raglan is aware of your arrival, and I will give orders for anything you may require in order to enable you to commence operations.'

After having conversed with several officers whom I knew, I was about to retire, when Colonel Steele said that he would write a note that afternoon to the Chief Engineer, ordering him to send me some carpenters, and give me all the assistance I might require. I thanked the colonel, and retired.

A short time after, Mr. Bracebridge came and informed me that Miss Nightingale wished to speak with me. Having passed a close review, I was about returning to our party, when I met Miss Nightingale coming towards this gipsy cooking encampment, in which there was considerably too much to do for so important an establishment. We promised to call next day, or the one following, to see Doctors Taylor and Mouatt, and retired through a long row of huts. Some of the men had found out that it was 'the good lady of Scutari,' as they called her; for Miss Nightingale was then but little known by name, it being her first visit to the Crimea. I heard afterwards, that some of them had been patients at the Scutari Hospital, and had experienced the full benefit of that benevolent lady's kind care and attention. A great number were waiting at the doors—sick and convalescent—and gave her three hearty cheers as we passed, followed by three times three. Miss Nightingale seemed much affected by so unexpected a reception, and, being on horseback, could only bow gracefully to them by way of returning thanks. Her horse being very restless, in consequence of the shouts of such a number of men, Mr. Anderson dismounted, and taking Miss Nightingale's nag by the bridle, led it gently along.

We then proceeded through the English and French camps, which, for miles, surrounded the doomed Sebastopol. The scene, though more extensive, was not nearly so picturesque as when beheld from the top of the hill at Balaklava. The afternoon was then drawing on, and Dr. Sutherland advised us to go home, as it was a very difficult matter for one to find the way in the dark through the camp; but Mr. Anderson proposed to have a peep at Sebastopol. It was four o'clock, and they were firing sharply on both sides. Miss Nightingale, to whom the offer was made, immediately accepted it; so we formed a column, and, for the first time, fearlessly faced the enemy, and prepared to go under fire. P.M. turned round to me, saying quietly, but with great trepidation—

'I say, Monsieur Soyer, of course you would not take Miss Nightingale where there will be any danger.'

We soon after reached the flag-staff at the head of the Woronzoff Road, and the sentry informed us we must dismount, as we were in danger, at the same time pointing to the marks of a number of cannon balls and splinters of shell, which, he said, they sent whenever they saw a group of people, especially on horseback. He added that they would send a shot or a shell in a moment. Fortunately, P.M. did not hear this, or we should have lost his agreeable company. I mentioned this to Miss Nightingale and to Mr. Bracebridge, who both laughed heartily.

We then dismounted. The sentry begged of us to go into a kind of redoubt, built of stone, where there was a telescope. 'There,' said he, 'you will be in safety, and have a good view of the town.'

This was true enough; the day being clear, and the sun pouring its rays on the city, we could plainly discern the large buildings, Greek temple, church, club-house, hospital, barracks, the harbour of Sebastopol, and the fortifications—viz., the Malakoff, Redan, Quarantine, Fort Constantine, and the Flagstaff batteries—and could see every shot sent by the allied armies as well as by the enemy. The bursting of shells could easily be distinguished. We were about to retire, when Mr. Anderson proposed going a couple of hundred yards further—to the Three-mortar Battery. Miss Nightingale immediately seconded the proposal, but the sentry strongly objected, saying it was too dangerous; that only a few days before those mortars had poured a very heavy fire into the city, and that the Russians kept a good look-out upon them.

'Oh, never mind,' said Mr. Anderson; 'I was there two days ago, and they have no powder to waste upon a few individuals.'

Although I was very anxious to get so far, and to go with them, I could not help observing to Miss Nightingale that there was a picket in the Woronzoff Road, to indicate the limits, and it was very imprudent of her to run such a risk for no purpose. I further remarked that, should any accident happen to her, no one would pity, but, on the contrary, blame her—that all the good she had done would fall into oblivion, and she would scarcely be regretted.

The sentry then repeated his caution, saying, 'Madam, even where you stand you are in great danger; some of the shot reach more than half a mile beyond this.' Mr. Bracebridge, though of my opinion, did not say much to dissuade her. The sentry then said, 'Well, madam, if you do not fear risking your life, I cannot prevent your going; but remember that, if anything happens, I have witnesses to prove that it was not through my neglect in not informing you of the danger you incur by going to the Three-mortar Battery.'

'My good young man,' replied Miss Nightingale, in French, 'more dead and wounded have passed through my hands than I hope you will ever see in the battle-field during the whole of your military career; believe me, I have no fear of death.' She then started with Mr. Anderson, who was very impatient at so much time being lost. Mr. Bracebridge and myself followed. P.M. was still in the redoubt, ensconced behind a gabion, looking through the telescope, when I suddenly called him. He came running out, as I had taken him by surprise, and he exclaimed, 'I say, where the deuce are you all going!'

'Oh, not far—only to the second trench.'

'But, my dear sir, there is a great deal of danger.' Taking him by the arm, Mr. Bracebridge and myself commenced talking upon indifferent topics, and so got him to advance. As he saw Miss Nightingale before us, he managed to raise courage enough to keep from running away, while the cannonading and bursting of shells was heard plainer, and could be seen much better. He again said, 'why should we go to the trenches? This is very rash to risk one's life for nothing; it is what I call giving a chance away.'

To comfort him, I called Mr. Bracebridge and Miss Nightingale. 'P.M.,' said I, 'seems to fancy there is some danger in the trenches, and I wish to impress upon his mind that there is much less danger there than where we are,' when a shell came whistling over our heads, and Mr. Anderson hearing it, cried out, 'A shell! a shell!' upon which P.M. immediately caught me by the shoulders with both hands, and placed himself in a crouching position behind me, which made us all laugh heartily at his expense, as the shell was not directed anywhere near us. I have frequently laughed since with Miss Nightingale at his idea that if the shell had struck me, he would have been any safer than if he had stood by himself.

At all events, we arrived in the Three-mortar Battery without accident. It contained three large mortars, and instead of being two hundred yards, as Mr. Anderson had called the distance, was full half a mile from the Flagstaff, going towards Sebastopol, and quite exposed to fire, had they thought it worth while to play upon us. We had, however, an excellent view of the besieged city, such as very few amateurs can boast of having obtained. Before leaving the battery, I begged Miss Nightingale, as a favour, to give me her hand, which she did.

As the *Robert Lowe*, Soyer's former vessel, was sailing from the harbour, he was given a berth on board another ship.

A quarter to eleven had struck when I made my first appearance on board the *London*. All had turned in and were asleep, and the lights were out in the chief cabin. The night watch showed me my berth, which I could feel, but not see; so I crept into it half undressed, the best way I could, and in a few minutes, from the fatigues of the day, I fell into a deep slumber. This lasted for several hours; and I was at last aroused by several persevering rats, who tried, at the risk of their lives, to pull a piece of Sardinian biscuit out of my great-coat pocket. This I had obtained on board the *Carlo Alberto* as a sample.

The presence of such unwelcome visitors made me spring quickly out of my slice of a bed, which is very judiciously called cabin-berth; and, as I found it too small for one, I had a great objection to extra lodgers. I therefore stood upon the offensive and the defensive, which caused my assailants to flee in the greatest confusion, and with such celerity that I was unable to make any of them prisoners. Relying upon the effects of their defeat, fatigue enticed me to try another dose of sleep, when all at once, with the perseverance of Zouaves, the rats returned to the assault, and running over my face, made me capitulate immediately, and leave them in possession of my nautical bedchamber. I spent the remainder of the night uncomfortably enough upon the narrow cabin benches, falling now and then on the floor by way of variation. The light at last began to peep through the cabin windows, and I could look after my garments, which I at once rescued from the teeth of my enemies, the Zouave rats. Not a morsel of the biscuit was left; they had gnawed two large holes in a new great-coat, no doubt to save the buttons, which they had not swallowed, but very nearly nibbled off. When I was dressed, I rushed upon deck, and began to breathe freely. The sun shone, and the morning gave promise of a fine day. At eight we had breakfast, and I related my night's sport to the captain, Mr. Bracebridge, and others. Everyone laughed heartily at my tribulation, which was poor consolation for such a victim as I had been.

A different cabin to the one I had occupied the night before was allotted to me. All the rat-holes had been stopped, and by special favour I was allowed a night-lamp. I had the pleasure of seeing the rats run about, which afforded me the opportunity of hunting them at my ease. I then perceived that several escaped through the bull's-eye, which I immediately closed, and so captured three. I then commenced killing them with a stick, and in so doing made noise enough to arouse everybody. Some of the crew came to see what was the matter, while the Captain, who was half asleep, and rather deaf, told the mate to send for the police and turn the drunken man out.

Having explained to the first mate the cause of my nocturnal disturbance, he told me that they were sure to come in at the bull's-eye, if left open, that being the easiest way for them when in harbour. 'And,' said he, 'they travel that way from one ship to another in bands of ten or twenty at a time.' He then showed me how to close and fasten the bull's-eye, after which he retired to his berth. All at once, one of the brutes, which had remained concealed, in attempting to escape upset the lamp upon the floor and extinguished it, and thus compelled me for the second time to seek to repose upon the hard and unsophisticated cabin bench, when the Captain made his appearance rather in a state of *négligé*, holding a rushlight in one hand and a sword in the other, with a nightcap tied round with a red riband upon his head. In great anxiety, he inquired what the row was about.

'The row, Captain,' said I, 'is nothing. It's only the bull's-eye in my cabin, which being half open, the rats have got in again.'

'What do you say, Monsieur Soyer?'

'Nothing,' again I shouted.

'Call that nothing? I never had such a row in my ship before. Bless my soul,' said he, 'what a nuisance those rats are! They make quite as free in my cabin; but, being used to it, I do not care so much about them. The worst of it is that we can never keep a bit of cheese or a candle; they eat them up as fast as I buy them.'

'It is certainly very provoking, Captain; but why not try and catch them?'

'Oh, bless you, we have tried everything—poison, traps, broken glass. We caught a few, but I would give the world to have them all caught.'

'I can give you a receipt which will enable you to have them almost all caught in a few days.'

'The deuce you could!' said he, coming and sitting opposite to me. 'Tell me how it is done—I shall be so much obliged to you; but I must go and put something on first, I am so cold.' As he said this, I perceived that the skylight over his head was open.

'Oh, never mind that; it won't take two minutes to tell you—listen to me.'

'So I will,' he said.

'The place where you keep your cheese would be the very spot to make the trial. The thing is quite easy. Have your cheese and candles removed.'

'So I will; but I wish you would let me put a coat on—I am getting so very cold.'

'Never mind about that; I shall not keep you a minute—listen to me.'

'So I will.'

'When the cabin is perfectly empty, have it cleaned and well scrubbed.'

'That will be done.'

'When it is dry, take half a pound of good Cheshire cheese, scrape it fine, and mix it with about two pounds of rough bread-crumbs.'

'Yes, I will.'

'Perhaps you think it is a pity to give them half a pound of good cheese.'

'Not at all, because the vermin eat pounds of it daily.'

'Mix both well together.'

'Yes, I understand—and make them into balls.'

'No, not at all—only spread the lot upon the floor, leave the door and window open, and go to bed. Of course they will come and eat.'

'I should say they would,' he observed.

'The next evening do the same, cutting the cheese a trifle larger. They will come again and eat it.'

'What next?' said he.

'The third night, leave the doors and windows open; go to bed as usual, and put nothing at all in the cabin.'

'What then?' he asked again, in a state of anxiety.

'Why, of course, when they come and find nothing to eat, and being in still greater numbers than the two previous nights, they will be all caught.'

'How,' said he, 'will they be all caught?'

'Why, of course, finding nothing to eat, they will be all taken in.'

'That bed—d! I have made a nice fool of myself, standing here half naked to listen to such rubbish as that.'

Having said this, he ran into his cabin, and for a long while I heard him sneezing and muttering to himself. The word 'fool' was all that I could catch; and soon after all was silent till daybreak.

In the days that followed, Soyer made himself known to the authorities, notably Lord Raglan.

Recollecting that I had not called upon Lord Raglan's *chef de cuisine*, I mentioned the circumstance to Dr. Hadley, stating how much I wished to do so, but that I had no horse. Dr. Hadley very kindly offered me his pony, a fine grey, smartly caparisoned, which I at once accepted. When I had mounted, Dr. Hadley said—'Soyer, if you fall off, mind and get up again; for,' said he, 'joking apart, though the pony is very quiet, recollect the road to Balaklava is a queer one, therefore take care of yourself. We should not mind so much if we had done with you; but as we really require your services, for our own sakes take care of yourself.'

'I will do so,' said I, laughing, 'were it only for the sake of your pony, which might get loose if I were to fall off, and you might not recover him again.'

'Never mind the pony,' said he: 'you may lose him; but, whatever you do, don't lose the saddle. We had better have a bit of supper on your return this evening, off that Yorkshire ham—you can cook it on your bivouac stove.'

'So we will, Doctor. I shall be back at six.'

'Don't stay in the camp after dark; I can assure you it is a very dangerous place. Robberies and murders are of frequent occurrence, though we hear but little about them. We have no police, and no newspapers are published here, so we know nothing about what passes in our own circle.'

'You are perfectly right, Doctor; though I am not afraid, as I never travel without a revolver; yet it is best to be upon the safe side.'

Having fixed upon six o'clock for my return, and seven for supper, I started. There were about twenty convalescents outside the wards, enjoying the warmth of the sun's rays. They were all in high glee at hearing our dialogue, which seemed to revive them from a state of lethargy to the consciousness of life.

The ride from the top of the Genoese heights to Balaklava harbour, by a new road, through mud, over rocks, rivulets, &c., and mounted upon a strange nag, was anything but pleasant to my feelings as a horseman. At all events, after numerous slippery evolutions of the part of my new charger, I found myself safe at the bottom of the ravine; but here another difficulty presented itself. The quay of the harbour was encumbered with French and Sardinian waggons, mules, and horses. The French, who had a wine depôt there for the troops, were strongly fortified with about a hundred pipes of wine, instead of gabions. So crowded was the road from the immense traffic and the unloading of shipping stores, that it took me nearly half-an-hour to ride a few hundred yards. This brought me as far as the Commissariat, where I had to call upon Commissary Filder. I found that he had just returned from head-quarters. We had about ten minutes' conversation upon business.

Having the best part of the day before me, I set off at a gallop towards head-quarters, intending to keep the promise I had made Lord Raglan respecting his dilapidated culinary department, and also to make the acquaintance of M. Armand, his *chef de cuisine*. As I was not well acquainted with the road across the country, I made up my mind to follow the high one which passes close to head-quarters. When about half-way, I perceived a group of officers standing by the road-side round a kind of tent much like a gipsy tent, but considerably larger. This excited my interest, and I was riding towards it, when, to my astonishment, several voices called out—'Soyer! Soyer! come here—come this way!' I readily complied with the invitation, and found two or three gentlemen whom I had the pleasure of knowing. During our conversation, an old dame of a jovial appearance, but a few shades darker than the white lily, issued from the tent, bawling out, in order to make her voice heard above the noise, 'Who is my new son?' to which one of the officers replied, 'Monsieur Soyer, to be sure; don't you know him?'

'God bless me, my son, are you Monsieur Soyer of whom I heard so much in Jamaica? Well, to be sure! I have sold many and many a score of your Relish and other sauces—God knows how many.'

'My dear lady,' said I, 'don't blame me for that; I assure you I am not at all offended with you for so doing, and shall allow you to sell as much more in the Crimea.'

'So I would if I could only get them. Bless me, I had a gross about ten days ago, and they are all gone; nor can I get any more for another month perhaps. Come down, my son, and take a glass of champagne with my old friend, Sir John Campbell.'

I immediately alighted, and Sir John came towards me and shook me heartily by the hand, saying, 'Welcome to the seat of war, Monsieur Soyer!'

'Many thanks, general, for your kind wishes. I had the pleasure of leaving my card at Cathcart's Hill the other day.'

'You did; and I was very sorry that I was out when you called; but mind, you must come and dine with me some day.'

'Thank you, general, I shall do myself the honour.'

'Now, Mrs. Seacole, give us another bottle of champagne.'

'Mrs. Seacole,' I exclaimed; 'is that lady the celebrated Mrs. Seacole?'

'Of course,' said the general.

She then came forth from her bivouac cellar, with two bottles in her hands, exclaiming, 'I shall stand mine, and no mistake.'

We all declared it would never do for a lady to stand treat in the Crimea.

'Lord bless you, Monsieur Soyer,' said the lady, 'don't you know me?'

'Yes, I do now, my dear madam.'

'Well, all those fine fellows you see here are my Jamaica sons—are you not?' said she, opening the champagne, and addressing the general.

'We are, Mrs. Seacole, and a very good mother you have been to us.'

'I have known you, general, for many years.'

'Well, here's a health to all.'

We emptied our glasses, and returned the compliment. The general then left, again expressing his desire to see me at Cathcart's Hill.

'Walk inside, walk inside, my sons; you will be better there—it is not so hot. Go in, Monsieur Soyer.'

No sooner had we entered than the old lady expressed her desire to consult me about what she should do to make money in her new speculation, in which she had embarked a large capital, pointing to two iron houses in course of construction on the other side of the road. She told me that her intention was to have beds there for visitors, which I persuaded her not to do, saying, 'All the visitors—and they are few in number—sleep on board the vessels in the harbour, and the officers under canvass in the camp. Lay in a good stock of hams, wines, spirits, ale and porter, sauces, pickles, and a few preserves and dry vegetables—in short, anything which will not spoil by keeping.'

'Yes,' said she, 'I mean to have all that.'

'In that case you will no doubt make money, as you are so well known to all the army.'

'I assure you, the last time Lord Raglan passed here, he spoke to me for more than ten minutes, and promised to do all he could for me.'

'That's right,' we all said.

'I know Miss Nightingale too. She was very kind to me when I passed through Scutari, on my way here; she gave me lodging and everything I required, in the hospital.'

'We passed this way a few days before Miss Nightingale was taken ill,' said I.

'I know you did; and I am sure, if the lady had known I was here, she would have called to see me. Thank God, I hear she is quite out of danger.'

'Yes, she is improving.'

'When you see her, present my best respects, and tell the dear lady that I shall go and see her.'

'I will, Mrs. Seacole. Good-bye.'

'Good-bye, my son.'

On getting up in a hurry to be off, I missed my horse, and found one of the officers' chargers, which had been left in charge of the same man to whom I had given mine, led by a Zouave. Upon inquiring of the Zouave where the man had gone, he informed me that he did not know, but that he had given him a shilling (which he showed me) to hold this animal for, as far as he could understand, about an hour, while he went on the grey in the direction of head-quarters. I called Mrs. Seacole out, and told her what had happened. She stepped up to the Zouave, and he began talking so fast, that I shall not forget the expression he made as long as I live. His speech may be thus translated: 'By the name of Jupiter! I have neither stolen nor sold your horse. Look at me! (showing his corporation.) If you like, captain, to lend me this quadruped, I will soon find the voyiou (meaning a low rascal). There is my name and the number of my regiment. We are encamped near the French head-quarters.'

All this time Mrs. Seacole had been looking about, and every grey pony she saw far or near was mine—at least in her eyes. The two officers mounted their horses, and went one one way and the other another, but soon returned, having found nothing. Having sent in all directions without being able to obtain any trace of the pony, we concluded that the animal was lost. I take this opportunity of publicly thanking those two gentlemen for the vivid interest they took in trying to find the borrowed steed. I very much regret that I do not recollect their names. They will no doubt remember the circumstance if this little works falls into their hands.

All our efforts to find the pony being useless, I made up my mind to walk back to Balakavla. Just as I was thanking Mrs. Seacole for her extraordinary exertions, Mr. Day, her partner, came in, and he advised me to go at once to the *Hue and Cry*, at head-quarters.

'How am I to do this?' I asked.

'Take my pony. It is not twenty minutes' ride from hence; and you will stand a good chance of getting it back, especially if the man who held it was an Englishman. He is sure to be found in the English camp.'

Thanking him for his kindness, I mounted, and started full gallop for head-quarters. I made inquiries at the Post-office, where I had the pleasure of meeting Mr. Russell, who introduced me to Mr. Angel, the postmaster. I then inquired for the *Hue and Cry*, and related the circumstances under which I had lost my pony. All seemed highly amused. They laughed heartily at my expense, and I could not help joining in the merriment. Mr. Angel invited me to dine with him, having a few friends that evening to join his popotte.

'I am much obliged, my dear sir; but I am staying at Balaklava, and I suppose you dine late.'

'About six o'clock,' replied Mr. Angel. 'You can sleep here. We have no bed, it's true; but I can lend you a blanket; and there is a small hut, which is empty, you can have all to yourself. Mr. Bracebridge slept there the night before last, when on a visit to Captain Boucher, a friend of his.'

'Oh, as far as that goes, I shall be comfortable enough.'

'Then you will dine with me?'

'I will,' said I, 'and am much obliged for your kind invitation.'

I thought by accepting it, I should have an excellent opportunity of looking out for my pony in the morning, if I did not happen to find it that night; I therefore went to the *Hue and Cry*, and gave the best description, to my knowledge, as I had not had the honour of this acquaintance long, and did not know of any private marks by which he might be recognised. They gave me but faint hopes of seeing it again, and by way of comforting me, showed me a long list of missing horses, mules, and ponies, enough to fill half a column of the *Times*.

'I don't care so much about the pony, as that can be replaced: but the saddle is a new one from London, and neither the animal or the saddle belong to me.'

'You may, perhaps,' said one, 'find the horse, but not the saddle, especially if it is gone to the French camp, for, believe me, the Zouaves are very fond of English saddles, as well as everything they can get hold of which does not require feeding; so they will probably keep the saddle and turn the horse loose. At all events, we will do what we can for you; but I advise you to look out for yourself.'

It was then about four o'clock, and I had an hour's ride about the camp, but it was all in vain. Every inquiry proved fruitless; and I could not obtain the slightest clue to the lost pony. I could not help smiling when I recollected Dr. Hadley's last words, 'You may lose the horse but don't lose the saddle.' Hoping for better luck next day, I returned to head-quarters, and begged Lord Raglan's groom to give Mr. Day's pony a night's lodging. Making sure Monsieur Armand would be in, I went to see him. He was rather busy, but he received me very politely, and showed me what he called his kitchen, though it had not the slightest claim to the title, as it was all but destitute of culinary utensils. The provisions were of inferior quality; but, as he told me, the best he could procure. I then offered my services if I could be of any use in getting stoves or a small oven erected.

'Ever since I have been here,' he replied, 'I have been asking for one or two charcoal stoves and a few shelves, but not a thing can I obtain for love or money.'

'Upon my word you surprise me! How can that be in the house of the Commander-in-chief? Truly, every one has much to do.'

'Such is the case.'

'Never mind; I think I shall be able to get something done for you, as his lordship has spoken to me upon the subject.'

'I shall be much obliged to you if you will,' said he; and then pointed out the principal things he required, which were soon afterwards furnished.

As it was nearly six o'clock, I left him, and returned to the Post-office, where a sumptuous table was laid out. There was actually a tablecloth and real plates, knives, forks, and various kinds of glasses. In fact, for the Crimea, it was as the French say, *épatant*. We sat down six to dinner; and had some very strong preserved soup, a very nice tough fowl—the remainder of the bill of fare was made from the ration meat. We had very good wine; and, perhaps, never was a dinner better relished, or accompanied with more mirth and jokes. Russell the great was the hero, besides having an Angel for the host. Towards eight o'clock, the party amounted to about fifteen, as far as we could discern through the clouded atmosphere with which the room was filled. Every one was smoking; some large chibouques, long and short pipes, a few cigars, but no cigarettes. The unexpected increase to our party, I must observe, was partly owing to our vocal abilities, several lively choruses having attracted Mr. Angel's illustrious neighbours, as the denizens of the woods were allured by the melody of Orpheus.

Our mirth at last became so boisterous that it not only brought around us men of all ranks, but attracted the attention of the Commander-in-chief, who sent to inquire what the noise was about. This we considered a rather inharmonious inquiry, but found that, by decreasing the pitch of our vocal organs from allegro to piano, we should produce as much effect, with less noise, as his lordship wisely called it; though I heard the next day, that Lord Raglan, who was sitting at his door enjoying the fresh air with several gentlemen of his staff, enjoyed it, and gave orders that we should not be disturbed. Complaints poured in from the numerous tents which surrounded head-quarters. It was then about ten o'clock, which is equivalent to twelve or one p.m. in London. The *mot d'ordre* from our chairman was, 'Tell those who cannot sleep to join our bacchanalian party.' So many took the hint, that no room could at length be obtained in the modern Crimean Temple of Momus.

At last the order took a more positive character, for the very Angel who was presiding, observed, and very justly, that they were all playing the devil with him, and still more so with his cellar, which being but meagrely stocked, could not long stand so severe an attack. He therefore begged all new comers to go back to their quarters, and bring or send the liquid requisite to keep up the spirits of the guests till midnight—which was done. Every one, like Cinderella, disappeared, by slipping quietly out at the most convenient opportunity.

Next morning, I found myself wrapped up in a horse-cloth, with a pair of top-boots for a pillow. The unfeeling and ungrateful board to which I had intrusted my precious limbs, had by the morning stamped his patron's seal upon my back. The following day we learnt that a terrible sortie had taken place in the night, and that there had been a severe loss of men on both sides. At an early hour the court-yard was thronged with officers; despatches were flying in every direction; the cannon was roaring as usual, but the fusillade had ceased. I then went to the stable for my pony, when I found the owner, Mr. Day, upon his back, just going home.

'Ah, Monsieur Soyer, I made sure that you had lost my pony as well as your own. I expected you back immediately, being in want of it.'

'I was not aware of that, or I would have walked from your place sooner than have deprived you of it.'

'Oh, never mind. Have you heard anything of your animal?'

'No! but I am going to look after him this morning. That is the reason why I slept at head-quarters last night.'

'I am going about the camp,' said he, 'and will inquire for you.'

He then started, of course leaving me without a horse, and with dreadful pains in my back and legs, which I attributed to the softness of the bed with which I had been favoured; though I could not boast of a single feather, like that Tocrisse of a recruit, who took one out of his master's feather bed, laid it down on the boarded floor of his hut, and next morning told his companions that his master must be foolish to sleep upon a feather bed.'

'Why?' asked they.

'Why, if one feather is so hard, what must the lot the captain sleeps upon be?'

The worst of my position was, how to get another horse, as it was impossible for me to walk all day about the camp, being so stiff and tired. I went to Lord Raglan's coachman, and inquired if he had one to spare. He replied—

'Monsieur Soyer, we can spare a pony for you, but you must ask permission of the master of the horse or Lord Raglan, as I have special orders not to lend one upon my own responsibility. I am sure his lordship will let you have it immediately.'

At this moment I caught sight of Lord Raglan's valet, and I begged him to make the request; which he did, and came to tell me that his lordship desired I should have it by all means. Once more mounted, I made an early call upon the friends of the previous night, most of whom resided round head-quarters. I had the pleasure of being introduced to General Estcourt, who took me to see the printing press where my receipts for the army were done—some of which have appeared in the public press. Afterwards I went with him to his quarters, which, though small, were very neatly arranged. The taste was not military, and I thought that I detected the work of a female hand, which I could not help remarking to the general.

'You are right, Monsieur,' said he, smiling—'it has only lately been arranged by ladies. Mrs. Estcourt and my sister are here, and this is a little bit of their handy-work. They are staying on board ship at Balaklava, and come here every day. Before they arrived I had only this small room (showing me his bed made upon boards) where I sleep as well as ever I did in my life. The only thing which awakes me in the night is when the cannon ceases firing—I am so used to it.'

'I believe that, general, and have no doubt you seldom miss hearing a report. In fact, you are the neaarest of those at head-quarters to Sebastopol.'

I then inquired about the sortie of the previous night. The general said he did not know the result of it, and very kindly invited me to breakfast, which I declined, having to go round the French camp in search of my pony.

'I shall be happy,' said General Estcourt, 'to do anything I can for you; and if you call in the afternoon, my wife and her sister will be here, and I will introduce you to them.'

Thanking him kindly, I retired, and proceeded round the French camp making inquiries; then to their head-quarters, where I met Captain Boucher, General Canrobert's aide-de-camp, with whom I had the pleasure of travelling. He promised to introduce me to the general, who, he said, would be very glad to see me. Upon my telling him about my pony, he remarked—

'If he is in our camp you are sure to get him back, for we have put a stop to that kind of piracy by very severe punishment. They used to come and steal our horses from our very stables; but tell me what sort of a horse he is, and I will advertise him with the others, and we shall know in less than five or six hours if he is in our camp? the plan we have adopted cannot fail.'

Having described the animal to the captain, I thanked him for his kindness.

Considering my French review terminated, I thought of returning at once to the English head-quarters, having to see several of the authorities upon business. On my way I happened to pass by a nice French canteen. I inquired if I could get any breakfast? A rather stout vivandière, dressed in the uniform of the Imperial Guard, very politely said to me:

'What a stupid question to ask! Do you think we have not everything required for that purpose here? Perhaps, Captain of the Lord knows what regiment, you think we have come out merely to thread pearls, sing 'Partant pour la Syrie,' and dance the Fandango.'

On my way I visited several regimental kitchens and tasted the soup. Some was better than at others. They had no vegetables excepting some vegetable marrow—more likely to spoil the soup than improve it. I made several important discoveries respecting the system of cooking pursued in the French camp, after visiting, with some of my new acquaintances, a row of twelve kitchens, which number, they informed me, was required for each regiment—being at the rate of one per company. One man was told off as cook for every squad or mess of sixteen. The buildings were composed of mud and stone, and covered an extent of about four hundred yards. I bade my brave companions farewell, and left them quite a happy man, having entirely forgotten horse and saddle, in making the discovery that in lieu of four hundred yards of space, a dozen buildings, and about eighty men for each regiment, an immense consumption of fuel, and smoke enough to blind three parts of the army—as the men were all cooks in turn—my system was simple, effective, and vastly superior to that even of the French, which had hitherto always been considered as preferable to the English. This was indeed the case, for all French soldiers understand a little cooking, and their canteen pan was far superior to that in use amongst the English trooops, which I condemned at first sight in the camp at Chobham.

Eventually, the perspiring Soyer reached the front line.

Six days had elapsed, and I had received no news of the lost pony. The endeavours to find his saddle were also fruitless; and the pony was quite a secondary consideration. This put me in mind of a most extraordinary case of absence of mind in a man who had been gambling, and unexpectedly found himself in great distress, having nothing left but his horse, which was starving for want of provender. On a sudden, a bright idea flashed across his mind. In order to save it, he went and sold the horse to buy some hay. Had the Doctor found the saddle, it was ten to one against his being able to purchase another pony, they were so scarce at the time.

On the seventh day, I happened to be riding triumphantly through the camp with my tall guardsman Thomas before me. He was carrying a fine piece of roast-beef— or at least beef for roasting—which I had begged of the captain of a vessel who came from Alexandria, and intended for Lord Raglan. But I must here observe that it would have been dangerous to cross the camp with such a precious treasure unguarded, as some of those marauding Jack Sheppards of Zouaves would have thought nothing of taking possession of it. They always went in strong bodies, and were ever on the look-out for prey. I said to myself, 'If, in the middle of the road, and under my own eyes, they will steal a horse, nothing is more certain than that they will try to borrow this'—the word 'steal' was not allowed to be mentioned in the French camp, the word 'borrow' sounding more genteel.

The loss of the beef, added to the rumoured loss of the four horses, would indeed have afforded abundant materials for fun; so I sent my avant-guard by the road on foot, instead of across country, and followed him on horseback. This plan gave me an opportunity of seeing Mrs. Seacole, to thank her for her kind exertions, although the missing pony had not been found. On reaching her place, I found several mounted officers taking refreshment; when Miss Sally Seacole (her daughter), whose name I have not yet introduced, called out—'Mother, mother! here is Monsieur Soyer!' This announcement brought her out immediately, and she exclaimed, 'Good luck to you, my son! we have found your pony: come down. Here are some officers who say they have had a grey pony like yours in the stables of their regiment these last few days. Didn't you say so, gentlemen?'

'Yes, Monsieur Soyer!' said one, 'but you must look sharp, for they are going to sell it to-morrow, if no one claims it.'

'Many thanks for the warning. I will ride over directly. Pray, what is the number of the regiment?'

'The 93rd—fourth division—near the Woronzoff-road. I am almost sure it is yours.'

'Well, my son,' said Mrs. Seacole, 'didn't I tell you that it would be found?'

'Really, Mrs. Seacole, I don't know what I shall give you for the trouble you have taken in this affair. At all events, here is something on account,'—saluting her upon her deeply-shaded forehead, at which every one present laughed and joked.

'Gentlemen,' said I, 'I knew you would be surprised; though it is very natural for a son to kiss his mother. At any rate, you cannot say that, upon this occasion, I have shown my love and taste for the fair sex.'

A hearty laugh concluded this innocent bit of fun.

My guardsman, Thomas, who had continued his journey, had by this time nearly reached his destination. After a sharp gallop I caught him, and just in time to rescue the piece of beef he had carried safely so far. I found him drinking brandy with several of the French Imperial Guard, at their canteen; and he was exhibiting the choice piece, which I had wrapped up so carefully in a cloth and packed in a basket. It was the admiration of all who formed the merry group. They said to him, 'Anglais roast-beef—bono Johnny.' This was all their conversation upon the subject previous to its capture, which I have no doubt would have been the case had I not made my appearance. Seeing the imminent danger in which the choice morsel was laced, and aware that nothing but a *ruse de guerre* could rescue it from the hands of the enemy—

'Thomas,' said I, in French, 'how dare you stay drinking in this way, when you know that General Canrobert must have that beef roasted for his dinner, and it is already past three o'clock. ('By Jupiter!' said one of them, 'it's no go—it's for the Commander-in-Chief.') Go along with you! (He began to inquire what I said.) Don't answer me, sir, or you shall have a night in the guard-house. Pray, my fine fellow, which is the nearest way to the French head-quarters? I had better carry it myself—I shall be there first. Give it me,' said I, taking the basket, and ordering Thomas to follow.

Bidding the astonished soldiers adieu, I galloped off with my prize. Upon arriving at head-quarters, I rated Thomas for his stupidity, and went to the kitchen to ask for a large dish to put the beef on. It quite astonished Monsieur Armand, as he had seen none of that quality before. Indeed, it contrasted strangely with some beef he had upon the table.

Some days later, Soyer is hailed by Lord Raglan, in jovial mood, who praises Emma's paintings:

'She was an Englishwoman, was she not, Monsieur Soyer?' said his lordship.

'Yes, my lord; her maiden name was Emma Jones.'

'Of course,' rejoined one of the group, 'her paintings were well known by that name.'

'So they were, captain, and fetched high prices too. I do not sell any now; on the contrary, I still have my gallery complete, and have bought in several since her death. I offered old Ude fifty guineas for the painting in his possession called 'La jeune Fermière;' but he would not part with it, as it was presented to him by her. Previous to my departure from England for the East, I was advised by the chaplain of the cemetery to insert on the monument the country of her birth, as many believed her to be a foreigner. The inscription was simply 'To Her.' I then composed the following laconic epitaph:—

"To the memory of Madame Soyer.
    England gave her birth.
    Genius immortality." '

'Very good indeed,' said his lordship. 'I myself have seen the monument, which is considered one of the finest in Kensal-green Cemetery.

'I was saying, Soyer, that I frequently visited Alvanley; and we always knew when Ude and his wife were at home, for they never ceased quarrelling. They kept five or six dogs, and what with their barking and the quarrelling of master and mistress, I never heard such a noise in my life. I often wondered how Lord Alvanley could put up with it; but he said he was used to it, and could hardly feel comfortable anywhere else.'

'Talk of quarrelling, I believe they could not exist without it—not even on birthdays; and if you will allow me, I will relate a singular birthday anecdote.'

'Pray do, Soyer.'

'You must know that the old gentleman, though very avaricious, now and then came out in first-rate style with his gastronomic parties; but the great day of all was the 15th of August in each year—being the fête and birthday of the illustrious and far-famed Louis Eustache Ude. Upon these occasions, about four-and-twenty of his most devoted and illustrious disciples were invited, with their wives, to a most sumptuous dinner at his house. The grandeur of the gold and silver ornaments was actually cast into the shade by the elegance and succulence of the *mets* they contained. The choicest articles in season—viz., fish, flesh, poultry, vegetables, and fruit—seemed to have been waiting to come to perfection for this high-priest of the gastronomic art, and many culinary invetions which still delight the scientific palates of the epicures of the day had their origin at that Lucullusian anniversary.

'Upon one of these great occasions, Madame Soyer and myself were invited. As it was the first to which I had been invited, I was very anxious to go. About a week previous, so strong was my wish to be present at this feast, I asked the committee to grant me leave of absence from duty for one evening, and they kindly acceded to my request. To the minute, *heure militaire*, we were there, and were saluted upon our arrival by the usual dogmatic chorus, which for a few minutes prevented our hearing a word that was spoken. At length we were all seated, Mr. Ude at the top of the table, and Mrs. Ude facing him.

'It was, I must repeat, a most superb and elegantly laid-out board. The best part of the dessert, which is always refreshing to the sight, 'particularly in the middle of Aguust,' had been made a perfect study. Soup was duly served, and highly praised by the culinary *convives* and judges. It was a *bisque d'écrevisses*. The Madeira was circulating cheerfully round the table, to the trinquing of glasses, after the old French fashion, when an unfortunate guest, having probably too far to reach a beloved friend, put his foot forward, and unfortunately deposited it upon the paw of one of the *enfans chéris de la maison*. Vermilion—that was the name of the plaintiff—being an *enfant gâté*, seized upon the leg, which happened to be bootless, as the unlucky guest wore thin shoes. The dog made a slight indenture with his teeth, causing him involuntarily to reply to the attack of Vermilion; three or four more of the four-legged tribe joined the battle-cry, and the noise was intolerable. The compliments which passed between the host and hostess were pithy and violent, though scarcely heard through the din, excepting by those who happened to be seated close to them. We were fortunately about the centre of the table, and all we could catch was—

'Oh, you stupid old man! why did you not lock the dogs upstairs, as I told you to do?'

'Be quiet, madam!' replied Mr. Ude. 'This is my birthday, and I will have no quarrelling.'

'No more will I; but why did you not lock up your dogs?'

'Well, madam, I am sure they were quiet enough till that stupid young man trod upon poor Vermilion's paw.'

'Stupid young man, did you say? Mr. Ude, pray how dare you insult my relation?

If any one is stupid here, it is you, Mr. Ude!'

'Will you be quiet, madam?'—'No, I shall not!'

'What, not on my birthday! There, take that.'

'As he said this, he threw some almonds across the table, and his wife replied with some projectiles snatched up at random from other portions of the dessert. The dogs joined in the fray, and entirely upset the party. All the ladies left the table. The young man who had been bitten attempted to apologize; in return for which concession on his part, the great Louis Eustache and his amiable spouse returned a volley of abuse. An hour elapsed before anything like order could be established, when several ladies returned to the table, while a few remained to console the victimized spouse. The great Mr. Ude had bravely retained his important position, and, still violently excited, commenced helping the fish—a magnificent crimped Gloucester salmon, procured at Groves's in Bond-street—which was by this time as cold as ice.

'Only fancy,' ejaculated the enraged Amphitryon, 'even on my birthday! Upon my word, she is a wretch! She never will—' Then, by way of parenthesis, to the waiter, 'Go round with the sauce, you stupid! don't stand there staring like a fool.'— 'Prosper! no, I'm sure she never, never will prosper!'

'At length something like harmony was restored; but only six ladies out of eleven returned; the others remained with Mrs. Ude's favourite pup..'

All laughed heartily at the anecdote, particularly Lord Raglan.

Eventually, Soyer returned to Scutari, where he took up residence in a newly-erected hut, designed (of course) by himself.

I went straight to the noble mansion called Soyer's House—a real kiosque, built of wood, very much like a cage. The proprietor was a Turkish carriage-builder, a kind of a duck of a fellow, who always retired to rest at dusk, and rose before daybreak to work. He and four bulky Turkish boys accompanied their incessant hammering by an Oriental chorus, which lasted from four till seven in the morning—their breakfast-time. We not only had the satisfaction of hearing them, but from my bed I could see them at work, through my sieve-like bed-room floor, the boards of which did not meet by about half an inch—no doubt to facilitate the ventilation of this Moslem edifice. The weather being hot, this was bearable; but the harmony of such inharmonious birds was not tolerable; so for several days, and while they were in full chorus, various accidents, in the shape of upsetting large buckets of water, occurred. The refreshing liquid at once found its way to the back of our illustrious landlord, and he changed his tone and air, to invoke the blessing of Mahomet upon our devoted heads: upon which I gave them to understand, through an Armenian groom, that if they dared kick up such a row, the General would turn them out of their house. After that we had less singing, but the same quantum of hammering. At all events, we were better than under canvas.

The house was very spacious: it contained nine rooms of a good size. I had left it tenanted by good company—viz., three civilian doctors—Burn, Ellis, and Howard—but found it deserted upon my return, by all but the rats and other vermin. I and my people preferred that to living and sleeping at the hospital, and, after a few days' sport, and stopping about three hundred holes, it became habitable. The landlord fortunately had the toothache, and the fat boy, to whom I gave a few piastres to hold his noise, was silent. The ablution of the other now and then with a jug of hot water

CHEF TO THE TROOPS

kept this extraordinary establishment quiet.

If the interior of this wooden crib was not all comfort, its outside was very cheerful, and rather elegant. It had the appearance of a large Swiss châlet. Vines grew round it; and if the windows were left open, branches of cherry and mulberry trees, loaded with ripe fruit, hung above one's head as one lay in bed. The strong morning sea-breeze made the house rock like a cradle, and in shaking the trees which were planted close to the house, forced the branches in. Such was, in a few words, Soyer's House, in Cambridge-street, Scutari, so much envied by almost all, except the man himself. Five of my people had kept possession in spite of several attempts to take it by storm during my absence. It appeared that lodgings were so scarce, they wanted to take it from them.

One evening, after supper, my man Jullien, who possessed a first-rate tenor voice, was delighting us with the modulations of it, when suddenly the house began to shake most awfully, and the branches of the trees outside the windows entered very abruptly, and much farther than usual, sweeping off all the goblets and bottles from the table, to our great astonishment, nearly upsetting us; when our friend P.M. exclaimed, 'Who is shaking the house?' Jullien, who had travelled much, replied, 'Don't be alarmed—it is only an earthquake.'

'Only an earthquake, eh!' said P.M., bolting.

In rushing to the street he upset my Greek servant, who was entering with a bowl of blazing punch, which gave both house and man the appearance of being on fire. We saw no more of P.M. till the next day, as he said he preferred being gulped up by mother earth at one nibble to being smothered beneath the ponderous timbers of my castle. The same day the Barrack Hospital shook so much, that the patients were actually seen in a state of nudity in the barrack-yard. Several jumped through the windows; one man was killed, and the others all more or less severely injured.

At length I found two tolerably good cooks, and re-established everything in the culinary department to my satisfaction. My presence being no longer required, I prepared for my departure. I had taught about a dozen soldiers my system of camp-cooking and the use of my new field-stoves. I also engaged a French Zouave, named Bornet, belonging to the 3rd Regiment, whose term of service was just out. He was to act as my aide-de-camp, écuyer, master of the horse, and shield, in case of blows. He knew the savate, single-stick, sword, foil, and could box well; was a capital shot and extraordinary good horseman; he could sing hundreds of songs, and very well too; had a good voice, danced excellently, and was altogether of a very happy disposition.

Among his other then unknown qualities, he was very quarrelsome; a great marauder à la Zouave; remarkably fond of the fair sex, in his martial way, running all over the camp after the heroic cantinières; and, though never drunk, seldom sober, always ready to fight any one whom he thought wished to injure or speak ill of me. In fact, he was, much against my will, my bull-dog, and kept barking from morning till night. He was allowed to wear his costume for twelve months longer. In fact, my Zouave was a model of perfection and imperfection. The doctor of his regiment, who admired him for his bravery and cheerful abilities, impressed upon me that he was the man I required. 'Very scarce they are,' said he; 'there are not more than one hundred left out of the whole regiment who began the campaign; and he is sound, although wounded at Inkermann.'

Upon this strong recommendation, and having to run so much risk about the camp, as well as for the curiosity of the thing, I engaged Bornet, the Zouave; had a new costume made for him; introduced him to Lord W. Paulet, Miss Nightingale.

203

&c. &c. Everybody found him extremely polite, good-looking, and intelligent. We bought four horses, and he had the sole command of the cavalry department. All admired his extraordinary good style of horsemanship, pazrticularly Lord W. Paulet. Thus, the illustrious François Bornet, late of the 3rd Zouaves, was recognised as belonging to the British army. He and twelve soldiers composed the brigade of Captain Cook—a title I had assumed in the camp.

We were now ready to enter upon our campaign. I had paid my respects to Lord and Lady de Redcliffe at Therapia, and to General Vivian at Buyukderé: he was then at the Palais de Russie. In this town I and my Zouave created quite a sensation. I had adopted an indescribable costume. It seemed to have attracted John Bull's particular attention on his supposed visit to the camp. Such, at least, was the case according to the *Times'* correspondent, who, in a dialogue with John Bull, says, 'I beg your pardon, but who is that foreign officer in a white bournous and attended by a brilliant staff of generals—him with the blue and silver stripe down his trousers I mean, and gold braid on his waistcoat, and a red and white cap? It must be Pelissier?'

'That! why, that's Monsieur Soyer, *chef de nos batteries de cuisine*; and if you go and ask him, you'll find he'll talk to you for several hours about the way your meat is wasted. And so I wish you good morning, sir.'

With Bornet in tow, Soyer set off once again for the Crimea, where he immediately visited headquarters.

My Zouave, whom I had brought with me, had disappeared, leaving word with the man at the entrance-hall that he would return in ten minutes, but that he could not resist paying a visit to his old comrades, who were encamped that day at the French head-quarters. He was *en petit costume*, as I did not wish him to attract too much attention. I expected, when I learnt he had gone, that the ten minutes would be doubled and tripled, and probably extend to hours: I therefore made up my mind to go about my business in the different hospitals and regiments. First of all, I visited Dr. Hall, the authorities, and my friends round head-quarters.

In the afternoon I returned, but no Zouave had been seen. A note was handed to me by the canteen-man, worded thus:—

My Dear Governor,—Your humble servant, Bornet the Zouave, is half drunk, and will feel much obliged if you will allow him to get quite so. He has met with a few old comrades, who very likely will not last much longer than the others who have died for their country.

Upon receipt of this, having nothing better to do, I started for the French head-quarters. I soon found the regiment. This was not enough—I wanted my man. My next inquiry was for the canteen, quite sure that the cantinière, whether blonde or brunette, no matter which, would have heard of him. It turned out as I had anticipated, and, not giving me time to ask twice, she said, 'Yes, Monsieur, he is here—the dear fellow!' And so he was, fast asleep. He no sooner awoke and saw me, than he came and apologized, seemingly almost sober. I say seemingly, for all at once he began to sing and dance like a madman, harmoniously introducing me to his friends, whom I had the pleasure of shaking cordially by the hand.

Some of these recollected my former visit, so I begged of them to sit down. At the same time I offered them something to drink. The liquid material—viz., two quarts of wine and one of rum—with tin cups, was brought, and the French and Jamaica nectar was poured out, with a certain elegance and graceful smile, by the Crimean Bacchanté, to these reckless children of Mars. In a short time many of them had fallen in the dreadful struggle. They were *enfans perdus*, and were all singing different tunes and dancing different steps.

The cantinière was elegantly dressed in her Zouave uniform, ready for starting to the trenches: she wore a red gown, and trousers of the same material, a jacket like that worn by the men, and a red fez cap with a long tassel. She carried a stoup full of spirits, a large basket of provisions, and followed her companions like a trooper.

The Zouaves gave me a pressing invitation to go and see them perform, which I promised to do that day week. They were perfectly satisfied, though I was not at all, with my Zouave, Bornet. As he was not fit to follow me, I gave him up, and, after seeing his horse right and him wrong, I left him, and started alone for Balaklava, returning in solemn solitude to my nautical home—the *Ottawa*.

At six the next morning he was on board, busily engaged preparing for our departure, so soon as a spot could be selected in the camp for us to pitch our tents. The horses were landed, and my military pupils sent to different quarters, and set to work cooking. I retained three with me for the opening of my field-kitchens. As I approached my deserter, the Zouave, in order to reprimand him for his conduct the preceding day, he remarked, by way of apology, 'I know, mon cher governor, what you are going to say—that is, if I play you any more such tricks, you will not keep me, as we agreed when you engaged me.'

'Certainly not,' said I.

'We will begin fresh to-day: but yesterday, you see, governor, the temptation was too strong for me. When I saw my old comrades Riflard and Franc Chatbeau, Panaudet, et la cantinière—Beni Zoug Zoug—des vieux amis de la tente, with whom I had braved all dangers, and so few of us left—not more than fourteen or fifteen of our company—why, voyez-vous, it carried me away, and I could not help standing the picton (which means something to drink), like a Frenchman and a man. And what a fine lass la petite Mère Jouvin is! Don't she look well in her Zouave dress?'

'Certainly, but did she go to the trenches?'

'Of course she did. She was on duty last night. Her husband goes one night, and she the other.'

'Did you see her this morning?'

'I did. The darling had just returned for more liquor. She told me they had a kind of sortie, and for twenty minutes were peppering one another like fun, and no mistake. Rabbit-shooting, governor—rabbit-shooting! We lost about seventeen men, besides the wounded. But that's nothing. Last year I saw three times as many knocked over in a sort of skirmish which only lasted ten minutes. We were half frozen and partly starved; and hundreds were found dead or nearly frozen, lying under shelter of those who had been shot, endeavouring to warm themselves before the bodies got cool.'

'Pray, Bornet, don't recal those things to my mind: they are too painful; but, after all, are only the chances of war, and must be endured.'

'Well, governor,' said he, while cording a large box, 'you have gained the esteem of the 3rd Zouaves; and should you require the services of the whole regiment, could it be spared, you would have them, including la petite Mère Jouvin.'

In uttering the last word he gave an extra pull at the rope, which caused it to break, and bang went my Zouave flat upon his back. A general laugh was heard upon deck. He picked himself up quickly, and, rubbing his back, said, 'By the explosion of a thousand shells, here is a stunning piece of straw.'

A gentleman present asked him if he had hurt himself. 'Very well,' he replied, being all the English he knew, except 'yes' and 'no.'

Seeing everybody laugh, he went on working at the box, and singing his favourite refrain—

J'aime le vin, l'amour et le gaité,
Les plaisirs, la gloire,
Et je suis, sans vanité,
L'enfant de la gaité.

I perceived some spots of blood on his shirt-sleeve, and pointed them out to him. 'Oh,' said he, 'that's no novelty. I've seen a sample of my blood before this, many times.'

On pulling up his sleeve, we found a deep scratch in his arm, from which the blood flowed pretty freely.

'You had better have it attended to,' said I.

'Bah! bah! nonsense! We Zouaves never trouble any one, particularly the doctor, about such trifles. Be kind enough to tie my pocket-handkerchief round it.'

This done, he kept at his work. Thus I discovered the determined character of these wild soldiers. They made up their minds to care for nothing—were ready either to fight or sing—be out all night without sleep, or comfortable under their tents— were content with much to eat and drink, or little—but so long as they had sufficient to sustain life, be gay, or at least appear so—never making a direct complaint, whatever might happen to them. In fact, though French soldiers like the rest of the army, they had created themselves a body of invincibles, and a company of very odd fellows, who would at all times much prefer robbing a man to wronging him; this being one of their mottoes:— 'Nous aimons mieux voler que faire du tort.'

The time had come for a grand demonstration of his new field stoves, despite various military interruptions.

Having fixed upon a spot for my kitchen, I immediately sent the stoves to the camp. As they happened to be close to the railway, they arrived early the next morning. In the course of the day I reached my field of battle, and to my great surprise found— what? Why, all my battery firing for the support of the Highland Brigade. The stoves had arrived early enough for the men to use them in cooking their dinners. Though I had given special orders that no one should meddle with them until I arrived, it gave me great pleasure to find that the men were using them to the best advantage and without instruction. In the first place, they could not possibly burn more than twenty pounds of wood in cooking for a hundred men, instead of several hundred-weight, which was the daily consumption. Although I had not given them my receipts, they found they could cook their rations with more ease, and hoped they should soon have them for every-day use, instead of the small tin camp-kettles, and their open-air system of cooking. The process was very unsatisfactory, being dependent upon good, bad, or indifferent weather, and the fuel was often wet and difficult to ignite. Colonel Seymour, whom I invited to see the men using the stoves without tuition from me or anybody else, can testify to the accuracy of this fact, having witnessed the process and interrogated them upon the subject.

My reason, reader, for relating this circumstance, is because it afforded me an assurance that I could render serve to the army, and that my exertions were of some use. I saw even further than that; for I inferred that if a soldier, who is not a cooking animal, being paid for other purposes—and that talent a peculiar gift conferred in a greater or less degree upon humanity—could without trouble or instruction cook well in the open air and in all weathers, the stoves would certainly be useful in all establishments, from a cottage to a college. I do not say anything of their use in hospitals, because they had been tried in those establishments with full success, as far as military cooking was concerned. The idea of connecting baking, roasting, boiling, and steaming crossed my mind; and this, I felt with confidence, would render them beneficial and useful to the public at large. This idea I at once communicated to the makers, and they have already acted upon my suggestion. I resolved upon my return to England to bring them out at as cheap a rate as possible for the use of small or large families. A really useful and economical cooking stove is as much wanted in England as sunshine on a November day—a stove by which all the usual domestic cooking can be carried on, without having recourse to bricks and mortar, and chimney-sweeps. Smoky chimneys, as well as other minor nuisances too numerous to mention, would be thus avoided. Twelve pounds of coal, or fifteen pounds of coke, will cook for one hundred men.

'War,' said I to myself, 'is the evil genius of a time; but good food for all is a daily and a paramount necessity.' These reflections led to a further communication with Messrs. Smith and Phillips, of Snow-hill. I took out a patent for the stoves. This I did not like to do before I had introduced them to the Government, as every one would have supposed that I wished to make money by the patent. The object of a patent, after such a decided success, was to secure the solidity and perfection of the article. As it was difficult to make, and certain to be badly imitated, my reputation must have suffered. Instead of being expensive, they will be sold at a reasonable price, sufficient to repay the manufacturers, and to leave a fair profit; thus placing them within the reach of all—the million as well as the millionaire.

The following day I was out very early at the Inkermann heights, with a numerous party, looking towards the Tehernaya Bridge. It was the 16th of August, the day of that memorable battle, which does not require a description on my part. From four till eight that morning I looked on, and saw the retreat of the Russians and the triumph of the French and Sardinians.

I remained at the camp till nearly three in the afternoon. About one, a long train of mules made their appearance, bearing wounded French and Russian soldiers—the latter prisoners. About twenty were wounded; the rest followed the mournful procession. Assisted by a few of my men, I gave them some wine, brandy, porter, &c.—in fact, whatever we could get at the canteen—which seemed to afford them much relief. I of course treated the wounded Russians in the same manner as the French; though two refused to take anything, fearing poison.

Not doubting that many more would pass, as I had some provisions in a tent for the opening of my kitchens, I made some sago jelly, with wine, calves'-foot jelly, &c. which unfortunately was not used, as the other prisoners went by a different road, though taken to the General Hospital at the French head-quarters. Upon leaving, I ordered my men to be on the look-out, and if any wounded or prisoners came by, to offer them some refreshment.

Just as I was going, I perceived a few mules approaching the Guards' camp. As they advanced, I and one of my men went towards some of the wounded with a basin of sago in hand, saying, this was a sort of half-way ambulance, where they might obtain all they might require. I was aware that some of the Russian prisoners in the first convoy would not accept any refreshment, for fear of being poisoned, of course not knowing better. The case of two poor French soldiers I cannot pass in silence. One had been severely wounded in the head, and was almost in a state of insensibility; the other had had his leg amputated on the field of battle. The first, after taking a few spoonfuls of the hot sago, asked for a drop of brandy, saying he felt faint. The conductor at first objected to this, but upon my asking him to take a glass with me and the patient, he agreed that it would do him no harm if it did him no good—adding, that very likely he would not survive the day. Having mixed it with water, he drank it, and thanked me warmly. The other was an officer. After giving him some wine-jelly, I conversed with him.

'How good this jelly is!' said he, in Fench; 'pray give me another spoonful or two, if you have it to spare.'

Having done this, he said that he suddenly felt very thirsty. This was, no doubt, owing to the loss of blood. I gave him some lemonade. He drank above a pint, and felt more composed, and proceeded to the hospital, near the English head-quarters. I accompanied him, and he told me that his leg had just been amputated; and, with tears in his eyes, added, in a low voice. 'All I regret is, that my military career should have ended so soon. I am but thirty years of age, and have only been two months in the Crimea.'

'My dear friend,' I replied, to cheer him, 'many thousands have done less, and died; but you will survive, and be rewarded for your gallant service—you belong to a nation which can appreciate noble devotion.'

'Ah!' said he, 'you have done me a deal of good, no matter who you are; if my life is spared, I beg you will let me see or hear from you.'

Though he gave me his name, not having my pocket-book with me, I could not make a note of it. Some time after, I visited the hospital, in company with Dr. Wyatt of the Coldstream Guards. We learnt that the man who had been wounded in the head had died, but that the officer whose leg had been amputated had been sent home to France.

Early in the morning the camp seemed full of life and gaiety. Mounted officers in full uniform might be seen rushing about in all directions; bands were playing, regiments filing past, and everything bearing the appearance of a great festival. I set cheerfully to work, and, in spite of difficulties which can only be understood by those who have been in the Crimea, I succeeded in getting all in tolerably good order for my great martial banquet *al fresco*. I made several messes with the soldiers' rations, and at the same expense, though I had introduced sauce and ingredients which could easily be added to the army stores without increasing the cost, thus making a nice variation in the meals, so important to the health of a large body of men like the army or navy, to the latter of which it is as easily applicable as the former.

The bill of fare consisted of plain boiled salt beef; ditto, with dumplings; plain boiled salt pork; ditto, with peas-pudding; stewed salt pork and beef, with rice; French pot-au-feu; stewed fresh beef, with potatoes; mutton, ditto, with haricot beans; ox-cheek and ox-feet soups; Scotch mutton-broth; common curry, made with fresh and salt beef.

By three o'clock my guests began to arrive. The stoves were in the open air, placed in a semicircle, and, though in a state of ebullition, no one could perceive that any cooking was going on, except on raising the lids. A material point I had in view was that no fire should be seen when used in the trenches. A common table, made of a few boards, and garnished with soldiers' tin plates, iron forks and spoons, composed my open-air dining-room.

About four o'clock my reception commenced. Lord Rokeby, accompanied by several French officers in full dress, was the first to honour me with a visit. This gave me an opportunity of fully explaining to him and his friends the plan and construction of the apparatus, as well as its simplicity, cleanliness, and great economy in the consumption of fuel. At the same time, I showed with what ease and certainty the men could regulate the heat and prepare the new receipts—which will be found at the end of this work.

I must also observe, for the information of those who only saw them upon that occasion, that the stoves, having been made for the General Hospital, were too lage and heavy for campaigning. That I might lose no time in making my trial before the authorities, I used them upon that occasion, as the process was the same as regards cooking in those as in the smaller ones. The sole difference was in the size, as it was understood that two would cook for a company of one hundred and twenty men, and might be carried by one mule while on march, with sufficient dry wood inside for the next day's cooking. This was of the utmost importance, in order to ensure the regularity of the soldier's meal, which ought always to be ready at the minute fixed by the rules of the service.

Thus I had surmounted every difficulty by the invention of this apparatus. In addition to its simplicity and economy, it had the merit of making cooks of soldiers, of which they had previously neither the inclination nor the chance. Smaller stoves on the same principle were also to be provided for picket and outpost duty, as first suggested to me by Lord Raglan. After giving the foregoing information to my illustrious visitors, we passed to the grand process of tasting the various messes. They all gave perfect satisfaction.

On September 8th, the battle for Sebastopol began.

Suddenly the batteries opened fire in every direction, shaking the very soil on which we stood. Clouds of smoke enveloped the besieged city. Not a thing could be seen or heard but a continuous rolling noise similar to that of an earthquake. All at once the noise ceased, and the rattle of musketry was heard, with, at intervals, cannon and mortar shot. By degrees, thanks to the heavy gale, the atmosphere got clearer, and by the aid of a telescope one could distinctly see the French flag floating from the Malakhoff, and the troops mounting to the assault. An hour had scarcely elapsed when the news was brought of the capture of the Malakhoff by the French, and of the Redan by the English. Aides-de-camp were flying in every direction; and numbers of wounded were on their way to the hospitals. We quitted our post to go to the General Hospital, in order to see whether our services were required. As we were crossing the English camp, a corpse was borne past us, carried by four soldiers. Upon inquiry I learned, with sorrow, that it was the body of Colonel H. R. Handcock, whom a few days before, I had had the pleasure of entertaining at my kitchens, with his young and very interesting wife.

The latter had been an eye-witness of the assault, and I was informed that, by the greatest imprudence, the mutilated body of her husband had just been uncovered before her. She fainted at the sight, and was borne to her residence, where she lay for some time dangerously ill.

The fight still raged, the weather was a little calmer, and we left the field of battle, intending to gallop at once to the hospital. On reaching the line of sentries, we met two naval officers who were trying to pass, in order to obtain a view of the action from Cathcart's Hill. They were having a rather warm discussion, the sentry doing his duty by stopping them. I pulled up my horse, and told them that unless they had an order from head-quarters they could not pass. Though much vexed, they thanked me, and submitted to the disappointment. I was about leaving them, when I heard one say to the other—

'What shall we do? I would give any money for a glass of wine or a cup of coffee.'

'So would I,' said the other. 'Where is there a Canteen, sentry?'

'It would be of no use my telling you,' the sentry replied, 'as they are all closed during the siege, or at least for to-day, in order to prevent men left in the camp from quitting their post. Several robberies were perpetrated in camp upon former occasions.'

I overhead their conversation, in which they stated that they had started without breakfast, and been a long way round—nearly seven miles among the hills—and had seen nothing after all, as the pickets would not let them pass the line of Balaklava.

'Gentlemen,' said I, 'if you will come with me to my tent, I think I can keep you from starving, and have no doubt you will fare there as well, if not better, than in a Canteen. I can also give you a description of the siege, having been an eyewitness of the same.'

They thanked me, and accepted my offer. On our way to quarters, I recounted the melancholy death of Colonel Handcock. My Zouave had by this time arrived— no one but the groom was at home, and he could speak neither French nor English, being a Greek—so I set my Zouave to lay the table; and with my magic stove I cooked some ration-mutton, made an omelette, brought out a piece of cold beef, bread, &c., and gave them a bottle of ale and a glass of sherry. In twenty minutes their hunger was appeased, and I told them they were welcome to stay, but that I must proceed to my duty. At the same time I informed them, that at six o'clock dinner would be ready, and they were welcome to partake of it if they happened to be about the camp. They thanked me for my hospitality, and said they would try and see something of the battle, and would be happy to return to dinner.

That evening, Soyer dined with Colonel Wyndham.

My description of the hospitals was the great feature of the evening, as none present had seen them, having other occupation at their posts with the various regiments. The Queen's health, that of the Emperor of the French, and of the Sultan, were toasted with three times three and one more cheer. In the midst of this, Buckingham!! the renowned Buckingham!!! who had displayed all his *savoir faire* in the *service de table*, acting upon that occasion as *maître d'hôtel en chef*, with a few utensils made a display worthy of a first-rate à la mode beef house, nothing to be laughed at in a Crimean popotte, rushed into the tent, crying 'Colonel! Colonel! the whole of Sebastopol is in flames.' It was true. In less than ten minutes streets had taken fire with the rapidity of a firework, and every minute the conflagration seemed to be upon the increase. Nothing but fire and smoke could be seen from the Guards' camp. I proposed that we should order our horses and go to Cathcart's Hill to see what was going on. To my surprise, no one seemed inclined to move. They all said that they had had enough of Sebastopol, and were tired to death. On urging the matter, the only answer I got from some of my gallant friends was, 'Not to-night, Monsieur Soyer, not to-night.'

'Surely,' said I, 'gentlemen! you don't expect the Russians will set a Sebastopol on fire every day at a few hours' notice to please you.'

'That is not likely,' said Major Fielden. 'But for all that I feel convinced that no one will go.'

As the fire seemed to extend and the sky became one lurid mass, I determined to go and get a sight of it. I bade my companions adieu, went back to my tent, ordered my horse, and tried to awake my Zouave in order to take him with me. He was so intoxicated I could not succeed. He had spent the day with some of his comrades, and completely lost his senses. As I could not find either groom or any of my men, I went to Mr. Mesnil's tent. My major domo being an old campaigner, had as usual turned in all dressed to be ready for any contingency. Rousing him, I requested him to accompany me. The eternal reply of 'Not to-night' was again heard.

'Oh, hang the place, let it burn,' said he.

As this was my last resource, I would not leave him. At last, in no very kindly mood, he turned out and agreed to go. The night was pitch dark, so we preferred going on foot. My friend was armed with a Russian sword and a night glass; I with a poignard-revolver and a lanthorn. Our intention was to get as near the city as possible, and we were prepared for any unpleasant encounter by firelight instead of moonlight. The purlieus of the camp were at this period anything but safe. With much difficulty, we reached Cathcart's Hill, having lost our way in trying what we thought would be a short cut. The camp was silent, and apparently deserted. Although only eleven o'clock, we did not meet a soul, with the exception of sentries, on our way.

By the aid of the night-glass we obtained so good a view that we did not deem it advisable to proceed further. The heat of the fire was felt even at that distance, and explosions were frequent. The cause of the solitude in the camp at that hour can only be attributed to the excessive fatigue consequent upon the tremendous exertioins of the previous day; the curtain had fallen on this grand drama—all was repose. We then returned to quarters through the same mournful solitude, not having met a soul either going or returning. This dreariness impressed me with the idea of chaos, after the destruction of a world and its empires.

Early the following morning, attended by my Zouave, who had recovered his sober senses, I started for the General Hospital.

We saw about thirty dead bodies laid out in a row, and stitched up in their blankets, with their name and nation marked upon each. I believe there was not a single case of amputation amongst them; they had all been mortally wounded. This speaks volumes in favour of the use of chloroform, the efficacy and safety of which, for a time, was much doubted, even by eminent medical men. Amputations were still being performed with skill and celerity worthy of a Guthrie or an Astley Cooper. The principal medical men were Drs. Mouatt, Lyons, &c. &c., who appeared to vie with each other in their kind attention to the sufferers.

Perceiving that nothing further was required for the present, and that all was going on well, I went to visit Sebastopol. My Zouave knew the road, as he had been there the day before. Our first visit was to the Redan, where we were refused admission. My intrepid Zouave, not contented with this rebuff, took me round another way, and, leaving our horses outside, we scaled the works and got in. The scene of death and destruction here was awful, and has been described too often for me to dwell upon it. Nothing but the effects of a devastating earthquake can give any one an idea of the *débris* of the interior, or of the destruction caused by the fire of the Allies, and the explosions that had ensued. We proceeded to the city by the Arsenal, on the British side. The town was still burning. On reaching the large barracks, we visited the kitchens and bakeries. In the former, some of the boilers contained cabbage-soup; others, a kind of porridge made with black flour. In the bakeries, loaves of bread were still in the ovens, and dough in the troughs. We removed a loaf from the oven and tasted it. As we had brought no provision with us, and there was none to be obtained in the burning city, we ate about half a pound of bread each, and finished our frugal repast with a good draught of water: the latter was retailed at the small charge of sixpence a pint. A quarter of an hour after, I looked my Zouave hard in the face, saying, as I placed my hand upon my stomach, with a rueful face and in a piteous tone of voice—

'Bless me, Bornet! do you feel anything wrong?—because, if you don't, I do!' Looking still more pitiful, I continued—'I *am* confident the bread has been poisoned!'

'The deuce it has!' he replied, turning pale, and putting his fingers in his throat in order to throw off the dreadful meal, but without success.

I laughed at him, and called him a coward.

'Coward!' said he; 'no, no, governor, I am no coward. I should not mind a round-shot, sword, or bayonet wound, in the field of battle; but, by Jupiter! to be poisoned ingloriously like a dog, would be base in the extreme.'

'You're right,' said I. 'Come, don't fear, let's go and taste the soupe-aux-choux.'

To this invitation he most decidedly objected, saying, 'No more of their relishes for me, if you please.'

Seven or eight days after, I was laid up with a very severe attack of Crimean fever. Not being aware of the nature of my illness, I thought rest was all I required, after the fatigue I had undergone: I therefore went to bed—but what kind of bed?—under damp canvas, with a muddy floor, as it had rained heavily for some days. I felt so ill, that I could neither lie, sit, nor stand, without great suffering. Imagining that I could conquer the disease, I did not send for the doctor. Fortunately for me, a short time after my attack, as I lay in bed, Dr. Linton, who often visited me, chanced to call at my tent. I told him of my indisposition, and he at once sent me some medicine, more blankets, and kindly offered his services; at the same time informing me that I had a serious attack of fever. I was in the Coldstreams' camp; and Dr. Wyatt claimed me as his patient, and paid me a visit. He immediately ordered me to keep my bed. For some days he watched my case most diligently, and under his skilful care I soon got better. During my illness I received visits and kind inquiries from almost all the heads of the forces, for which I shall ever feel grateful; their attention was most gratifying to my feelings, and I am proud of the consideration evinced for me by that noble band, the British army.

Directly I recovered and was allowed to go about, I felt anxious to have a decided answer respecting the stoves—for the matter was at that time in abeyance. I also wished to visit the various regimental hospitals in which my men were engaged teaching the soldiers. In my eagerness to attend to these things, I overfatigued myself, and brought on a second attack, much worse than the former. Dr. Wyatt was almost in despair, and privately informed Mr. Mesnil that I was in great danger. However, owing entirely to his great care and kind attention, in three weeks I had partly recovered, but was so much altered that scarcely anybody could recognise me. I one day visited Lord William Paulet, who had left Scutari, and was on board the *Leander* in Balaklava Bay. I was so much changed, that neither Admiral Freemantle nor his lordship knew me. Miss Nightingale had returned, and was much in want of my services. Not being aware of my illness, she sent for me; and as soon as I recovered, I waited upon and accompanied that lady to the Monastery Hospital. The fatigue consequent upon my exertions brought me so low, that Dr. Wyatt insisted upon my leaving the Crimea, saying he would not be responsible for my safety any longer in that climate.

A few days before my departure the following laughable circumstance occurred, which has already been related in the columns of the *Illustrated News* by an amateur correspondent:—

An Unexpected Visitor and a Conversation.

I had an amusing adventure the other evening. A stranger visited me, and I entertained a late distinguished *attaché* of the Reform Club unawares. It was getting dusk, and I was very tired, having been engaged in the hospital marquees all day—for we had a very sudden and violent outbreak of cholera. Phillipo, my Maltese servant, was down on his hands and knees, blowing the lighted charcoal in my fireplace, with the intention of expediting dinner. My fireplace, I must tell you, consists of a hole dug in the earth, with three pieces of iron hooping stretched across by way of grate; and a very admirable kitchen-range it is. Phillipo had just afforded me the agreeable information that dinner would not be ready for nearly an hour, and I was in the act of lighting my pipe, when I heard an unaccustomed step climbing up the rock side, close to my tent, and a musical and hilarious voice exclaimed, 'Is Guy Earl of Warwick at home?' I laid down my pipe utterly astounded; and in another moment a hand drew aside the canvas, a head appeared at the entrance of my tent, and the portly figure of a man speedily completed the apparition. For a moment my visitor surveyed me, evidently as much astonished as I was. 'Ah! I see, I have made one grand mistake!' (he spoke tolerable English, but with a decided French accent). 'You will think me strange. I was looking for my old friend Warwick, and made sure this was his tent. We call him Guy Earl of Warwick. Ah! ah! badinage. It may be you know him?'

By this time I had fully surveyed my visitor. He was a tall, stout, rather handsome-looking man, aged about fifty years. He wore a drab-coloured 'wide-awake' wrapped round with a red scarf, and a white blouse, heavily braided about the sleeves. His hair had been black, now rapidly changing into grey; and his whiskers, moustache, and beard (the latter primly cut), were of the same 'Oxford mixture.' Observing that the walk up the hill had slightly affected his breathing, I invited him to take a seat on one of my bullock-trunks, the only 'ottoman' of which my Turkish tent could boast. (It is no slight exertion to get up to my tent, as I have pitched it almost at the top of a hill, in order, if possible, to evade the rats, which swarm in the Crimea; indeed, I scarcely know whether rats, flies, or fleas are the greatest nuisance.) In a few moments we got into conversation.

'I am going to Balaklava shortly,' said the stranger; 'I am going on board ship. I have been out here some few months; my health has been gone ever since I came. They tell me I am older ten years this last five months. I am going to England.'

'And I am only waiting till this Crimean drama is over to follow your example,' said I. 'I must see the Russians finally driven out, and then I go home too. As to campaigning, the curiosity which brought me here is gratified; as to the moving accidents of war, I have supped full of horrors!—But here comes Phillipo with the dinner.'

The Maltese entered, and placed upon the table a piece of beef baked in an iron pot, also some boiled potatoes. I observed that my visitor eyed the dinner curiously, and I was almost angry to observe the instantaneous elevation of his eyebrows, when with great difficulty I succeeded in whittling off with a sharp carving-knife a slice of the outside.

'Nice beef, but not done quite enough,' said my visitor.

He might well say so; it was almost raw. I stuck a fork into the potatoes; they were as hard as pebbles. I was in despair. The stranger laughed aloud. I was rapidly getting sulky.

'I see you have a good fire outside,' said my visitor; 'that charcoal gives a beautiful heat. Now, if you will take my advice, I should say, cut a slice or two—'

'Excuse me,' I replied, 'but if there is one thing more than another that I pride myself on, it is my cooking. I can cook with any fellow in the Crimea, perhaps excepting Soyer; and some people say that he is a great humbug.'

'Do they indeed?' said he. 'Well, he must be rather a clever humbug to sell 40,000 of his books.'

'I must confess,' I said, 'that his shilling Cookery-book is a great invention. I have made many capital dishes by its direction. The fact is, I generally superintend the cooking myself.'

'And your politeness to me has spoiled your dinner. Now look here.'

And, almost before I could interpose a word, my potatoes were in slices, a large onion was dissected piecemeal, my beef was submitted to the knife, a pinch or two of ration salt and pepper completed the preparations, and my little canteen-pan was on the fire. I looked on, regarding these proceedings with much astonishment, and not a little jealousy. After a few minutes the stranger gave the pan a graceful wave or two over the fire, and then replaced it on the table. There was a dinner fit for Sardanapalus! Never shall I forget the elegant curl of that steam, or the exquisite odour which soon pervaded the atmosphere of my tent. I could not help thinking of and half excusing a certain hairy man who lived in the first ages, and who for just such a mess of potage disposed of his estates.

'How do you like it?' said the stranger.

'Don't talk at present,' I answered; 'I consider dinner one of the most serious duties of life.'

'Ah! ah! then you would not call Soyer a humbug to make this?'

'Soyer!' I said in disdain—'Soyer never made or invented a dish half as good in his life! Talk about French slops in comparison with prime English beef and onions! Bah!'

I was carried away by my enthusiasm, and quite forgot that I was at that moment eating part of the carcase of a wretched Armenian beast, that would not have fetched 50s. in an English market. At last dinner was over.

'One more glass of sherry,' said the stranger, 'and then I go. I am very glad to have made your acquaintance, and I hope you will come and see me when you come down to Balaklava. I shall be on board the ship *Edward* in the bay. I am going to stop there a little time for my health. Come on board and ask for me.'

'With very great pleasure—and your name'

'Oh! my name—*Soyer*,' said he; and he sat down and laughed till the tears stood in his eyes.   W.C.

Despite this anecdote, Soyer's health was still very poor.

Nothing is less likely to restore a man when he is half dead than trying to persuade him that he must succumb. Thanks to my lucky star, I have deceived them all; and some richly deserve it, as they had laid bets upon my chance, particularly my Zouave and another of my men. The former answered all inquiries respecting the state of my health by, 'The governor, you see, is in a very bad way. His hash is settled; it is all over with him. It is a pity, for he is a good man, and he had promised to take me with him to London, a place I very much wish to visit.'

A few days after my arrival in Constantinople my health again failed me, and having no further need for the services of my Zouave, to his great regret we parted, but on such friendly terms, that he afterwards often observed, 'Look ye, governor, you have been a good master to me, and if you ever recover from your serious illness, which is not very probable, send for me—I am still your man, and will follow you anywhere and everywhere, even to England; and if any fellow annoys you, here is the arm (showing it to the shoulder) which will make them bleed to death and bury them after.'

I took up my residence at Soyer House, where I enjoyed the gay and interesting prospect for an invalid of the monster lugubrious cemetery, or Grand Champ des Morts, on one side, and the hospital on the other. The weather was wet and wretched—the house, as usual, splendidly ventilated, and had been robbed of its furniture by a Greek servant I had left there. It was, moreover, populated by rats and other vermin. Before I could set it in order, I fell ill for the third time, and had, in addition to my former malady, a severe attack of dysentery. I left my dismal abode, now become unbearable, crossed the Bosphorus to Pera, and took up my lodgings at an hotel for a few days, as I then anticipated, having determined upon my departure for England. However, instead of improving in health, I grew worse and worse, and was laid up for three months; in fact, I began to fear my Zouave would win his wager. During this time, I received notice that the order had been given for four hundred stoves, which were to be forwarded as fast as they could be made. I therefore decided upon remaining at Constantinople, in the hope of being able, in the event of getting better, of returning to the Crimea, and distributing them to the different regiments.

One day I had crossed over the Scutari, in order to visit Miss Nightingale, who had just arrived from Balaklava, when I met the celebrated Dr. Sutherland, who, like the rest, gave me a very encouraging view of his scientific opinion upon the state of my health. 'For God's sake, Soyer,' said he, 'do leave this country, and go immediately to Malta—not England—or you are a dead man.'

'Not so, doctor,' I replied; 'I am much better these last few days. In fact, I am going back to the Crimea; my stoves are expected daily, and I must go and distribute them.'

'In that case, don't forget to take your tombstone with you.'

'A very interesting thing to do, doctor; but I shall chance the voyage for all that, if I improve; and as to the tombstone, I shall leave that to friendly hands in case it is required.'

However, there was still plenty of work to be done.

After having started them in person, I sent my cooks every morning on their rounds to see if the men followed my instructions, and I visited each regiment daily. The hospitals, thank God, were at this time almost empty. When a division had made use of the stoves about a week, I requested the general commanding that division to inquire of the colonel, officers, and men, their opinion of the results of my labours; and in that manner I acquired the above-mentioned numerous letters of commendation, having in my possession many others, but space will not allow of their insertion.

One of the days on which salt rations were issued, I requested General Garrett to go round his division and ask the men what they did with the fat. This he very kindly did, accompanied by his aide-de-camp, Major Dallas. The first cook we visited, in the 18th Regiment, had rations for 94 men (the whole of his company). They were being cooked in one stove: the two stoves for the same quantity would have been much better, as the more water the meat is boiled in, the more salt is extracted from it. The boiler was filled to the brim, the contents simmering gently: the meat was beautifully cooked. There were about four inches of clear fat, as sweet as butter, floating on the top. The stove was in the open air, and the cook only burnt from ten to fifteen pounds of wood (or hardly so much) to cook for that number—viz., the whole of his company. The allowance of wood had been reduced from 4½lbs. to 3½lbs. per man daily. The advent of peace gave me a full opportunity of thoroughly instructing the men, and thus I was enabled firmly to establish my new system. The saving in wood alone, supposing each company to consist of one hundred men, would, at the former rate of allowance, amount to 450lbs. per company per diem, allowing 25lbs. for cooking, which is ample. This in a regiment of eight companies would make a daily saving of 3600lbs. of wood, independent of the economy of transport, mules, labour, &c. In an army of forty thousand men, it would amount to the immense figure of 180,000lbs., or 90 tons, per day saved to the Government, or 32,850 tons per annum.

General Garrett asked the man what he was going to do with the fat.

'Throw it away, general,' was the answer.

'Throw it away!—why?' said the General.

'I don't know, sir, but we always do.'

'Why not use it?'—'The men don't like it, sir.'

I observed that when the salt meat was cooked in the small canteen pans, the fat was lost for want of the necessary quantity of water to allow it to rise to the surface, as well as to purify it of the salt. Asking the man for a leaden spoon and a tin can, I removed the fat as I had before done in the Guards' camp. On weighing it the next day, I found upwards of 14lbs. of beautiful clean and sweet dripping, fit for use as described in the receipts. Thus about 800lbs. of this were wasted weekly by each regiment—salt rations being issued four days a week.

General Garrett expressed a decided opinion that my apparatus was much superior to the old canteen pan, and gave me a letter, which I append in the Addenda.

The signature of the treaty of peace changed all the proceedings in the camp, except mine; for in anticipation of the distribution of the remainder of the stoves among the various regiments in the camps at Aldershot barracks, &c., as well as to those on foreign stations, I continued my daily course of instruction, in order that the men, upon arrival at home or elsewhere, might be well acquainted with their use, and be able to impart their knowledge to others. I have since hit upon a plan by which I shall introduce an oven and steamer, and thus do all that is required to vary the cooking of the daily meals in barracks—a subject of great importance.

War having ceased, the camp bore the appearance of a monster banqueting-hall. 'We have done fighting,' said every one, 'so let us terminate the campaign by feasting, lay down our victorious but murderous weapons, and pick up those more useful and restorative arms—the knife and fork.'

'What can I do,' said I to myself, 'for an event of historical importance?' Neither Mr. Crockford nor the captain could assist me, when an idea struck me:—'If you can't give me an idea,' said I to my friends, 'at any rate lend me a dish.'

'That I will,' said the captain.

'Recollect, I want a large one.'

'You had the largest for your salad yesterday.'

'That one will do; it will hold enough for twenty-five persons.'

'Then here goes,' said I, writing. 'To-day I shall dress in it the *Macèdoine Lüdersienne à l'Alexandre II.'*

'A very good name in honour of the event,' said Mr. Crockford. 'But pray, of what is it to be composed?'

'Oh! for that,' said I, 'if I were to implore the Genius of Gastronomy, from Lucullus to Apicius and Vitellius, or Vatel to Ude and Carême, I could get nothing from them but inspiration; while what I require is something substantial, and not artificial. It strikes me that a word from you to your head man at Kadikoi (as you will not be there to-morrow) would do more for me in a few minutes than the whole of those defunct celebrities, whom I am not now inclined to trouble upon so material a subject. Pray give me *carte blanche* to get anything you may have and I require for the composition of this modern Babylon, which must be constructed upon a base sufficiently strong to resist the joint attack of the heads of three of the most powerful armies in the world, and only be destroyed after having conquered the conqueror's *place d'armes*, the stomach, so called in military parlance.'

The order was readily given by my friend Mr. Crockford, and we then lay down to sleep, being both completely exhausted with the fatigues of what was called a day of pleasure. We had hardly closed our eyelids, when morning caused them to be reopened; so up we got. My friend started for Constantinople, and I for head-quarters. I started immediately—bought a few things in Balaklava market—called at Crockford's store at Donnybrook, which I ransacked and despoiled of condiments of every description. Instead of going direct to headquarters I changed my mind and went home to prepare, having decided, as the time was so short, to produce one good dish only, instead of several small and insignificant ones. This was, however, to be worthy of the occasion. I was well aware that General Codrington's cook, under the liberal management and command of Captain Ponsonby, would turn out something worthy of the event. Upon arriving at my hut, I sent two of my cooks to assist him, despatched my groom on horseback to Kamiesch for various things, and then began the construction of my *Lüdersienne* upon the lid of my new field-stoves, the dish I had brought from the *Alar* being too small.

My novel dish was completed, and carried to headquarters by two soldiers; and at a quarter to two I personally placed my culinary wonder upon the table. It was called

Soyer's Culinary Emblem of Peace,
The Macédoine Lüdersienne à l'Alexandre II.

This monster dish was composed of—

12 boxes of preserved lobsters	1 bottle mixed pickles
2 cases of preserved lampreys	1 bottle Indian pickles
2 cases of preserved sardines	1 bottle pickled French beans
2 bottles of preserved anchovies	2 bottles pickled mushrooms
1 case of preserved caviar	½ bottle pickled mangoes
1 case of preserved sturgeon	2 bottles of pickled French truffles
1 case of preserved thunny	2 cases of preserved peas
2 cases of preserved oysters	2 cases of preserved mixed vegetables
1 pound of fresh prawns	4 dozen cabbage lettuces
4 pounds of turbot clouté	100 eggs
12 Russian pickled cucumbers	2 bottles of preserved cockscombs.
4 bottles preserved olives	

The sauce was composed of six bottles of salad oil, one of Tarragon vinegar, half a bottle of Chili vinegar, two boxes of preserved cream (whipped), four ounces of sugar, six eschalots, salt, cayenne pepper, mustard, and a quarter of an ounce of Oriental herbs which are quite unknown in England.

The dining-room, decorated under the artistic superintendence of Captain

Ponsonby, presented a ravishing *ensemble* well adapted to the occasion. It was hung, ceiling and all, with the Allied flags, to which the Russian standard, so long absent, had been happily reinstated in the bond of friendship and civilization. Those few pieces of printed cloth spoke volumes to my mind. These adopted colours of different nations had not waved together for a long while, and their playful movements, caused by a fresh breeze, which seemed to have purified itself in passing swiftly over the cheerful vineyard attached to head-quarters, pleased me very much. The god of war had put his seal and autograph upon them, just in the same manner as we see a name upon a bank-note, which only acquires value from national convenience and conventionality. Still these rags, which the will of mighty empires had favoured with their high regard, were so proud of their post, that they appeared to float and flutter in the air with more grandeur than a common piece of stuff just brought from the loom, as was the case with them before their glorious national christening, would have done. They appeared as proud and superior to their brothers and sisters as a race-horse is to one of his less fortunate fellows—a cart-horse.

I was left almost alone in that ever-memorable spot (every one having gone to the review), giving the last *coup-d'œil*, with Captain Ponsonby and the maitre d'hôtel, to the well-provided table. The illustrious guests were momentarily expected. Volumes, indeed, could I read in those printed sheets—symbols and emblems of glory. Upon them seemed engraved, in letters of gold, 'L'union fait la force,' and 'Regeneration instead of destruction!' Such were my sentiments on that memorable occasion. The world at large was interested in this mighty fusion; the end of this grand drama I could plainly read, though merely printed upon pieces of common calico.

Professionally, I was doubly proud of the honour of contributing my mite of industry to this California of grandeur and great events. My monster Macédoine was placed in the centre of the table, and, though only a few persons were present, was much admired. 'In a few minutes,' said I to myself, 'those great men whose names are echoed and re-echoed throughout the world by the trumpet-blast of fame will be here, not only gazing upon my impromptu *chef-d'œuvre*, but, I hope, also freely partaking of it—and, while enjoying the pleasures of the table, cementing the sentiments of peace and of friendship.'

So much was my mind absorbed by the superficial, that I had almost forgotten the material. The words, 'the review is over, and the generals are coming,' recalled my wandering senses. A gorgeous cavalcade was seen approaching, headed by four generals-in-chief in full uniform, and their respective Staffs, wearing their decorations, followed by above thirty generals. A few minutes after, I was attending upon Generals Pelissier, Lüders, and Sir W. Codrington, who were sitting together— General Pelissier on the left and General Lüders on the right of Sir William. The following persons were sitting at the same table:— General della Marmora and Sir Colin Campbell were facing; and at the same table sat Admiral Freemantle; Generals MacMahon, Martinprey, Wyndham, Garrett, Barnard, Lord Rokeby, Lord W. Paulet, Cameron; Colonels Scariatini and M. Amazzoff, aides-de-camp to General Lüders; and the aides of the other generals.

My anticipations were realized; for no sooner had the guests taken their seats than the conversation became more animated. I had placed at the apex of my pyramidal Macédoine a small card, with the dedication written upon it. Sir W. Codrington handed it to General Lüders, who, after showing it to several of his suite, requested permission to keep it as a reminiscence of the day. This request was granted by Sir William with a smile.

The entrées, roasts, and the entremêts had been handed round, and a serious attack upon my Lüdersienne commenced, almost every guest partaking of it twice. Captain Ponsonby requested me to remove it, as several gentlemen on the other table wished to taste it. General Pelissier, with whom I had the honour of conversing longer than with any one else, was in an excellent humour, and full of that vivacity and wit so characteristic. He bantered me several times for not having stoned the olives which formed part of the Macédoine. I told him that time would not permit of this, as I had received such short notice of the banquet, and that I went the evening before on an excursion by water to Lukan.

General Pelissier again addressed me: 'You may say what you like, Monsieur Soyer, but you might as well have stoned the olives.'

'Very true, general, if time had allowed. It is all very well for you to take the Malakhoff in a few minutes, but it took me four hours to make that dish.' At which reply he could not help laughing.

'Your friend General Barnard,' said he, pointed to that officer, who was sitting at the bottom of the table, 'would like to taste it. Go and offer him some.'

I did so; but the general had been served. I then made a tour round the table, asking each guest, above thirty in number, whether he had been attended to.

The time was getting short, and another review—that of the English army—had to come off. The iced champagne had performed a grand *rôle* during the repast; all seemed highly gratified and full of animation. What a burst of enthusiasm was elicited when General Lüders rose, and proposed the health of her Majesty the Queen of England and that of the French Emperor! which enthusiasm was renewed when Sir William Codrington responded by proposing that of the Emperor Alexander.

After the festivities, the British began thankfully to return home. Soyer, however, found it hard to tear himself away. He visited a nearly deserted canteen for a bottle of ale, and strolled on to the ruins of a troop theatre.

Female attire, including wings, ringlets, caps, bonnets, bunches of flowers, crinolines, and toilets of all fashions, bedaubed with chalk, bismuth, vermilion, and red brickdust, instead of carmine, were scattered about the stage in such a state that a French *chiffonnier* would not have disgraced his hamper by including them amongst its contents. The painting-room floor was like a rainbow; all the powdered colours had been kicked in every direction, forming a mulligatawny of shades enough to puzzle an Owen Jones and his disciples. The benches in the stalls and pit were piled up into a formidable barricade. Nothing had been respected but her Majesty's royal arms, which ornamented the centre of the proscenium. These had been painted by Major Dallas, General Garrett's aide-de-camp.

By the aid of a ladder, I carefully removed them, with the intention of placing them amongst my Sebastopol trophies, as a memento of the dramatic art in the Crimea. Upon leaving this desolated skeleton temple of Melpomene, I inquired of Mr. Stuart's bottle-breaker the cause of this awful disorder. He told me, frankly enough, that so far as the wardrobe was concerned, the rats had taken possession, but that for the remainder, himself and a few friends had done the work of devastation by way of closing the season. Thus terminated the dramatic performances in the Theatre Royal of the Fourth Division; and it was, no doubt, a fair specimen of what happened in other divisions, if left in the hands of similar good managers.

Indeed, I could not but feel hurt at this sudden devastation, for it was only a few evenings before that this tumble-down temple of Momus was gloriously shining through the resplendent glare of a dozen brown candles, and that the celebrated band of the Rifles (by permission of Lord A. Russell) was delighting a crowded audience numbering upwards of five hundred soldiers, when, at the end of the first piece, to the astonishment of all, and myself in particular, a distinguished artist and 'non-*commissioned*' poet came forward, who, though not in the style of Victor Hugo or Moore, but rather in the poet-*less 'or you-go-not style,'* poured forth the following song, to the amusement of the audience, who at its conclusion encored it most lustily. The *'poetry'* (?) ran as follows:—

Soyer's New Invention

A trifling thing, gentlemen, I am going to mention;
Oh tell me, pray, have you seen this great and new invention.
To cook in camp I believe it is their intention;
For Soyer's patent, I confess, it is a perfect creation.

Steam!   Steam!

For in it you can burn coal, wood, or patent fuel,
Put in your meat, and then you'll find it will soon be doing;
And when lighted, away it goes, and everything in motion;
For Soyer's patent, I confess, it is a perfect creation.

Steam!   Steam!

They gather round for to see the wonderful man who made it,
And stand in amaze and have a gaze, and then begin to inspect it.
All the cocked hats, I believe, say it's a stunning notion;
For Soyer's patent, I confess, it is a perfect creation.

Steam!   Steam!

It's greatly approved of, I believe, by all the nation,
And they are about to contract for this great new invention.
I sincerely hope that there's no harm in anything I mention;
For Soyer's patent, I confess, it is a perfect creation.

Steam!   Steam!

Composed by A. Thos. Price,
Lance Corporal 20th Regiment.

My presence being discovered, the whole of the troops rose *en masse*, and favoured me with three cheers, when, mounting a bench, I addressed them as follows:—

'My worthy friends and brave fellows, allow me to express to you my most profound gratitude for the honour you have conferred upon me thus unexpectedly. My humble services have often been approved of by your superior officers, but believe me, nothing can be more gratifying to me than your genuine and spontaneous approval of my endeavours to improve the cooking of the soldiers' rations; and now that peace has re-established order amongst us all, I shall only be too happy to devote my time in instructing you in the plain art of cookery; for, believe me, it is the desire of her Most Gracious Majesty the Queen, and your superiors, that you should live well, long, grow fat, and die happy.'

Shouts of laughter and rounds of cheers terminated this unexpected dramatic impromptu. The performance in consequence terminated twenty minutes later than usual.

To my joy the time had arrived to sail for England's happy land, which two years previous I had so unexpectedly left. Double pleasure was attached to my return, for I felt assured that within its sea-girt shore thousands of true British hearts were wishing me well, to use his Majesty the Sultan's term. And indeed I was not disappointed, for in less than forty-eight hours after my arrival in its mighty metropolis, I had been so fervently shaken by the hand, that I could not but help exclaiming for a short time, 'Save me from my friends.' Added to this, my kind reception by the home authorities was to me more than gratifying: then the last, though not least, reminiscence of my late campaign which occurred in Hyde Park, on the occasion of the distribution of the Order of Valour by her Most Gracious Majesty, when, being recognised amongst the thousands assembled in the stand by the valiant general, Sir Colin Campbell, the elevation of my hat was not sufficient for the impetuosity of the major-domo of this grand and imposing ceremony—the last link of the late memorable Crimean Campaign. On my going towards Sir Colin I was greeted with a hearty shake of the hand, and the usual kind and affable inquiries so peculiar to the amiable General having passed between us, I could not help expressing to the gallant warrior how highly gratified I had been by the admirable and perfect manœuvring of the troops. Shortly after he bade me adieu, and, accompanied by his staff, left the ground. At this time I much regretted not having had the opportunity of paying my duty to one of the generals in command, as it would have closed, in a most *apropos* manner, the last page of this work, my 'Culinary Campaign;' but, thanks to my star, an hour after the termination of the proceedings, while walking along Piccadilly towards my residence, a friend's voice behind me exclaimed—'Halloo, Monsieur Soyer!' On turning round, who, to my astonishment, should I perceive, mounted on his Balaklava charger, and followed by his aide-de-camp, but the very gallant general whose absence I had just been regretting. It was no other than Lord William Paulet, who was turning the corner to enter his chambers in the Albany. 'I have,' exclaimed his lordship, 'been looking out everywhere for you, having learned from Sir Colin Campbell that you were upon the ground.'

'So have I been looking for you, my lord, and with great anxiety, but unfortunately I was deprived of the pleasure of meeting you.'

'By-the-bye, Soyer, I saw your portrait in the historical Scutari painting, by Barrett, this morning at Buckingham Palace, and I consider it an excellent likeness.'

'I am glad you think so, my lord, and for my part I consider the whole of the picture remarkably well executed. At the same time allow me to inform your lordship, that as you are so near home, I should have been very sorry to have had the pleasure of meeting you in the Park.'

'Why so, Soyer?' remarked his lordship, leaning over his charger, and still retaining my hand in his.

'Well, my lord, the reason is simple. Having so prosperously commenced my culinary campaign under your command and very kind assistance, while your lordship was Brigadier-general of Scutari, nothing could be more in accordance with my wishes than that the last page of a work which I am now about completing, in anticipation of perpetuating the style of cookery introduced by me both at Scutari and in the camp before Sebstopol, should terminate at the very threshold of your door, and while you were returning from the last national ceremony relating to the great Crimean campaign.'

'Well, upon my word, it is very remarkable; and I am happy to think, Soyer, that you have written a work upon so important and interesting a subject.'

We then parted. A few minutes had thrown a curtain over this grand military display, which will ever be remembered in history, as well as graven on the memory of man.

The Author, after his laborious campaign, in bidding adieu to his readers, does not intend to remain *Soyer tranquille*, as he is most anxious, after having chronicled his culinary reminiscences of the late war, to put his views into action by simple practice; and as he had no other object in writing this book, he sincerely hopes it may be the means of causing a lasting amelioration in the cooking for both army and navy, and all public institutions. Such a result to his labours, after his long culinary experience, would make the author happy indeed, and he would for the future be found as traced below.

Epilogue
'Farewell, dear Friend'

Soyer's health was broken beyond repair by his privations in the Crimea. Years of rich food, devoted work and hectic play had burned him up, but the damp and the cholera were his death warrant. His life was shortened still further by a riding accident in the summer of 1857, shortly after he had returned to England. A restive horse threw him and dragged him by one leg for some distance along the Kensington Road. No bones were broken, but Soyer took many weeks to recover from the battering.

Yet still his inner dynamo drove him on. He wrote up his *Culinary Campaign*, composed a pamphlet of *Instructions to Military Hospital Cooks, in the Preparation of Diets for Sick Soldiers*, and lectured on military dietetics. He designed a cook-wagon for armies on the march and a sea-going coffee pot for emigrants on board ship. His final triumph was the erection of a model kitchen at the Wellington Barracks in Birdcage Walk. Here, using only the standard rations for three hundred men, he created a delicious meal of soup, salt pork, beef dumplings, roast mutton, liver and bacon and much more, before an astonished gathering of military top brass. Once again, he was showing what could be produced from the humblest of materials.

By the middle of 1858 he was seriously ill, coughing blood and spending most of his days in bed. Yet even at this melancholy pass, a spark of the old creative mischief can be glimpsed:

During these later days he would occasionally spit blood, and this increased to such a degree that he began, from mere custom, to think nothing of it, and, when remonstrated with by his friends, he would laugh it off. The fall from his horse seems to have materially aggravated his already acquired complaint. Still he took no heed of the advice so freely given him, but ran on in a mad career of gaiety. No constitution, however strong, could stand this self-inflicted taxation; and soon poor Soyer was laid on his bed, terribly ill and shaken. His medical adviser suggested change of climate, diet, and regular living, as the only method likely to once more make him a man again. Promises were made, and so soon as he was patched up, ready for the intended journey, so soon would he find something that would only detain him 'just' one day. He would say, 'You know, my dear fellow, how necessary it is that I should finish the 'Hospital Dietary,' and open my kitchen at the Wellington Barracks, before I leave England; and then I can live quietly for a few weeks, and come back and find my system in full operation.' So fully was Soyer bent on his purpose, that he would not be dissuaded from it.

June came, and still Soyer got thinner, despite the efforts of his attendants. Yet still he hoped on; and how merry was he when enabled once more to get into his kitchen, and personally attend to his *'batterie-de-cuisine!'* Then would he rate the servants for their carelessness; then would he dive into stew-pans and kettles; and then would he drink that which he should not have drunk, namely, wine; and then would he go to bed and feel so much exhausted, and the next morning complain of so much weakness, that the doctor was sent for, and the usual remedies applied; and so was Soyer again patched up, and thus matters went on until his death.

Memoirs of Soyer by Volant & Warren

Alexis Soyer died on the evening of August 5th 1858. A week later he was
buried beside his beloved Emma in Kensal Green Cemetery. Due to a last-
minute change in the arrangements, there were fewer mourners present than
had been expected. However, the crowd was still large:

In the morning, his burial took place in Kensal Green Cemetery, and was attended
by a number of sorrowing friends; much greater than might have been anticipated
from the change in the hour appointed, the early hour of the day ultimately fixed
upon, and the somewhat unusual and unnecessary exactitude by which that time was
observed to the moment. Assuredly those who thus ordered the change could not
possess the proper feelings and spirit of the occasion, else ample opportunity would
have been given for the collection of a greater number of his intimate friends.
However, the sight was (as the *Morning Chronicle* said), 'a very interesting one,
from the deep sympathy which affected all who attended the last obsequies of one
whose brilliant wit and social spirit made him the most genial companion, while his
largeness of views, in regard to his art, and the generous philanthropy with which he
studied to make his skill and judgment useful to all, elevated his character and
ennobled his actions to a degree which the outer world, who regard him only as Soyer
the cook, would perhaps find it difficult to realize. None great and noble stood around
his grave; no soldier mourned, with grateful tear, one whose health had been shaken
in continued efforts for the comfort of the British army; but the literary man, the
journalist, many who had been the friends of his earlier life, and many who had but
enjoyed a brief sunshine of his acquaintance, thronged round his tomb to bear
testimony to their affection and esteem for a friend.'

Memoirs of Soyer by Volant & Warren

At the end of the service, one of Soyer's oldest friends stepped forward and
addressed the coffin with great emotion:

' "Oh! dear friend, my long-loved friend, Soyer! we may not part from thee thus
without giving utterance to our deep regrets at losing thee, and pouring forth our
blessings on thy memory, and praying fervently for thy future happiness. Oh! friend,
Oh! companion, often tried and never found wanting—great in heart—fresh in
spirit—bright in genius, and simple-minded, who can tell thy worth? who can hope to
repair thy loss?
   ' "Yet may we reflect that, couldst thou come to life at this moment, it would be
thy joy and gratitude to find thyself surrounded by those you always loved, thus
engaged in honouring thy memory.
   ' "Farewell, dear friend! Farewell! Adieu, Alexis, thou kindest and dearest of
men! thou noblest of Frenchmen!" '

Memoirs of Soyer by Volant & Warren

Other tributes followed swiftly. Amongst the most affectionate came from
George Augustus Sala, who had first spied the arresting figure of his friend
eight years before, bargaining animatedly for lobsters in Hungerford Market:

'He was a vain man; but he was good, and kind, and charitable . . . He was but a cook; but he was my dear and good friend. He quacked, certainly—puffed himself and his eccentricity in all kinds of ways—in dress, manners, speech, mode of life; but he never derogated one iota from his dignity as an honest man . . . He was an original. He didn't do anybody any harm. He did, on the contrary, a vast amount of good in his generation; and even those who laughed at him, loved him for his simple childlike ways and generous candour.'

Soyer très hereux

Bibliography

Délassements Culinaires (1845). Alexis Soyer.

The Gastronomic Regenerator (1846). Alexis Soyer. Simpkin, Marshall & Co., London.

The Poor Man's Regenerator (1857). Alexis Soyer. Simpkin, Marshall & Co., London.

The Modern Housewife (1849). Alexis Soyer. Simpkin, Marshall & Co., London.

Soyer's Shilling Cookery for the People (1854). Alexis Soyer. Geo. Routledge & Co., London.

The Pantropheon (1853). Alexis Soyer. Simpkin, Marshall & Co., London.

A Culinary Campaign (1857). Alexis Soyer. Geo. Routledge & Co., London.

Memoirs of Alexis Soyer (1859). Compiled and Edited by F. Volant & J. R. Warren. W. Kent & Co., London.

Portrait of a Chef (1938). Helen Morris. Cambridge University Press, Cambridge.